Extreme Ghosts

Extreme Ghosts

Disturbing and Dangerous Paranormal Cases

A. N Bird

WHITE OWL
AN IMPRINT OF PEN & SWORD BOOKS LTD.
YORKSHIRE – PHILADELPHIA

First published in Great Britain in 2026 by
White Owl
An imprint of Pen & Sword Books Limited
Yorkshire – Philadelphia

ISBN 978 1 03619 754 4

A CIP catalogue record for this book is available from the British Library.

Typeset by Mac Style
Printed in the UK by CPI Group (UK) Ltd, Croydon, CR0 4YY.

FSC www.fsc.org
MIX
Paper | Supporting responsible forestry
FSC® C013604

The Publisher's authorised representative in the EU for product safety is Authorised Rep Compliance Ltd., Ground Floor, 71 Lower Baggot Street, Dublin D02 P593, Ireland.
www.arccompliance.com

For a complete list of Pen & Sword titles please contact:

PEN & SWORD BOOKS LIMITED
47 Church Street, Barnsley, South Yorkshire, S70 2AS, England
E-mail: enquiries@pen-and-sword.co.uk
Website: www.pen-and-sword.co.uk
or
PEN AND SWORD BOOKS
1950 Lawrence Road, Havertown, PA 19083, USA
E-mail: uspen-and-sword@casematepublishers.com
Website: www.penandswordbooks.com

Contents

Introduction

What you are about to read is not fiction.

☽✧†✧☾

Extreme Ghosts is a collection of true stories – genuine, terrifying and often deeply disturbing accounts of paranormal encounters that have profoundly affected the people who lived through them. These aren't the kinds of experiences that can be easily dismissed as tricks of the mind, sleep paralysis or the creaking of old floorboards in the night. These are not light brushes with the unexplained or fleeting moments of uncertainty. These are intense, drawn-out, and at times harrowing experiences that leave a deep and lasting impact on those unfortunate enough to find themselves caught in the middle of them. Some have suffered emotional and psychological damage. Others have seen their relationships strained or broken entirely. Families have been divided. Lives changed. Beliefs shattered.

Each account within these pages has been thoroughly documented, with many involving extensive interviews, follow-ups, and – when possible – corroborating evidence. These stories are not simply retellings; they are the raw, unfiltered memories of people who never expected to find themselves dealing with the unexplained. These are real people, real experiences – and what they went through is what I would describe as extreme.

But this book is more than just a chronicle of supernatural phenomena. It is also a deeply personal account. It is the story of my own journey into the world of the paranormal – a journey that began long before I ever thought of documenting other people's stories. I was born and raised in Nottingham, and from as early as I can remember, there was something about our family home that didn't feel right. As a child, I couldn't explain it. I didn't have the vocabulary or the understanding to put it into words. But something was wrong. It wasn't just fear of the dark or childhood imagination running wild. There was a genuine sense of unease that permeated the house.

There were the usual signs at first – small, subtle things that you could easily overlook. Strange noises in the night, doors that creaked open on their own, items that would go missing and turn up in places we knew they hadn't been. There were sudden cold spots in the house, areas where the air seemed unnaturally still, where you'd get that unmistakable feeling of being watched. Our family dog, Harry, would often bark furiously at corners of rooms where nothing visible was present, his hackles raised, his body tense. Sometimes he would refuse to enter certain areas of the house altogether.

At first, we told ourselves it was just the quirks of the building. Old houses do strange things. They settle. They creak. They have draughts. But over time, the occurrences became harder to rationalise. The feelings grew stronger. Shadows seemed to move where there should be none. Whispers were heard when no one else was home. You start to question yourself – your sanity, your memory, your grip on reality. But the truth was, it wasn't just me. Other members of my family were noticing it too. What began as a series of odd happenings gradually turned into something much more troubling. Something that affected our daily lives. Something that couldn't be ignored.

And then came the realisation: this wasn't just a haunted house. I was beginning to have experiences that were different from those around me. I was sensing things, seeing things, feeling things that others couldn't. Over time, I came to understand that I had what many would call a psychic sensitivity – a natural openness to the energies and presences that exist beyond the veil of our everyday world. It wasn't something I asked for. It wasn't something I understood at first. But it was there, and it wasn't going away.

Living with that kind of sensitivity is both a gift and a burden. On one hand, it opened up a path that would define my life – a path of discovery, investigation and helping others. On the other, it came with a heavy cost. You don't get to switch it off. You don't get to choose when or how the experiences come. The paranormal doesn't work on a schedule. It intrudes, it disrupts, and sometimes, it terrifies. But for me, turning away from it was never an option. It was something I had to confront. Something I had to understand. And eventually, it became something I felt compelled to study and share with others.

That path led me to become a paranormal researcher – someone who investigates hauntings, documents eyewitness accounts and tries, as best as anyone can, to make sense of the things that defy explanation. Over the years, I've travelled across the UK, meeting people from all walks of life who have had experiences they cannot explain. I've spent time in some of the most notoriously haunted locations, spoken with families living in fear, and witnessed phenomena that still baffle me to this day.

In this book, I'll take you through some of the most disturbing and unforgettable cases I've encountered – cases that challenge our understanding of reality and force us to confront the possibility that we are not as alone as we think. These are hauntings that push the boundaries. Some involve malevolent forces. Others present more mysterious, even tragic, patterns. Alongside these tales, I'll share my own childhood story in full – the experiences I lived through, the strange abilities I came to understand, and the stories passed down through my family that helped shape the person I became. None of it is exaggerated. None of it is fictionalised. What you'll read is exactly how it happened, to the best of my memory and the records I've kept.

This book isn't for everyone. It isn't a collection of spooky campfire tales or harmless ghost stories to read with a torch under the covers. These are the real deal. Extreme hauntings. The kind that changes lives. The kind that forces people out of their homes. The kind that leaves you questioning everything you thought you knew about life – and death.

If you're still with me – if you're ready to face what lies beyond the edge of explanation – then turn the page.

The haunting begins here.

My Haunted Life

Part One

Where the Fear Started

The Beginning

My story begins in the early hours of 28 January 1983. It was 12.40am when I arrived – born in the Queen's Medical Centre in Nottingham (known to us Nottinghamites as the 'QMC' and now famous for featuring on the reality television series 24 Hours in A&E). Outside, the city was cold and sodden with rain. Inside, my mum and dad were starting a new chapter they never could've predicted.

They hadn't been together long – barely a couple of years by the time I came along – but their story stretched back further than that. They first crossed paths as teenagers at Manvers Pierrepont school. My dad, 16 years old, was already a bit of a character, the sort who had a cheeky grin and a way of getting noticed. My mum hung around with a different crowd, but he always had his eye on her. He and his mates would follow her and her friend Jane home from school, trying to catch their attention while the girls giggled and pretended not to care. Nothing came of it back then – just teenage glances and missed chances.

Years later, in 1981, fate nudged them back together. They both ended up at the Lord Alcester pub one evening when the landlord handed out tickets to a Boots work party. A sort of blind date, really. They never even made it to the event. Instead, they got drunk on cheap lager and spent the evening talking, laughing and connecting. And that was that. From that night onwards, something clicked. They got together in a time when the world was shifting – Nottingham, too, was changing. It was a city built on layers: cobbled history and concrete estates, lace factories and nightclubs, a place full of promise and rough edges. That backdrop would shape the two of them, and eventually, it would shape me too.

Dad was what you'd call a proper ladies' man back then – full of confidence, always with a story, always the centre of attention. He'd told his mates for years he'd never settle down, that marriage wasn't for him. But something changed when he saw my mum again. He used to tell me, over and over through the years, that he just knew – she was the one. And you could tell he meant it. It was there in his eyes, the way he looked at her like she was the only person in the room.

Mum's path to him was harder. She'd been married before, young and full of hope, only to find herself trapped in a relationship that turned sour. It took a long time for her to climb out of the shadow of that first marriage, and when she did, she built walls around her heart. She was wary, guarded. So when my dad came along with his big heart and even bigger intentions, she didn't make it easy for him. But he waited. And slowly, piece by piece, she let him in.

They got married on 21 October 1982. Mum was heavily pregnant with me, glowing in a cherry red maternity dress. Dad wore a marl-grey three-piece suit with a matching tie. I've seen the photographs. There's joy in them – proper joy. Not just smiles for the camera, but something deeper. Two people who had lived a bit, who had hurt and healed, and somehow found each other anyway.

My early childhood unfolded primarily in their first home, a two-bedroom upstairs flat on Wray Close in St Anns, where my parents nurtured me through the formative first five years of my life. We did not possess the trappings of wealth – no extravagant holidays abroad or luxuries – but what I had was something far more profound: the nurturing love and devotion of my parents, who instilled in me the values of kindness and respect.

Life on Wray Close was a vibrant kaleidoscope of happy memories, punctuated by the laughter of family and friends. My parents moved between three different flats (all on that same street!) during those early years, yet each flat was a haven filled with warmth. My paternal grandparents, Joan and Frank, lived only a stone's throw away, just a few doors across the road, and their presence added a rich layer of security and familiarity to my childhood. Summers turned into vivid tapestries of joy as I spent countless afternoons playing with my cousins, who were almost my age. Together, we transformed the modest surroundings into a kingdom of imagination, whether we were playing games such as 'Dobby' and 'What time is it, Mr Wolf', immersing ourselves in make-believe adventures, or simply enjoying the lazy warmth of a sunny afternoon.

As I reflect on those moments, I recall an element that my late father often mentioned when I had grown up – there appeared to be something spiritual about me, a sense of depth in what I perceived. My mother, on the other hand, has always approached such notions with scepticism, notwithstanding her own ghostly encounter (which I'll get to in the future). I remember my dad sharing stories of how, even as a baby, I would fixate on one particular corner of our living room, staring wide-eyed as though there were a world only I could see. It fascinated him, and as I grew, his curiosity turned into an acknowledgment that perhaps I was more sensitive to the ethereal than most. At night I'd lie in my cot, gurgling softly in the dark, as if conversing with an unseen visitor, my laughter echoing gently through the walls, to the curiosity of Mum and Dad.

When I turned 6, a new chapter in our lives unfolded as we moved off Wray Close to a larger, 1930s semi-detached red brick house. The move was to become the start of my paranormal life. In the summer of 1989, we moved to Serlby Rise.

Moving In

Moving to Serlby Rise now feels like a twist of fate, an unexpected connection to my family's history that seemed to beckon my mum back. In 1954, my Nana Audrey and Grandad Don had been living in another house on this same hilltop street when my mother was born. For the first twenty years of her life, this house, which belonged to my great-grandfather, Andrew Amos, was her home. It was a place filled with memories, laughter, and perhaps, a few shadows…

As I think back on my parent's decision to relocate, I recognise now that my mum had a deep affection for her childhood on Serlby Rise. She often reminisced about her life that unfolded during her younger years, the friendships forged, and the sense of comfort that enveloped her. So, when the opportunity arose for us to move onto that very same street, she leapt at the chance, eager to recreate the warmth of her upbringing for her own family. What I would later come to discover was that Mum herself had experienced certain brushes with the supernatural while living in that original house. Those stories (which I'll get round to later in the book, I promise) would reveal a lineage of peculiar events woven into the fabric of our family's fascination, and encounters, with the supernatural. It is a narrative that deepens my understanding of the haunting presence that lingered within our own home.

When you turn off Carlton Road, a main road that runs from the city centre, right to Carlton, onto Linnell Street, you come to the bottom of Serlby Rise, at the south end. From there, the road rises steeply and curves to the left, reaching its peak in the centre. My house was located as you reach the brow of the rise. Then, from the centre, the road curves to the right as it climbs up to the highest point at the north end, where you turn onto Gordon Road.

The house we moved into was modest, yet filled with potential and promise. It boasted a spacious living room that went from the front of the house, right to the back, a large kitchen, dining room and three bedrooms that promised sweet dreams – and, unfortunately, some nightmares. The loft space became a sanctuary for my dad, a personal retreat where he could potter around and create, an early prelude to what is nowadays referred to as a 'Man-Cave'.

Serlby Rise offered us more than just a new address; it seemed to present a continuity of sorts, an unbroken thread that connected my mum's past with mine. In a way, this house marked the beginning of my journey in life. Much happened here, both amazingly positive, and distressingly negative.

Not long after we settled into our new home on Serlby Rise, I started making friends with a few of the local kids. Warren, Sasha and Claire (I've changed their names here to protect their privacy) weren't just the neighbours' children – they quickly became a huge part of my life. It happened naturally. Our parents had started chatting over garden fences, bumping into each other in the street, eventually becoming friends themselves, and before long, we kids followed suit. Warren was the first one I got to know. He lived just a couple of doors up the street from us – a lively, adventurous lad with a cheeky grin and an endless supply of energy. It wasn't long before he introduced me to his younger sister, Sasha, and then Claire, who lived directly across the road. It felt easy, right from the start. Like we were supposed to find each other. Before I knew it, they became my closest companions during those early years on Serlby Rise. We pretty much grew up side-by-side, spending hours just hanging about, making our own fun like kids did back then, long before phones and tablets took over.

One of our favourite things to do as we got older was simply sit out on the steps in front of Claire's house. We'd spend what felt like endless afternoons just hanging out there, chatting about anything and everything. It didn't matter what the weather was like – we'd still find ourselves perched on those steps, talking about school, TV programmes we liked and what things we wanted our mum and dads to get us. It sounds so simple now, but at the time, it felt like the best place in the world.

We'd often wander off together to Lou's, the little corner shop just around the corner on Gordon Road. It was the sort of place where you could smell the newspapers and the sweet jars the moment you walked through the door. I still remember clenching my 20p piece tightly in my hand, carefully picking out a bag full of one-penny chews, counting them one by one. Flying saucers, cola bottles, blackjacks – all the classics. If we were feeling flush, we might even splash out on a packet of crisps or a can of pop. Those trips were a regular part of our little world, back when it was safer to let a group of young kids go off to the shop by themselves, and it became a ritual that felt just as important as any of our bigger adventures.

As we got older, our interests started to change a bit. Warren and I got really into computer games. We'd spend hours at each other's houses playing on our Atari computers – games like Crystal Castles and Centipede that, even now, bring back a flood of memories. Sitting in front of those bulky screens, controllers in hand, battling pixelated enemies and trying to beat each other's high scores, we were completely lost in our own little universe.

One of the best parts of those long afternoons on Serlby Rise was hearing the distant jingle of the ice cream van making its way up the street. We all knew him simply as 'Mr. Whippy' – a kind old man with a smile as warm as the summer sun. We never did learn his real name. No matter what we were doing, we'd drop everything and race to the curb, clutching whatever coins we could scrape together. I always went straight for my favourite, an ice cream Mars. Warren usually chose a Strawberry Split and the girls would go for '99s', with a flake. Mr. Whippy would chat to us as he served, never rushing us along, always treating us like we mattered.

Looking back now, I realise just how important those friendships were. They weren't just a way to pass the time – they were a lifeline. Those ordinary days and silly little traditions gave me some of the happiest memories I have of living on Serlby Rise. We were just kids, doing what kids did best: living in the moment, without a care in the world. No pressures, no responsibilities, just the pure joy of being young and surrounded by people who mattered. When I think about Serlby Rise, it's not just the strange things that come to mind – it's also those sunlit afternoons, the laughter echoing down the street, the rustle of sweet wrappers in our pockets, and the endless hours spent together. Those were the good times. And for all the eerie memories that were there, I'll always be grateful that I had those bright, simple moments first.

But even with all the good times we had in those early days, there was always a shadow hanging over us as a family. Right from the moment we first moved into the house at Serlby Rise, something didn't feel right. It wasn't anything you could put your finger on straight away – it was just ... a feeling. My mum and dad noticed it almost immediately. The house was freezing cold, and not just during winter. It was a kind of chill that crept under your skin and stayed there, no matter how high you turned up the heating.

They still talk about that first winter. No matter what they tried – turning the radiators up full blast, using portable heaters – the cold just wouldn't shift. It wasn't normal. It had this damp, heavy feel to it, like the walls themselves were sucking the warmth away. Ice would build up on the inside of the windows, spidering across the glass in jagged patterns. Even when summer rolled around, you'd get condensation running down the windows like it was still the middle of December. It made no sense. They got people out to check the place – looking for draughts, checking the insulation, anything that could explain it. But there was nothing wrong. Nothing anyone could find, anyway. That same coldness seemed even worse upstairs, especially in my mum and dad's bedroom. I'd catch them sometimes, exchanging looks when a cold breeze swept through the room even though all the windows were shut. They'd talk in quiet voices about feeling like they were being watched, like there were eyes on them that they couldn't see. It wasn't constant – things would happen in fits and starts – but it always left this heavy feeling behind, like a weight pressing down on the house.

That wasn't all, either. Little things started happening, small enough at first that you could almost brush them off. But they niggled at you, unsettled you without you really knowing why. Our dog Harry – a lovely Rough Collie-German shepherd cross, full of life and daftness – started acting odd. He would point-blank refuse to go into the dining room. He'd just stand there at the doorway, tail tucked between his legs, ears pinned back, staring like he could see something we couldn't. You could call him, coax him, even try and pull him gently by the collar, but he'd dig his paws in and whine, terrified.

As for me, even back then I hated sleeping in my own room. I always had a bit of this fear like most kids do, but after we moved into Serlby Rise, it went from bad to worse. It wasn't just childish fear anymore; it felt real. Like there was something there with me when the lights went out. And no matter how tightly I pulled the covers over my head, that feeling never really went away.

Escalation

As the months turned into years and I grew older, the strange goings-on inside that house didn't fade away – they got worse. The disturbances became stronger, more frequent, harder to explain away with the usual excuses. One of the first things that really started to rattle my dad was the noises from the loft. Early on he just shrugged it off, telling himself it was just the house settling – the kind of thing you expect in an old place. But as time went on, that explanation started to wear thin. The sounds weren't creaks or groans like timber contracting in the cold. These were heavy, deliberate footsteps. Pacing. Moving. Shifting. As if someone – or something – was walking around just above our heads. I think it genuinely unsettled my dad more than he let on at the time, but he tried to keep a lid on it. Tried to stay rational.

I was lucky, in a way. Being young, I didn't notice half of what was going on. A lot of the weirdness passed me by, hidden behind the simple distractions of childhood. I was more interested in my toys, my friends or what was on TV. But looking back, I can see now just how much tension there was simmering beneath the surface in our house.

Looking back, those early days at Serlby Rise feel like the beginning of something quietly unravelling. The cold that never went away. The footsteps overhead when no one was up there. It hadn't yet become frightening – not truly – but something about it felt wrong. Like the house was watching, waiting. And at the time, I thought we were alone in that feeling. I thought this strangeness was ours and ours alone.

But over the years, I'd learn that these things weren't unique. I've heard many stories since. Stories from people who lived in different towns, in different houses, but who felt the same quiet dread pressing in at the edges of their lives.

The first I'm going to share with you came from a woman named Vanessa.

She told me about a flat she lived in, in Cambridge.

And about a sound that followed her through the darkness……

Vanessa's Story

The Whistling

I've always found that hauntings seem to find people when they're most vulnerable. There's something about emotional upheaval – grief, heartbreak, big changes – that seems to open the door to experiences most would rather not have. Like wounded animals, we become easier to follow. Easier to reach. Maybe it's our energy, or maybe it's something more spiritual than that. But the pattern repeats time and again.

Vanessa was 43 when her story began – not with a ghost, but with a breakup. By the time we met on video call in December 2021, she'd long since put the experience behind her. At least on the surface. She was well-dressed, well-spoken and carried herself with the kind of quiet strength that often hides deeper scars. Her eyes, though – they gave her away. There was a heaviness behind them, the sort of weight you only really notice when you've carried it yourself.

We became acquainted after she watched one of my YouTube Live investigations. She waited until the end, hung back from commenting while the others were chatting away, then contacted me via Email, where we arranged a video consultation. She came across with a strange mix of defiance and caution.

'I don't normally talk about this,' she said. 'But I've never been able to explain it. And I think you might understand.'

She was right. I did.

Vanessa had spent most of her life in Cambridge. She'd built a steady career in arts and cultural management, the kind of behind-the-scenes work that keeps galleries and events running smoothly. It was a job that suited her – organised, thoughtful, precise. She had a close-knit circle of friends, kept in regular contact with her parents, and had always been independent by nature.

She met Mark at a friend's birthday dinner. He wasn't her usual type – more relaxed, a bit rough around the edges – but he made her laugh, and he had that easy charm that made things feel uncomplicated. For the first year, they were good together. He'd stay at her flat above a bookshop near Parker's Piece. They'd go to comedy nights, order takeaways, spend lazy Sunday mornings in bed together.

But after two years, things began to fray.

'It was like … we stopped being a team,' she said. 'We were still together, technically, but it felt like we were moving in different directions.'

He started staying out more. She started noticing silences stretching longer. Conversations turned to friction. The warmth had gone, and neither of them could seem to get it back. In the end, she made the decision to split up with him.

'I knew it would be hard, but staying would've been harder. I needed space. Something of my own.'

It was around this time she found the listing for the flat. It was part of a grand old Victorian villa on one of the quieter streets off Mill Road. The building had been converted into four separate units in the 1980s, but the original architecture remained. High ceilings, long sash windows, arched doorways, and those narrow, slightly creaky corridors that only older homes seem to have. There was something appealing about it. A sense of history, of quiet dignity. And for Vanessa, it represented something more than just a new home – it was a reset. A place to rebuild, reflect, and start over.

She moved in during late August 2020. The summer was tapering off. The trees lining the street had begun to lose their vibrancy, and the air had that early-autumn edge to it – still warm by day, but cool enough at night to make you reach for a jumper. Her parents helped with the move. They brought boxes, bags, a little kettle for the first night. Her dad fixed the curtain rail in the living room while her mum unpacked mugs and arranged them neatly by the sink.

That first evening, after they'd left, Vanessa sat on the living room floor with a glass of wine, surrounded by boxes, and let the quiet settle around her.

'It felt … peaceful,' she told me. 'A bit lonely, maybe, but not in a bad way. I was proud of myself. I'd done something scary. I'd chosen myself.'

She unpacked just the essentials. A few clothes, her toiletries, her phone charger. Made the bed with fresh sheets. Opened the bedroom window a little to let the breeze in. The room smelt faintly of old paint and dust, the kind that clings to Victorian buildings no matter how much you clean.

That night, she fell asleep with the sounds of the city drifting through the window – distant traffic, the occasional laugh from the street, the familiar hum of life continuing around her. Normal sounds. She slept deeply.

Until 2.37 am.

She remembered the time exactly – not because she looked at the clock, but because she'd made a habit of checking the time whenever she woke in a new place. Something she'd done for years, almost subconsciously. A quirk of her mind. Her phone, dimly lit on the bedside table, told her the time.

But, what woke her wasn't a dream. It wasn't a sound from outside.

It was whistling.

Low and soft. Not musical. Just a few notes. Drawn out. Repeated. The kind of whistling you do when you're thinking, or pacing, or lost in thought. It seemed to be coming from the kitchen.

At first, she thought it might be a neighbour. The walls were old. Sound carried. Maybe someone above or next door had come home late and was making a snack or pottering about.

She waited.

The sound stopped.

The silence felt heavy. She lay there for a while, listening hard, her ears straining in the dark.

Then she got up.

The hallway light flickered slightly when she switched it on – a quirk of the ancient wiring, she assumed. The kitchen was empty, of course. Quiet. No windows open, no signs of anyone.

She made a cup of tea, sat at the little kitchen table, and tried not to let her imagination run away with her. That night, she told herself, it was just a blip. She was tired. She was adjusting. Old houses make noises. Sound travels. She was logical enough to believe all of that.

But deep down, something had shifted. A sliver of unease had slipped through. And by the second night, that unease had found a foothold....

☽✧†✧☾

The second night came quickly. Vanessa kept herself busy during the day – unpacking, rearranging furniture, setting up little routines to make the place feel like home. She'd always been the sort of person who found comfort in order. Even as a child, her books had to be arranged by size or colour. Her workspace at the gallery office had always been neat, her inbox zeroed out before the end of each day.

But that second night, something had changed.

'I didn't feel alone,' she said, over a year later. 'It was like there was an awareness in the air. Not threatening, exactly. But watchful. Like I was being observed.'

Vanessa tried to dismiss the feeling. Ate dinner on the sofa, watched the end of a drama series she'd been following. Even laughed out loud at one point – though she'd later admit that it felt forced. She went to bed around 11 again. This time, she made sure all the windows were shut and locked. Her keys and phone were next to the bed, a glass of water on the side table. The second bedroom door was closed.

At 2.37 a.m., she woke again...

Same sound...

Whistling...

But this time, it was closer. It was coming from the second bedroom. That door had been shut when she went to bed. She was certain of it. But now, in the moonlit hallway, it looked ajar. Only by a few inches, but enough.

The whistle was different too – more deliberate. Not tuneful, but not random either. As though whoever was doing it wasn't quite human. Like they didn't fully understand the purpose of the sound but were mimicking it anyway. She lay frozen for a long time, not daring to move.

'I told myself it had to be from outside. A neighbour again. Thin walls, right?'

But the problem was, there weren't any neighbours on that side of the building. The flat next door was empty. And the second bedroom didn't share a wall with anyone.

It stopped as soon as she sat up. This time, she didn't go to investigate. She stayed in bed until morning.

The next day, she left the flat early. Took herself to the cafe near Parker's Piece where she used to meet Mark. Sat in the corner by the window and drank two coffees back-to-back. The waitress asked if she was alright.

'I lied and said I was tired from the move,' she told me. 'But the truth was, I already didn't want to go back.'

Still, she did. That evening, she kept the lights on longer. Played music while she made dinner. Moved more of her things into the second bedroom to make it feel less eerie. Books, an old armchair, a standing lamp she hadn't used in years. She thought maybe giving it a purpose – making it part of her life – might help.

It didn't. Night three was colder. A sudden drop in temperature, sharp enough to see her breath when she brushed her teeth. The radiators were on, but the air in the hallway was icy.

At 2.37 a.m., she woke to whistling in the bathroom. Now it was just feet away from her bed. She heard it echo slightly, bouncing off the tiled walls. And again, it stopped the moment she moved.

But this time, something new happened. She thought she heard a shuffle. Not from the floorboards. Not a creak. A distinct movement. Like someone brushing their arm against the doorframe. It was so slight, so quick, that she told herself she must have imagined it. She got up, walked to the bathroom and stood there for a moment. The mirror was fogged, oddly – like someone had been in there with a hot shower running. But it was bone dry.

She didn't sleep again that night.

☽✧☥✧☾

By the fourth day, she was exhausted. Everything felt muted. The light outside seemed greyer. Her appetite had vanished. Her friends texted to ask how the new place was, and she didn't reply.

She considered calling her parents but didn't want to worry them. What would she even say? 'I'm being whistled at by an invisible someone every night at exactly the same time'?

No. She wasn't ready to say it aloud yet. Saying it made it real.

That night, she left the hall light on. It flickered again as she turned it on. She unplugged the TV before bed. Made sure every window was locked. Checked the second bedroom, the bathroom, the kitchen. Everything was still.

And yet, when she lay down, she felt it again.

That pressure in the air.

That sense of attention.

Tonight, it came from the hallway. The whistling didn't even start this time – it was already in full flow when she woke. She sat up straight, heart pounding, and stared at the gap under her door.

She could see movement. A slight shadow. Like someone pacing just outside. She didn't move. Couldn't.

'I've never known fear like that,' she told me. 'I've been through heartbreak, through hospital scares with my mum … but that night, I truly felt preyed upon.'

When the sound finally stopped – abruptly, as if snapped off – she lay there in absolute silence, straining her ears for even the tiniest creak or whisper.

There was nothing. Just that awful quiet.

And somehow, that was worse.

By the fifth day, Vanessa felt completely untethered from her life. It wasn't just the lack of sleep – it was something more profound, more invasive. A sense that she was no longer in control of her own environment. The flat, once filled with potential, now felt like a trap. Its high ceilings and ornate cornices no longer looked elegant, but cavernous and cold. The rooms seemed to loom. The corners of each ceiling carried a strange darkness that didn't quite lift, even in daylight. Vanessa spent most of that day trying to stay out. She went into the city centre, wandered aimlessly around the shops, then walked along the Backs, pretending she was just enjoying the late summer weather. But everything felt dulled. Detached. Even the sound of the river seemed too quiet. She checked her phone obsessively, almost hoping for some distraction, some reason to go somewhere else. But there were no urgent messages, no forgotten jobs. Just silence.

As dusk rolled in, she made herself walk back to the flat. Her legs felt heavy. She stopped twice on the walk, unsure whether she was just tired or if part of her – some deeper part – was trying to delay the inevitable.

By the time she opened the front door, it was fully dark. The hallway greeted her with a heavy stillness. She left all the lights on that night. Every single one. Even the little lamp in the second bedroom, which she hadn't switched on since the first day.

She made herself a tea and didn't drink it. Dinner was a sandwich she couldn't finish. She didn't want to go to bed – but staying up seemed worse. Like she was waiting for something to arrive, and to be awake for it would somehow make it more real.

She went to bed fully clothed. Hoodie. Joggers. Slippers left on. She lay stiffly under the duvet, phone gripped in one hand.

She didn't remember falling asleep.

But at 2.37 a.m., she was awake.

This time, the whistling was right outside the bedroom door. No longer faint. No longer distant. It was there. Loud, clear, purposeful. There was something awful about the sound. Something unnatural. The pitch was off – too low in places, too breathy in others. It had the same lilt as before, but it dragged. Like whoever was making it didn't have lungs. Like they were imitating breath.

The hallway light she'd left on was flickering again. Through the gap under the door, she could see it blinking in and out. A stop-motion strobe. And with each flicker, she thought she saw a shadow move. Back and forth. Slowly. Pacing.

'I knew if I made a sound, it would come in,' Vanessa told me.

She lay there frozen, holding her breath, tears starting to form. Every instinct screamed to run, to scream, to do something. But her body wouldn't move. The air in the room was leaden. Pressed down on her chest like a weight.

Then, the handle on the door twitched…

Not a full turn. Not a creak. Just a slight, unmistakable jolt, as though someone had gently tested it.

She didn't sleep at all after that. Just lay there, listening to the hallway until dawn began to bleed faint light into the room. Only then did she dare move.

Vanessa didn't go to work the next day. She didn't even call in sick. She sat on the edge of her bed for hours, trying to convince herself to pack a bag and leave – but she couldn't bring herself to move. Something had been outside her door. Something had been inches from her. The flat had crossed a line. And she knew, deep down, that whatever was happening was escalating.

What frightened her most wasn't just the proximity – it was the intention. She felt it more clearly than ever. This wasn't residual energy. It wasn't a confused spirit.

It was deliberate.

It was moving closer…

And tomorrow night, it would be inside…

The next night, Vanessa once again didn't remember falling asleep. But she remembered waking up. It was night six. And from the moment she opened her eyes, she knew.

The air in the room felt wrong. It was dense, unmoving, as if the atmosphere had solidified into something too thick to breathe. The shadows on the walls were too dark, the edges of everything too sharp. A strange pressure filled her ears, like the moment before a thunderstorm.

Vanessa didn't check the time. She didn't need to. The silence was absolute.

There was no whistling this time. No pacing outside the door. Only a stillness so deep it made her heart pound against her ribs like a warning drum. She lay frozen, afraid to move, afraid even to blink. And then – very slowly – she became aware she wasn't alone…

Something was in the room…

Not just a sense, not just a feeling – she could see it. At the foot of the bed, partially obscured in a low-lying mist that hadn't been there seconds before, stood the figure of a man. He was old – at least, the face was. Gaunt and sunken, with deep-set eyes that seemed too large, too black. His features were collapsed inward slightly, like a dried apple or a face left in water too long. His skin had a greyish pallor, almost blue around the lips, and though his expression was still – almost innocent – it didn't read as harmless.

The body was strange. Wrong. It wasn't just that it was shrouded in a grey mist – it lacked definition. As though his presence didn't fully belong here. His shoulders faded away into smoke, and where legs should have been there was only more swirling fog, like steam rising from a sewer grate.

But it was the eyes that held her.

They stared at her with a kind of knowing. Not wide and wild like something mad, but focused. Intent. Not a memory, not a loop. He was looking at her.

For a long moment, neither of them moved. Vanessa's mind was racing, heart hammering so fast she thought it might tear itself from her chest. She tried to scream. Tried to move. But her body wouldn't respond. It was as if the very force of the entity had pinned her in place…

And then it changed.

The stillness broke.

The figure tilted its head …… and screamed! The sound was unnatural – piercing, animalistic, like a human scream pushed through broken vocal cords and torn from a throat not meant to make noise anymore. It rose up in the room like a siren, vibrating the glass in the windows, forcing Vanessa's hands to her ears even as she convulsed with terror.

The man's face twisted – not in anger, not in rage – but in sheer, manic delight.

He was enjoying this.

The scream lasted no more than five seconds. But it shattered something inside her. At that moment, Vanessa broke from the paralysis. She flung herself out of bed and bolted from the room, not even stopping to grab shoes. The hallway was ice-cold and flickering with the harsh overhead bulb she'd left on. As she passed the bathroom, she caught a glimpse of her reflection in the mirror – wide eyes, pale face, mouth half-open in terror – but didn't stop. She threw the front door open and ran. The night outside was freezing. In her slippers, wearing only her pyjamas and hoodie, she ran down the front path, across the gravel drive, and didn't stop until she was in the middle of the road. She stood there panting, arms crossed tightly against her chest, staring back at the flat.

There was nothing in the window. No sign of movement. But the silence felt watchful.

She walked, then half-ran, the ten minutes it took to reach her parents' house. It was nearly three in the morning by the time she arrived, knocking frantically, face streaked with tears and throat raw from gasping sobs she didn't remember making.

Her dad answered the door in a dressing gown, alarmed, confused. Vanessa couldn't speak at first. Just threw her arms around him, shaking, unable to form the words. When she finally told them what had happened, they didn't ask questions. They didn't try to reason it away, even if they were sceptical and worried about her mental wellbeing.

They simply let her stay.

Vanessa never set foot in that flat again. She arranged for her things to be collected while she was out of town, and the lease was quietly terminated.

The flat has since been re-let. She's never returned to the street, never even walked past. When she speaks of it now, her voice remains steady – but her hands tremble slightly, and she doesn't make eye contact during the details.

'I don't know what it was,' she told me. 'But it wanted something from me. I could feel it. It moved closer each night, feeding off something I didn't realise I was giving it. And I honestly believe… if I'd stayed one more night, I wouldn't be here to tell you this.'

'You honestly believe that, don't you?' I ask.

She nods gravely. 'Yes.'

Vanessa stayed with her parents for a few weeks after that night. They didn't press her for details. They didn't need to. Her mum quietly made her cups of tea without asking, while her dad checked the locks each night and left a lamp on in the hallway – just in case. They didn't say the word ghost, or spirit or haunting. But they didn't dismiss it either.

'I think they could tell something had happened,' Vanessa told me. 'Even if they didn't understand it, they could feel it on me.'

The trauma lingered in ways she hadn't expected. For months afterward, she struggled to sleep. Not just from nightmares – though those came too – but from a deeply rooted fear that she might wake up and hear that whistling again. That the thing from the flat might have followed her. That somehow, by seeing it, she'd given it permission to return.

She eventually moved in with a friend temporarily before finding a new place – modern, open-plan, purpose-built. 'Something with no history,' she said with a half-laugh. 'No draughty hallways. No sash windows. No ghosts.'

Even now, Vanessa still doesn't like being alone at night. She sleeps with a fan on, for the noise. She avoids documentaries on the paranormal and horror films. She doesn't entertain conversations about spirits at parties or let people tell ghost stories if she's staying over.

And she's never whistled again……

☽✧☥✧☾

When she first shared her experience with me, I could see the weight it still carried. Not in the way she spoke – her voice was calm – but in the subtle gestures: the way she wrapped her cardigan tighter around her, how her eyes moved to corners of the room when certain memories surfaced. She hadn't told many people.

'I didn't want people to think I'd gone mad,' she said. 'Because honestly, for a little while … I thought maybe I had.'

But she hadn't. I've spoken to dozens – possibly hundreds – of people like Vanessa over the years. People who didn't ask for anything paranormal, who didn't believe in it, who only came forward because something happened to them that they couldn't explain. Something that rewrote their understanding of reality in a single, terrifying moment.

There are different theories, of course. Some would argue that Vanessa experienced what's known as a residual haunting – a non-conscious imprint of traumatic energy replaying itself in a kind of loop. The classic 'stone tape theory' which suggests that certain materials, especially stone, brick or wood, have the ability to 'record' emotional or traumatic events from the past. Like a kind of psychic tape recorder, the theory proposes that these materials somehow absorb intense human energy and replay it under the right conditions.

It's not a haunting in the traditional sense. There's no spirit trapped or conscious intelligence at work. Instead, it's as if a moment in time has been imprinted into the fabric of a place — a violent argument, a death, or even an overwhelming sense of loss — and every so often, it plays back like a film reel. Witnesses might see a figure walking across a room, hear old footsteps on the stairs, or catch the echo of a long-ago voice, always repeating the same action, never aware of the living.

The term itself was popularised in the 1970s, following a BBC play *The Stone Tape*, but the concept is far older. Many of the cases I've investigated over the years seem to fit this pattern: the same apparition appearing at the same spot, the same sounds at the same time each year, as though the walls themselves remember. If the theory holds any truth, it paints an eerie picture of the world around us, one where buildings are not merely bricks and mortar, but living archives of emotion. Places steeped in tragedy might literally remember what happened within them, silently replaying those moments to anyone sensitive enough to notice.

But I don't believe that applies here. This wasn't a tape. It wasn't repeating without awareness. Whatever was in that flat watched her, approached her and escalated deliberately. It knew she was there. It waited for her to be alone, vulnerable, emotionally raw.

And then it moved.

Sceptics might suggest it was a psychological projection – the product of grief, anxiety, the psychological fallout of a painful breakup. But Vanessa wasn't fragile. She was composed, analytical and rational about splitting with Mark. This wasn't stress or a nervous breakdown. This was a haunting.

I believe she encountered something real.

Something intelligent. Perhaps something that had lingered in that building long before it was converted to flats. Something attached to the house itself – or more chillingly, something that latched onto her, drawn to the crack in her defences left behind by heartbreak.

Sometimes, when people ask me what ghosts really are, I tell them this: They are not always echoes. Sometimes, they are watchers. Waiters. Listeners.

And if you listen too long to their tune … sometimes, they come closer.

Vanessa survived whatever it was. She escaped. But I'll never forget the way she said it – quietly, firmly, without melodrama:

'If I'd stayed one more night … I wouldn't be here to tell you this….'

My Haunted Life

Part Two

The Haunting Continues

Back to my childhood and our home on Serlby Rise, we were living with shadows of our own, and ours hadn't gone anywhere. The cold was still there. The unease still sat in the corners. And slowly, almost imperceptibly, things were beginning to escalate.

The Front Door

One of the things that became almost a running joke – though deep down, it wasn't funny at all – was the front door. It had this unsettling habit of swinging open all on its own. It wasn't like it was being blown open by a gust of wind or left on the latch. Time and again, my dad would come downstairs first thing in the morning and find it wide open, as if someone had walked straight out in the middle of the night – or worse, walked in. I can still picture it: the door hanging ajar, the early morning chill seeping into the hallway, and Harry standing there, tense as anything. His body would be rigid, his tail down, his teeth bared in a low, rumbling growl, eyes fixed on a spot none of us could see. You could feel the fear coming off him in waves. Whatever he was seeing – or sensing – was enough to put a fully-grown, loyal family dog on high alert.

My parents tried to make light of it for my sake, tried to pretend that these strange happenings were nothing to worry about. But you could tell. You could hear it in the forced laughter, see it in the way they checked the locks two and three times before bed, the way they would glance over their shoulders when they thought nobody was looking. There was an unspoken understanding between them that something wasn't right. An atmosphere had settled over our home, thick and heavy, like a fog you couldn't shift. And deep down, no matter how much they tried to deny it, I think we all knew – we weren't alone in that house.

The Keys

One of the most confounding things that would happen was the disappearance and reappearance of objects. One memorable episode of this happened during one of my mum's annual girlie weekends away to Blackpool with her friends, leaving my dad and me to our own devices. I can still picture that Sunday morning vividly. The sun was shining. My dad, determined to make the day enjoyable, asked me to help him with chores while he prepared breakfast.

However, things began to take a bizarre turn the minute my dad realised his door keys had gone missing. He searched high and low, rummaging through pockets, turning the contents of drawers upside down – all to no avail. They had simply vanished into thin air. This was peculiar enough on its own, but what followed was nothing short of extraordinary. Once we finished breakfast, we washed the dishes together, an act of normalcy that contrasted sharply with the atmosphere of our home. After drying the plates, he folded the tea towel, placing it neatly on top of the cooker.

With every intention of securing the house before heading out, he used an IRONING BOARD (Yes, really! That was Dad all over!) lodged against the front door before we headed out. We spent a few hours out down what is locally named the 'Bottle Pond', doing some fishing. My dad was an avid fisherman – hooked, you could say, from the age of 12. Growing up in St Ann's, he and his mates Pete and Rob would haul their rods, tackle boxes and bait and set off on long walks across Nottingham, heading for the River Trent, hidden ponds, and quiet lakes in search of carp. Fishing wasn't just a hobby to Dad – it was a passion, a way of life. They'd walk for miles without complaint, driven by the simple thrill of the cast and the hope of a catch.

He was a brilliant fisherman, too, my dad. Patient, knowledgeable and instinctive – he just knew where the fish would be. In later years, he'd often head out with his good friend Victor, or Simon, who was married to our cousin, Maria. They had their spots, their routines and their stories – laughing, planning and sometimes just sitting in contented silence as the water rippled gently before them. Fishing was his escape, his therapy, his joy. Of all the pleasures in life, I think it was the one that gave him the most peace. He took me a few times when I was a kid. We'd camp out overnight by West Lake, in Colwick Park, tucked away in the bivvy with the rods propped up and the mist rolling in at dawn.

I didn't appreciate the hobby back then – not really. I didn't quite get the patience, the stillness, the way time seemed to slow down. But I did appreciate being with him. Those nights by the lake, just me and Dad, are etched into my memory with a kind of quiet reverence. Looking back now, I realise I wasn't just learning about fishing – I was learning about him.

Upon our return that day from fishing, we entered through the back door, into the kitchen. The tea towel that Dad had used on the pots, that had been resting peacefully on the cooker from earlier, was now crumpled on the floor. Dad bent down to pick it up, and as he did, his front door keys clattered to the ground from within the folds of fabric. How had they ended up there? Neither of us had the slightest clue. I watched him, perplexed, his expression a mixture of disbelief and irritation as he grappled with the unexplainable.

Such episodes spurred countless conversations between my parents and they would often clash over it, my mum remaining cynical and insisting there was a rational explanation. But the unexplained continued. It was as if the very walls of our house held secrets we were never meant to uncover. The haunting chill remained, an unshakable reminder of the mysteries that lingered within. Though we continued to live in the house, the oddities transformed our existence there, changing the way we perceived our surroundings. Our home became a character within my childhood, and the shadows of those untold stories accompanied us throughout our years. There was something strange, but like a good book, it was a story we were bound to explore.

Of course, I'm not the only one drawn into a story like that – one that starts quietly, with shadows and whispers, and ends in something far more terrifying. Over the years, I've heard from others who also lived out strange chapters in their youth. Some stumbled into it by accident. Others went looking.

The next story is one of those.

It begins with a charity shop find, a group of friends, and a Ouija board.

And what followed would leave a lasting mark on all of them…

Carly's Story

The Ouija Board Kids

Back in 2012, Dad and I went to a paranormal convention in Surrey. It wasn't a huge affair, not one of those glossy, stagey-style things with camera crews and merchandise stalls – this was a bit more understated, more intimate. A proper British gathering. The kind of weekend where people came together out of shared fascination and experience rather than spectacle. We weren't giving a talk or appearing on any panels. We were just there as attendees – curious and hopeful that we might meet some like-minded people who shared similar experiences and interests.

And we did.

What made that weekend special wasn't the venue or the speakers or even the subject matter. It was the people. You just got to meet different people. Some we already knew of from social media. These events always attract a range: from seasoned paranormal investigators with equipment cases and case files, to the shy, hesitant individuals who've had something happen to them and don't know where else to turn. That's how we met Carly.

She was sat in the same row as us during one of the afternoon talks. I can't remember the speaker, but I do remember her. In her early thirties, quietly spoken, polite. She had driven up from Kent for the weekend. We ended up chatting during the break, and something about her stood out. Carly wasn't trying to impress anyone. She wasn't selling anything. She was just there, listening – absorbing everything. She told us she was an artist, painting pet portraits for people. Married, with a young child, living a quiet life in Gravesend. She'd never joined a ghost group, didn't know much on the subject at all to be honest. But she had come to the convention for a reason.

She'd had an experience – one that had haunted her for years – and she was hoping to find some sort of explanation. Or at least to be around people who wouldn't laugh at her for sharing it. We spent a fair bit of time with her over that weekend. Dad and I both took a real liking to her. She was warm, easy to talk to and completely sincere. There was no bravado in how she told her story. No dramatics. Just a calm, honest retelling of something that had left a permanent mark on her life.

She told us she'd only ever shared it with a handful of people. She didn't even tell her husband all the details, because even after all these years, saying it out loud still made her feel uncomfortable. But she trusted us. And when she finished telling it, I looked her straight in the eye and told her the same thing I've said to a few others over the years:

'One day, I'm going to write this down. Because people need to hear it.'

This is Carly's story.

It happened in the summer of 1998. She was 15 years old. Back then, Carly lived in Cobham Village, a small rural community in Kent. For those not familiar with it, Cobham is one of those places that seems unchanged by time. Lots of old cottages and country lanes, with a quiet, well-behaved atmosphere. The sort of place where everyone knows each other's business and not much ever really happened. Carly lived in a decent-sized four-bedroom house with her mum and dad and her younger sister, Danielle, who was 13 at the time. The house was set back slightly from the road, with a long driveway and a patch of trees down at the bottom of the back garden.

She was at comprehensive school in Gravesend at the time and had a close little group of friends – Brett, Sarah, Dawn and Lewis. They were typical teenagers of the late nineties. No social media, no smartphones. They passed notes in class, phoned each other's landlines and hoped nobody's dad ever answered, met up in parks, and wandered the streets with bottles of alcopops or warm cider when they could get their hands on it. They weren't bad kids, just full of mischief and energy. They'd smoke behind the bus stop, mess about in shops, and dare each other to knock on the door of the local weirdo. It was all part of growing up.

Carly described them all with a fondness that comes from surviving your teens together. Brett was the loud one, always trying to impress the girls but a bit of a mummy's boy underneath it all. Sarah was Carly's best mate – fiery, sharp and loyal. Dawn was quieter and more considered, but when she laughed, she laughed with her whole body. And Lewis – Lewis was the odd one out. Bit nerdy, loved horror films, the sort who would sit and draw monsters while everyone else bunked off PE. In fact, Lewis sounded a lot like me at that age!

Their friendship group had a routine. After school or at weekends, they'd gather together, usually in Gravesend, sometimes in Cobham. There was a patch of land near Carly's house where a thin trail of trees curved round into open farmland. A bit out the way, not near any main roads. It wasn't a wood exactly, just a band of dense trees that created enough shelter to feel like your own private den. That's where they'd go. Sit on fallen logs, listen to a bit of music on someone's portable tape player. Talk about nothing and everything.

'I think that's what makes what happened so frightening,' Carly told me. 'We were just being kids. And then it just … changed.'

When Carly sat down with us at the convention in 2012 and started recounting what happened that summer in 1998, it was clear she'd gone over the memories a thousand times in her head. She spoke slowly and carefully – not because she was unsure, but because every detail mattered to her. You could tell by her voice that she was someone who didn't like drama, someone who didn't embellish. She was telling us the truth, and she wanted to get it right.

'There was this one day,' she said, rubbing her palm along the side of her coffee cup. 'Danielle and I were in a charity shop, just messing about really. We weren't looking for anything.'

It had been in a neighbouring village, not far from Cobham. The kind of place that still had a small high street with a butcher, a greengrocer and a charity shop run by women who seemed to have lived there forever. It was just a little afternoon out – two sisters killing time, flicking through old clothes and leafing through battered paperbacks, laughing at 1980s dresses and ceramic figurines that looked like they'd haunt your dreams.

Carly told us she wasn't expecting to find anything. And then she saw it.

'It was just there,' she said, shaking her head as if still confused by it. 'On a shelf between some old board games. The box was a bit battered, but it was definitely what I thought it was.'

A Ouija board.

Not a fancy one. Not one of those modern paranormal investigation ones with gothic lettering and glossy finishes. This was old. Cardboard box.

Yellowed edges. A faded planchette that had clearly seen better days. And a sticker on the front: £1.50. She looked at Danielle. Danielle looked at her.

'We just thought … for a laugh,' Carly said. 'That's all it was to us. A laugh.'

I remember glancing at my dad as she said that, and we both knew what she meant. Most teenagers who mess with these things don't do it because they're trying to summon something evil. They're not practicing rituals or contacting spirits of lost loved ones. Most kids do it for a laugh. Curiosity. Something to pass the time. Something to impress their mates.

And that's exactly how it was for Carly.

'It just didn't seem like a big deal,' she said. 'We'd heard of them, obviously. Everyone had. But I don't think we really believed they worked. It was just something you messed around with.'

They paid for it, walked out of the shop with it in a plastic bag, and took it home. Carly tucked it under her bed, almost forgetting about it in the days that followed. There was no grand plan. No rituals. No strange happenings. It was just an odd little thing she'd bought for one and a half quid and pushed out of sight … until the school holidays came.

Carly said the summer break that year had been typical to start with – hot weather, late nights and endless boredom. Her group of friends – Brett, Sarah, Dawn and Lewis – were still spending most of their time together. They'd hang out at each other's houses, sometimes just sitting around in bedrooms listening to music and daring each other to call people they fancied on the phone. But one day, they made a plan that stuck out. Carly's mum and dad had, somewhat reluctantly, agreed to let the whole group sleep over at their place.

'I think they knew we'd just do it anyway,' she said, Smiling. 'So they decided it was better to have us under one roof than sneaking around.'

It was a big deal. A full night of freedom. They all brought sleeping bags and snacks. A CD player and piles of CDs. They were excited, loud, full of that teenage energy that buzzes through your body when you feel like you're about to make memories.

That afternoon, they wandered the village. Carly remembered it vividly – the way the sun was still bright but starting to dip, the way the village felt familiar and safe. They'd gone to the recreation ground for a bit, then walked the lanes around the edge of the village, daring each other to run across fields or climb over gates. They stopped in the shop to buy sweets and cheap lip balm, sat under a tree near the school and shared a cigarette, joked about people at school, swapped stories they'd heard about who fancied who and who might have kissed.

By the time they headed back to Carly's house the sky was beginning to fade into that strange shade between blue and grey that signals evening. And then they passed the church.

Cobham's village church was old. It had that slightly hunched-over look that old buildings get when they've stood still for too long. Its walls were discoloured, its windows tall and dark. The gravestones outside leaned at odd angles like they were trying to listen to what was being said. Dawn stopped and looked at it. 'That place gives me the creeps,' she had said.

The others laughed. Brett made a joke about ghosts hiding in the bell tower. But Dawn didn't smile.

'I'm serious,' she said. 'It looks haunted.'

Carly had then turned to her and said it almost without thinking. 'We should do the Ouija board there later.'

The others paused.

'What Ouija board?' Sarah had asked.

'I bought one. Couple of weeks ago. Me and Danielle found it in a charity shop. It's under my bed.'

There was silence for a second. And then Lewis said what they were all thinking.

'He said "No way." Carly told us.

But of course, they were going to. That was the thing about being that age. You don't believe in consequences – not really. Fear only goes so far. And curiosity always wins.

They got back to the house, ate, waited for Carly's parents to go to bed, then sneaked out the back door with the board tucked into a carrier bag. The village was quiet. Streetlights glowed orange. The air had that unmistakable summer-night coolness to it, the kind that makes your skin tingle when you're walking in short sleeves. When they got to the churchyard, everything felt different.

'I can't really explain it,' Carly told us, staring down at her hands. 'It just felt wrong. Straight away.'

They sat on the grass between the gravestones, choosing a spot where they wouldn't be easily seen from the road. Carly unfolded the board and placed the planchette in the centre. Sarah and Dawn giggled nervously. Brett tried to act brave, but his voice was quieter than usual. Lewis hovered at the edge of the group, not quite sitting down. Carly began the session, not really knowing what to say – just copying what she'd seen in films or heard from others.

'If there's anyone here, please make yourself known…'

They waited for around twenty minutes and nothing happened.

And then the planchette moved.

Not fast. Just a slight nudge. Carly said it felt like someone else was guiding her hand – gentle but deliberate. It began to spell out letters.

R
I
C
H
A
R
D

'Richard,' Carly said aloud. Then it spelled again:

D
E
A
T
H

Followed by:

S
O
U
L
S

That was when things shifted. That's when everything turned.

'I felt the change,' Carly said to us, eyes fixed. 'The air went heavier. We weren't just playing anymore. Something had joined us.'

Sarah flinched first. 'Ow – what the – 'She jerked away, hand flying to the back of her head. Her voice cracked with panic. 'Someone just pulled my hair.'

It wasn't a playful tug. She said it was sharp, violent – like a fist had yanked a thick clump from the root. She winced, rubbing her scalp as her eyes darted around the graves, trying to make sense of it. There was no one behind her. No branches. No wind. Nothing.

'I thought maybe Brett had done it,' she said later to Carly. 'But when I turned, his hands were right there on the board.' She had looked at Carly, her face pale. 'Something's not right.'

Brett didn't answer. His nose had started bleeding. A single drop at first, then more. He swiped it with the back of his hand and stared at the blood, confused. Carly watched as his bravado slipped away. The blood kept coming, quick now, dark and steady.

'I think I'm going to be sick,' he said, standing up and stumbling away a few steps. He looked dazed – like he wasn't really in his own body. The others stared, unsure of what to do, the weight of what was happening settling in.

Then Lewis gasped – loud and guttural. He doubled over, clutching his side. 'It stabbed me!' he shouted. 'Something just stabbed me – bloody hell – '. His hand gripped the left side of his torso as though trying to hold something in. His face had gone grey. Carly said he didn't even look like himself anymore. He sat there frozen, rocking slightly, face twisted in pain.

'Are you messing about?' Dawn asked everyone, still trying to find some control in the chaos. But Lewis didn't answer. His breath came fast and shallow. He said he could feel something under his skin, deep and sharp – like a blade had slid between his ribs, quick and without warning.

Dawn was next. She suddenly screamed and leapt to her feet, arms flailing.

'Oh my God – get them off me – get them off!' She was shaking her hands wildly, spinning on the spot, clawing at her legs. 'Spiders! They're all over me!'

But no one else could see them.

'There's nothing there,' Carly said, voice cracking. 'Dawn – there's nothing there!'

But Dawn was hysterical, slapping at her arms and legs, stamping her feet, whimpering through her cries. She had a lifelong phobia – proper, deep-rooted arachnophobia. And she was seeing them everywhere. On her knees, her arms, her neck. Her voice broke as she kept repeating, 'They're on me – they're all on me – '

'I wanted to help her,' Carly said to us. 'But I couldn't move. I was frozen. I was so scared.' She said it felt like the whole graveyard had changed shape. Like the ground under them wasn't real anymore. Like something invisible had risen up and wrapped itself around their little group and was watching them fall apart.

Panic set in fully then. The shouting, the screaming, the sudden noises must have carried, because lights started flicking on in houses across the road. Front doors opened. Someone called out, 'What's going on over there?'

Carly's heart dropped. 'If they tell my mum and dad, I'm dead,' she thought.

But even that fear didn't seem real anymore. Nothing did.

Eventually, the hysteria faded. The night air was still cold, and the churchyard had gone deathly quiet again. Whatever had stirred itself during that terrifying session had seemingly withdrawn, at least for the time being.

The group were pale and shaken as they left the churchyard, barely speaking as they made their way back through the dimly-lit lane of Cobham. The excitement that had buzzed between them earlier that day was gone. Replaced by something else. Something none of them had words for.

'I don't know how we even walked back to my house,' Carly told me, all those years later, when she and I sat down and talked through it all again in detail. 'We were just … drained. Still shaking. Everyone was in their own head.'

Back at the house, the reality of what had just happened was still sinking in. Carly thinks that on some way they were all in denial. They came in through the back door quietly, not wanting to wake Carly's parents. Brett, still shaken, ducked into the downstairs loo to clean himself up. The nosebleed had stopped during the walk home, but the blood had dried across his lip and chin in thick streaks.

'He looked grey,' Carly said. 'Properly pale. Not like someone who'd had a laugh and a shock – he looked ill.'

They all regrouped in the Carly's large bedroom, where they'd set up their sleeping bags and pillows earlier that evening. No one turned the lights off yet. No one dared. They didn't say much at first. Just sat or lay there, jittery, eyes darting to every shadow in the corners of the room. Eventually, Sarah broke the silence.

'What the hell was that?'

No one answered.

'I'm not being funny,' she said, her voice more insistent now, 'something was there. That wasn't us. That wasn't just the board.'

Carly nodded slowly. They started going over it all again – piece by piece – trying to understand, trying to make sense of it. Sarah was adamant that something had pulled her hair. She said it had felt like a full-fisted yank, not a tap or a tug.

'I thought it was Brett,' Carly had told them. 'But then I saw his face. He looked as shocked as me.'

Brett, now sitting cross-legged in his sleeping bag, looked down at the floor. He had never had a nosebleed in his life, he had told them. 'It just started. Like someone had punched me but I didn't feel anything.' were his words.

Lewis described the sensation like being jabbed deep between the ribs but that it wasn't just pain. He said it was cold. Like … like something went through him.

Dawn, still visibly shaken, kept repeating: 'There were spiders on me. They were crawling up my back. I could feel them.'

The rest of them insisted they hadn't seen any spiders.

'I know what I saw,' she had snapped. 'You didn't feel it.'

Carly told us: 'When it spelled out souls,' she said quietly, 'I asked the others if they had felt … a strange tingle. That's how I described it.'

They had all nodded in agreement.

'The board felt hot under my fingers,' she added. 'Like it was pulsing.'

Nobody slept straight away that night. They sat up for ages, speaking in low voices, flinching at every creak of the floorboards. The weight of what they'd experienced hung thick in the room, unspoken but ever present.

Eventually, they drifted off one by one. Carly said she must have fallen asleep sometime after three. She was in her bed, laid on her side, facing the others. The quiet hum of her hi-fi system on standby was the only sound. Someone was lightly snoring.

Carly woke up suddenly. Not from a dream. Not from a noise. But because the air felt wrong. She opened her eyes, expecting to see the same dim room she'd fallen asleep in.

But instead, she saw *it*. Standing at the far end of the room was a figure. Tall and black, cloaked in some kind of thick robe. It had a long cowl over its head, obscuring its face entirely. It carried what looked like an old cane in one hand, and as it moved around the sleeping bodies, it dragged its left leg behind it like it was injured. Carly lay frozen. Her heart thudded in her chest so loudly she thought it would wake the others. But they didn't move. They were fast asleep.

She watched in utter terror as the figure leaned over Brett's sleeping form … and then she heard the sound of sniffing.

It moved on to Dawn. Then Sarah. Then Lewis.

Sniffing.

Deliberately.

As if taking them in.

Its movements were slow and deliberate, almost ritualistic. Carly said she felt physically sick watching it. Her stomach twisted in fear. The room was freezing cold, though the room had been warm when they went to sleep.

She couldn't take it any longer. She screamed; A deep, throat-tearing scream that jolted the others awake in a panic. The others scrambled out of their sleeping bags, disoriented, heartbeats pounding.

The figure was gone. Just like that. As if it had never been there. But Carly's scream had already echoed through the house.

Footsteps thundered down the landing. Carly's mum and dad burst into the room, half-asleep, confused and instantly on edge.

'What's going on?! What happened?!'

The truth came out. Not all at once – but enough. The Ouija board. The churchyard. The message. The things they'd seen. Carly's vision. Her parents were furious. They told her she'd scared herself. That she'd worked herself up into a state. That these things weren't real, and that bringing something like a Ouija board into their home was irresponsible and dangerous for Danielle. Carly's mum confiscated the board immediately. Threw it in the wheelie bin the next morning.

But Carly knew what she'd seen. And her fear didn't go away.

In fact, it deepened.

The next day, one by one, the friends went home. The usual post-sleepover tiredness wasn't there. No giggling goodbyes or plans to meet up again that evening. Everyone left looking pale and quiet, barely making eye contact. Carly felt different. She couldn't explain it. It was like something had followed her home – not physically, but emotionally. Something heavy.

☽✧✝✧☾

The rest of that day went by quickly. Carly hardly spoke. Danielle was quiet too. Withdrawn. When Carly spoke to her, she barely answered. She didn't eat much at dinner. She seemed jittery – scared, almost.

That night, the house was subdued. Carly's parents noticed something was off. They asked if she was alright. She nodded. Said she was just tired.

But she wasn't tired.

She was on edge. She couldn't shake the image of that figure sniffing her friends. That dragging leg. The cane. The mist around its shoulders. She could still hear it – feel it – moving around the room in her mind.

That night, she went to bed early. She lay awake for ages, listening to every creak and groan of the house. Eventually, she fell into a shallow, restless sleep.

Somewhere after midnight, she woke up.
She needed the toilet.

She walked down the hallway to the bathroom. The air felt heavier again. Cold. The kind of cold that wraps around your skin and clings. After she had done she was washing her hands. Carly looked up into the mirror. And saw him.

A man.

Standing in the bath.

His grin was wide, too wide. His wide eyes were sharp, staring and menacing. His hair was long, down to his neck; a thick brown mop that fell down the side of his head. He had a beard – unkempt, tangled. He looked like he'd been pulled from some dark corner of the past. His stare went straight through her.

He didn't speak.

He just grinned.

Carly screamed. Not just a startled yelp or a panicked cry – but a full, guttural scream that ripped through her throat and echoed violently off the bathroom tiles. It was instinctive, primal. The sound of someone who had seen something so fundamentally wrong that the body reacted before the mind could process it.

The man in the bath had vanished the instant her scream broke the silence. One moment he was there – smiling, still, terrifying – and the next, nothing. Just the empty bathtub, the cold taps, the damp curtain half-drawn. As though he had never been there at all.

But Carly knew what she'd seen. Her chest was heaving, her breath coming in short, panicked bursts. Her legs threatened to give way beneath her, and for a few seconds she had just stood there, paralysed, eyes still fixed on the spot where he'd stood.

Then the bathroom door burst open.

Her dad was first through, wild-eyed and half-dressed. Her mum was right behind him, pulling her dressing gown tighter around herself, looking equally stunned.

'What happened?!' her dad shouted, looking from Carly to the empty room.

'There was someone—' Carly had gasped. 'In the bath – he was just there—'

Her mum and dad had looked in the bath. Nothing. Just the usual tiled wall and porcelain tub.

'There's no one here, love,' he said, trying to stay calm but clearly unsettled.

'I saw him!' Carly insisted to us now, her voice shaking with frustration as much as fear. 'He had long hair, a beard … he was smiling at me. He was just standing there, like he was waiting for me to notice him. I think I described him at the time as looking like Shakespeare. That's the only person I could liken him to.'

Her mum's face darkened at the time. 'This is because of that bloody board,' she said. 'You've worked yourself up into a state. You scared yourself and now you're seeing things.'

'I'm not seeing things,' Carly had insisted, louder this time. 'I saw him. He was real. He was just standing there, staring at me through the mirror!'

Even years later I could see how upset she was about being doubted. Carly admitted to us that she had never quite gotten over the fact that her parents hadn't believed her and that their reaction had made her feel so isolated and alone.

Her dad looked between them, clearly torn between trying to keep the peace and make sense of what had just happened. He tried to calm her down but Carly wasn't calming down. Her heart was still pounding, her hands clammy, her stomach churning. She felt like the walls were closing in.

'I didn't want to go back in there,' she whispered to me. 'I couldn't fathom why they were not listening to a word I was saying.'

But she had no choice. Her parents guided her gently back to her room, made sure the lamp was on, and left the door slightly ajar.

'Just try to sleep,' her mum said, placing a hand on her shoulder. 'You'll feel better in the morning.'

Carly nodded but didn't believe it. Not for a second. She sat on the edge of her bed for a long while, hands folded in her lap, staring at the carpet. Her eyes stung. Her throat felt raw. Her whole body was tense, like she was braced for something else to happen.

Because it didn't feel over.

Not at all. The house felt wrong now. Not just uncomfortable – inhabited. Like there was something unseen in the corners of the hallway, or behind the wardrobe door, or just beyond the reach of the bedside lamp's glow. She lay back eventually, curling on her side with the duvet pulled up to her chin. She didn't close her eyes. Couldn't. She watched the dark corners in her room, too afraid to blink, too afraid that if she let her guard down for even a second, he might come back. It was about half an hour later when she heard the soft knock at the door.

Not loud. Not panicked.

Just three gentle taps.

She didn't answer at first. Just stared at the door, heart racing again, her breath caught in her throat. The handle turned, and the door creaked open a couple of inches.

Danielle's face appeared in the gap! She looked pale. Her eyes were wide, glassy, the way someone looks after they've been crying without letting the tears fall.

'Can I sleep in here?' she whispered.

Carly nodded quickly and moved over, lifting the duvet without saying a word. Danielle climbed in beside her, shivering. Neither of them said anything for a moment. Then Danielle spoke, voice barely above a breath.

'There were people in my room.'

Carly turned slightly. 'What do you mean?'

'I could see them. Shadows. All around the bed. And I heard them. Whispering. Talking in voices I couldn't understand. Some of them were just … mumbling. Like they were trying to talk through me.'

Carly reached out and grabbed her hand.

'They were just there,' Danielle continued, trembling now. 'Not looking at me. Just standing there. Like they belonged there more than I did.'

Carly said nothing. She just held her sister's hand tighter, as if that alone might keep whatever was happening at bay.

They lay like that for hours.

Neither of them slept.

They just listened.

And waited.

Because whatever they'd let in that night – it wasn't finished with them yet.

☽✧✝✧☾

It had taken time for Carly to get to this point – years, actually. She needed to take a small break before she could continue. We decided to finish the story over a drink at a pub just around the corner from the convention. She started slowly.

'The day after,' she said, stirring her tea absently, 'we went out as a family. Into Gravesend. Just for something normal.'

Carly had barely slept. Neither had Danielle. They'd spent most of the night clinging to each other in silence, flinching at every creak and whisper of wind, haunted by what they'd seen. By what they'd felt. There'd been no resolution. No closure. Just a kind of quiet, creeping dread that hung over them like smoke.

'I remember staring out the car window the whole way there,' she said. 'Just watching trees blur past, feeling like none of it was real. Danielle was dead quiet. She wasn't sulking or tired – just … off. Mum and Dad kept giving us sideways glances, asking if we were okay. We said we were. But I don't think either of us believed it.'

They parked up in town and stopped off at a café not far from the river. Nothing fancy – just a standard high street place with plastic menus and those little white milk jugs that somehow never pour right. But even in that safe, everyday setting, things weren't right.

Carly said she could feel the tension from her and her sister. The way Danielle kept looking around, as if expecting to see something. The way she barely touched her toast.

Then they heard someone calling. It was Dawn and her mum.

'They were walking past and just happened to see us through the window,' Carly told me. 'So they came in. Mum, Dad and Dawn's mum sat at a separate table, chatting, and the three of us got our own table further down near the back.'

That's when things began to shift again.

Dawn looked tired. Pale. Not like she'd just had a late night – but like something had drained the life out of her.

'She sat down and looked straight at me,' Carly said. 'And the first thing she said was, "I've been seeing things."'

Carly looked at me across the table now and shook her head, as if still disbelieving it all, even after all these years. 'She told us that after she'd gone home, she got into bed and tried to sleep. But she couldn't stop thinking about what happened at the church. Then, sometime in the early hours, she sat up and there he was. Standing, at the foot of her bed. Just watching her.' Carly looked down, then met my eyes.

'She described him exactly the same way I'd seen him. Exactly. Male. Messy brown hair. Big, staring eyes. And that horrible grin. And she said he didn't move. Didn't speak. Just stood there like he was waiting for something.'

I didn't say anything. I knew that look. The expression on Carly's face as she told me. I've seen it in countless people who have had real encounters. There's a weight to it. Like they're trying to translate something too big for words.

'She said she couldn't move,' Carly continued. 'That it felt like her body had turned to stone. And then, just like that – he was gone.'

That was the moment Carly knew it wasn't just her. Wasn't just Danielle.

Something had followed all of them.

'I can't even remember if we finished our food,' she said. 'We just left, and as soon as I got home, I called Sarah. I got her straight away and the second I mentioned Dawn, she went quiet. I could tell by her voice she'd been crying.'

Sarah had experienced something too.

'She said she didn't know how to explain it, but … she thought she'd left her body.'

Sarah had been in bed, listening to her Walkman. She must have drifted off, but when she 'woke up', she wasn't in her room anymore. She said she was in the churchyard again. But it wasn't a dream. She was adamant about that. She said it felt too real. More real than being awake.

Sarah saw the séance happening again – like it was playing back in front of her. Carly, Brett, Lewis, Dawn – all of them were there. Even herself.

'But there was someone else,' Carly said. 'An extra person. She said he was walking in a circle around us. Just laughing. That same horrible, breathy little chuckle.'

Sarah had watched, frozen in place, unable to move or speak.

'And then he looked right at her,' Carly said. 'Stared straight into her eyes. And then he ran at her. Full pelt.'

Sarah screamed. And just like that – she was back in her bed, soaked in sweat, heart racing.

'She didn't sleep again after that,' Carly said. 'She just lay there waiting for him to come back....'

☽✧☨✧☾

After hearing that, Carly knew she had to speak to the others. She contacted Brett and Lewis, arranged to meet up somewhere local. Somewhere familiar. They didn't want to be alone.

'I think we ended up in a little shelter by the river in Gravesend,' she said. 'It wasn't private, but it was quiet. Safe. We just sat on the benches, knees up, heads down, and ... we told each other everything.'

She looked at me, her voice quieter now.

'And that's when I realised... it had touched every single one of us.'

She started with Brett. He looked awful, she said. Like he hadn't slept in days. He wasn't his usual self – no jokes, no cocky grin. Just tired. Hollow. Brett had been having dreams. The same dream, over and over. He would walk into his house and find his parents lying in the hallway. Dead. Their eyes open. Their bodies stabbed. And standing over them was him – the same man. Smiling. Holding a long, blood-soaked knife.

'But the worst part for him,' Carly said, 'was the laugh.'

Brett told them that he could hear it all the time. At school. At home. In the bath. Sometimes faint, like it was coming from another room. Sometimes loud, right by his ear. But no one else ever heard it. Brett thought he was going mad and Carly herself was concerned that he was starting to.

Then there was Lewis.

'He didn't want to talk at first,' Carly told me. 'He just sat there with his arms crossed, looking at the floor. But eventually, he opened up....'

Lewis had been reading in bed that night, book balanced on his chest. And then he felt it...

Something sat on the end of his bed.

Not lightly.

Not imagined.

He said the mattress dipped, and he could feel the shift in weight.

He lowered the book.

And there he was.

The Smiling man. Sat on the end of his bed. Just watching him.

'Lewis said he couldn't move,' Carly said. 'He tried. But his body wouldn't listen. He said it was like being buried in mud.'

He closed his eyes…

Counted to ten…

And when he opened them … the man was gone.

'But the weight was still there,' Carly added, voice shaking. 'The mattress was still dented.' She paused. 'We didn't sleep after that meeting,' she said. 'Any of us.'

I asked her what she thought it was. She stared at the wall behind me for a long time.

'I don't know,' she said. 'But it didn't just scare us. It attached itself to us. Like it fed off what we gave it. It was … intimate. Personal.'

She looked back at me.

'It knew us.'

☽✧†✧☾

I sometimes think about how differently this chapter would play out if it were a horror film. You know the type – *Insidious*, *The Conjuring*, any one of those carefully packaged, popcorn-drenched versions of the supernatural. If Carly's story had followed that path, the events that followed their terrifying encounter would have built to a crescendo: books flying off shelves, possessions, violent attacks, frantic calls to psychic mediums, and eventually, some desperate final act of spiritual warfare. Maybe someone would have died. Maybe the evil would have passed into someone else.

But that's not what happened. Because this isn't fiction. This is real life and what happened next... was nothing.

Not a single thing.

The laughter stopped. The dreams faded. The shadowy figures that had tormented them that night after the séance simply... vanished. One by one, the kids returned to their normal routines – school, homework, long evenings in the park. No more sightings. No more cold bed sheets or disembodied voices. Whatever it was that had broken through during that session in the graveyard – whatever they had invited in – left as suddenly as it had come.

Carly leaned forward when she told me this. We were sitting in the same pub as before, the sky outside turning dark in that gentle, late-autumn way.

'I think that's what made it even more unsettling,' she said. 'It didn't end with a bang. There was no explanation. It just stopped.' She looked at me across the table, her voice quiet.

'But it didn't feel over.'

That's the thing about some hauntings – some encounters. They don't come with answers. There are no credits rolling. No final battle. Just a strange, heavy presence that invades your world, leaves its mark, and then slips away like it was never there. But make no mistake – it leaves something behind.

I asked Carly what changed for her afterwards. She thought for a long moment.

'I think,' she said slowly, 'it made me feel seen. Not by other people – by something else. I've never been able to shake the feeling that I'm being watched. Even now. Not all the time. But in quiet moments. When I'm alone, when everything's still ... I get this feeling, right between my shoulder blades, like there's something just out of sight.'

She tapped her sternum with one finger.

'It's not fear. Not anymore. It's like a ... connection.'

She told me that after the events of that summer, she started noticing things. Changes in her sensitivity. An awareness that hadn't been there before.

'I'd get a feeling when I walked into someone's house. A heaviness, or sometimes a warmth. I started dreaming of people I hadn't thought about in years – only to find out they'd passed away. I'd just know things before they happened. Nothing dramatic. Just ... small things. Subtle.'

I didn't find that surprising. It's something I've heard before – many times. It is something that I've encountered all my life, and when I informed her of this, she seemed relieved. When people have a brush with something other, it can sometimes leave a kind of opening. Like a door left slightly ajar. And through that gap, things can be felt. Sensed.

That doesn't mean the person becomes psychic. But it does mean they're changed. They're no longer closed to that frequency. Something in them resonates a little more closely to the strange. For Carly, that meant years of feeling slightly off-centre. A low hum in her life that she couldn't fully tune out. I asked if she ever spoke to the others about it. If they kept in touch or shared similar feelings.

'Not really,' she said. 'We all kind of drifted apart after school. But I've spoken to Sarah a few times over the years, and once or twice we brought it up. And she said the same thing. That it never really went away. That it's like something stayed with us.'

She paused……

'I think we were marked,' she said. 'Not in a scary, dramatic way. Just … marked.'

I nodded. There's a quiet tragedy in stories like Carly's. Not because of what happened – but because of what was left behind. People want answers. They want arcs and climaxes and redemption. But hauntings like this don't always give you that. They don't give you anything. Just a feeling. A memory. A deep, slow echo that lingers for years. That night in the churchyard changed all of them.

None of them were ever quite the same.

And yet – by morning – it was like nothing had ever happened. No possessions. No broken furniture. No evidence to show the world. Just six teenagers who had glimpsed something impossible … and then had to carry on like everyone else.

Carly finished her drink. We sat in silence for a little while, letting it all settle. Then she looked at me with a wry smile.

'You still want to write it all down?'

I smiled back and tapped my head. 'I already have.'

☽✧✝✧☾

The Smiling Man: A Possible Identity

After Carly finished telling me everything that happened that summer, I found myself haunted by her story. Not just because of the intensity of the events she and her friends had endured, but because of one detail – one very specific and consistent detail that had been echoed by every single one of them: the man who plagued them.

There was something about the way they all described him – that awful, sinister, fixed smile, the wild staring eyes, that each of them had seen – whether in dreams, in their bedrooms, or from the end of a bed at night. It stuck with me. Got under my skin. It was like I could picture him myself, despite never having seen him. A face stitched together from six teenage memories.

And I couldn't let it go.

So I started researching.

Dad and I decided to visit the location ourselves on a day trip out, and we went to the village first: Cobham, Kent. A historic little village that, by all appearances, shouldn't have been the setting for something so disturbing. But like many English villages, it had its fair share of age – and age, I've learned, often hides things. Forgotten things.

Unexplained things.

We did visit the house itself but for the privacy of Carly's parents, who still reside there, we won't share its location or photograph. It was a very normal, everyday home, large and quite grand looking. Not at all what you would expect from a house that a very dark encounter had occurred. We visited the church and had a wander around. Again, it was a village church. Nothing stood out that said it was another other than normal.

After our visit, I dug through public records, historical societies, online archives. It wasn't quick. It wasn't easy. I chased dead ends, followed up on false leads. But then I stumbled across something that stopped me dead in my tracks: Cobham Village had a connection – however small – to one of Victorian England's most infamous tragic art figures.

Richard Dadd.

Even writing the name now gives me a chill.

I recognised it instantly, and I remembered why. I had read about him years earlier in connection with the so-called 'mad artists' of the nineteenth century. But something made me look again. Deeper this time. Not just at the headlines, but at the face. I opened a photograph of Dadd – one of the few known surviving images of him.

And I froze.

There he was.

The same wild, staring eyes. The same facial structure. A dishevelled mop of brown hair. A beard that looked uncannily like the one described by Carly, Danielle and the others. But it was the mouth that really got me.

That small, sinister smile.

Not a pleasant smile. Not a grin of joy or laughter. It looked like someone trying to smile – someone forcing themselves into the shape of a human expression and not quite getting it right.

My blood ran cold.

I emailed the image to Carly and Danielle without comment. Just the photo. I didn't want to lead them. Didn't want to influence what they saw. Carly called me almost immediately. Her reply: 'That's him! That's the man! Oh my God!'

That was all the confirmation I needed. And so, I went deeper... discovering there was even more to be found.

☽✧☥✧☾

The Life – and Madness – of Richard Dadd

Richard Dadd was born in 1817 in Chatham, Kent, just a short drive from Cobham. By his early twenties, he had become one of the most promising young painters of his generation. A prodigy of the Royal Academy and a favourite of the London art scene, Dadd was known for his fine detail, his dreamlike subjects, and his deep fascination with fairy folklore, mythology, and the occult.

But in 1842, during a trip through the Middle East with his patron, something changed.

Dadd began to unravel.

What started as erratic behaviour soon morphed into full-blown delusions. He became convinced that he was under the influence of the Egyptian god Osiris. He believed demons were trying to manipulate him, and that people around him were impostors or possessed. He grew paranoid. Withdrawn. Dangerous.

A year later, in 1843, Richard Dadd brutally murdered his own father with a knife, stabbing him and slashing his throat in a savage and sudden attack. This occurred in the village of Cobham.

He fled to France, where he attempted to kill a tourist with a razor before being captured and returned to England. He was committed to Bethlem Royal Hospital – known infamously as Bedlam – where he was diagnosed as criminally insane. Later, he was moved to Broadmoor Hospital, where he spent the rest of his life painting.

And it's those paintings that still unsettle people today.

They're beautiful. Meticulous. Fantastical. But look closer, and there's something … off about them. The figures are too rigid. The eyes are wrong. The smiles – too wide. His most famous work, *The Fairy Feller's Master Stroke*, took him nine years to complete. It's crammed with minute details, tiny people, strange proportions. A painting that seems to whisper as you stare. Dadd died in Broadmoor in 1886.

His body was buried.

But maybe … not his spirit.

But, if you need even more convincing that it was this tortured artist's spirit that tormented them, surely we have to be convinced by what came next. Yes, it was only after all my research was done – after I'd looked through every photo, every piece of history – that something clicked, and the full weight of it hit me. Back on that night in 1998, in the churchyard, it had spelt out the name RICHARD. At the time, the group hadn't thought too much of it. It's a common enough name. It could've been anybody.

But after everything that had been uncovered – after seeing that photo of Richard Dadd and having her scream 'That's him!' – I realised what we'd missed.

The board had told them.

It had given them his name from the very start. The smiling man who walked the circle; The one who whispered in dreams, and stood at the foot of beds.

Richard.

Richard Dadd.

It was never random. Never anonymous. They hadn't summoned a nameless spirit.

They'd summoned him. And that was when I truly understood: they hadn't opened the door to a ghost – they'd opened it to a man whose mind had shattered long ago, whose tormented legacy had bled into the spirit world … and who, for one reason or another, chose to step back through it, grinning. In Cobham, he went there to convalesce after his breakdown. He would have walked the same lanes as Carly and Danielle. Knew the same fields. It's likely they walked in his footsteps, in the very place where he brutally murdered his dad. The connection is there.

Maybe something of him remained…

☽✧✝✧☾

So what happened that night in 1998? There is no doubt in my mind that what those teenagers encountered was the spirit – the presence – of Richard Dadd. Or at least, something that wore his face.

But why? Why would the ghost of a nineteenth-century artist, however disturbed he had been in life, return to torment a group of modern-day teenagers? Why did it react so violently to the séance? Was it summoned?

Triggered? Or had it simply been waiting – a latent echo tied to the land, the village, or even to the energy of adolescence?

Was his tormented soul never put to rest? Had a lifetime of mental anguish and spiritual confusion warped him into something darker?

Had the agony of guilt and madness twisted his essence into something… demonic?

So many questions, so many unanswered mysteries … and the truth is, I don't know the solution.

The truth is, I don't have the answers.

Not to this one.

This isn't a clean-cut case. There's no nice conclusion. Just a group of teenagers who came face-to-face with something they couldn't explain – and never saw again.

But that doesn't mean it wasn't real. In fact, I'd argue it makes it more real. Because real hauntings don't follow a script … They don't give you resolution.

They just leave a mark.

And that summer in Cobham … Richard Dadd seemed to have left his……

My Haunted Life

Part Three

Beyond Serlby's Walls

The story of those teenagers and their Ouija board left me thinking about how easily we can invite things in – sometimes without realising we've done it. Curiosity, fear, grief, even boredom … all of it can open doors.

But not all hauntings begin with an invitation.

Some just begin…

And back at Serlby Rise, ours was still unfolding – quietly, steadily – like something biding its time. The house hadn't finished with us yet.

During the strange and unsettling events that would come to shape so much of my later life, there were summers that also felt like magic – sun-drenched, laughter-filled, and brimming with the boundless energy of childhood. And at the very heart of those golden days were my beloved cousins, Eleri and Nathan. We were inseparable – three peas in a pod, thick as thieves from the time we were toddlers right up into our teenage years. Ours wasn't just a cousinly bond; it was a deep friendship that pulsed with love, mischief and a shared imagination that knew no limits.

We practically grew up together, hopping between each other's houses, but our favourite playground – the place that became our own little kingdom – was Nana and Grandad's flat at the top of Wray Close. Out the back of their flat stretched a large grassy patch of land that, to us, might as well have been a whole world of possibilities. That grass saw more adventures than most children ever dream of.

Just behind the flat was a little incline, a grassy hill we treated like our personal theme park ride. We'd roll down it until we were dizzy, or grab an old wooden board that belonged to a neighbour and take turns sliding down, shrieking with laughter. It was simple, it was silly – and it was perfect.

One day, during a game of footy, one of us booted the ball a bit too hard and it sailed over the fence into the grounds of the care home that bordered the back of the land at Wray Close. We groaned in unison – until one of the elderly residents, sitting quietly in a garden chair, stood up, ambled over and kicked the ball back to us. Only, when he did, his slipper came flying over the fence with it! We were howling with laughter, absolutely beside ourselves. I got so carried away with the hilarity that I sprinted off laughing, tripped over my own feet, and went sprawling, grazing my knee on the grass! Even that didn't stop the laughter.

As we got a bit older, the games matured into sleepovers at their house. I spent long stretches of the summer holidays with them, and it was a welcome escape from Serlby Rise. Those weeks were a haven – light-hearted, safe and full of harmless adventures. One summer, we even formed our own Spy Club – a sort of kids pint-sized Neighbourhood Watch! Armed with notepads (and a lot of imagination!), we spied on what we decided must be suspicious goings-on with the neighbours. We'd report back to each other with dramatic flair, convinced we were uncovering major mysteries.

Looking back, growing up with Eleri and Nathan wasn't just fun – it was one of the happiest parts of my entire childhood. No ghosts, no shadows, no fear. Just sunshine, laughter, and two of the best friends a kid could ask for. But looking back on my childhood with my cousins, there was one experience that involved them, when I was 9, that still gives me chills to this day. Because, as it transpired, beyond the walls of Serlby Rise, other things began happening to me – things just as strange, and just as hard to explain...

A Weird Occurrence

The December nights had drawn in thick and early, smothering the sky in a shroud of deep navy that bled into black. The kind of night that seemed to swallow the world whole, casting even the familiar into something more secretive, more watchful. It was one of those cold, damp evenings – where the streetlights glistened on wet tarmac and your breath came out in ghostly puffs. Christmas was edging closer, and with it came the comforting rituals that helped carve a little light into the darkness. That particular evening in 1992, we decided to visit Nana and Grandad.

It was only a short drive from Serlby Rise to Wray Close, no more than a few minutes, but to the 9-year-old me, it always felt like a journey to happy feelings. Wray Close held warmth and safety for me.

We pulled up just outside, headlights cutting briefly across the row of buildings. I leaned forward in the car seat, craning my neck out of instinct, my eyes searching for the amber glow of my grandparents' window. That was always my ritual – before I even opened the car door, I'd peer through the window and give them a wave, even though I know they probably couldn't even see me!

But that night … something else met my gaze. My eyes locked on the corner of the living room, just beneath the standing lamp with its yellowed shade and frilly trim. Sitting there – calm, still – was my cousin Nathan.

My heart leapt. 'Eleri and Nathan are here!' I shouted, practically bouncing in my seat. 'Eleri and Nathan, they're down!'

Mum laughed at my excitement, turning to Dad with a knowing smile. 'Your Diane must be visiting then,' referring to Dad's sister.

I couldn't contain the grin spreading across my face. It was like being handed a surprise gift – an unexpected evening of games and giggles with my cousins. Any moment with them felt golden.

But then … I looked again. Nathan hadn't moved. He was still sat there in Grandad's chair, completely motionless. His frame was nestled into the cushions, his arms limp at his sides. His face – usually quite animated – was slack. Blank. Sombre. Something about his eyes…. They were staring directly out of the window. Directly at me. Not vaguely in my direction, but at me. Through me. There was no emotion, no smile. Just a steady, cold gaze. As if he was looking deep into my soul.

A chill prickled across my arms despite the car's heater still humming. For a moment, I felt frozen to the spot, as though the world outside that window had changed its rules. But I brushed the feeling off. My childhood joy was stronger than whatever instinct whispered warnings in the back of my mind. Maybe he'd been told off or something. Maybe I was just seeing things through the window.

I was already out the door, running up the path, Mum shouting at me to not rush. I flung open the flat's front door and bounded down the long, narrow passage that smelt faintly of tobacco and cheap air freshener. The hallway opened into the living room and I burst in, grinning ear to ear – ready to greet my cousins.

But they weren't there. No Eleri. No Nathan. No Auntie Diane. Just Nana, sat in her usual spot at the end of the settee, cigarette perched between her fingers, a curl of smoke drifting lazily upward. Grandad was in the kitchen, his back turned as he filled the kettle, his silhouette framed by the frosted glass of the door.

I stopped dead, the breath catching in my throat. My smile faltered.

'Where are they?' I asked, frowning.

Nana looked up. 'Who?'

'Eleri and Nathan!' I said, scanning the room.

Grandad came through, wiping his hands on a tea towel. 'Eleri and Nathan aren't here,' he said with a puzzled expression, looking over at Nana as if checking whether she'd heard it too.

I blinked. 'But … I just saw Nathan. In your chair!'

They both exchanged a glance. Not a joking glance – no smirk, no teasing. Just confusion. My heart began to race.

'You must've been seeing things, ya daft bleeder,' Grandad said jokingly.

'No!' I insisted. 'It was Nathan. He was sitting there.' I pointed to Grandad's chair. 'He was looking right at me. Where are they hiding?' I laughed, convinced they were having me on.

My insistence must have been more than just the usual childish stubbornness, because neither of them laughed. They didn't try to play it off. Still convinced it was a trick – or that they were hiding in the flat somewhere – I went through every room. The hallway, the bedrooms, even the tiny bathroom. I checked behind doors, in the airing cupboard, behind the settee.

Nothing.

No cousins. No sign of anyone else in the flat. It took nearly twenty minutes before I finally gave up and realised it wasn't all a prank. My brain was still trying to make it make sense. Had they just left? No. I would have seen them. No extra coats or shoes near the door. The silence of the flat confirmed it – there had been no guests that evening.

I couldn't explain it then. I still can't. Even now, over three decades later, the memory remains razor-sharp – etched into my mind with all the clarity of something profoundly real. I saw Nathan. I know I did. I saw the expression on his face. I saw the way he looked at me – not through me like a ghostly figure, but into me, like someone desperately trying to say something without speaking. But if that wasn't really him … then what was it?

I learnt years later after becoming a paranormal investigator that in the world of the paranormal, we talk of things like 'mimic spirits': Beings that take on familiar forms – faces of those we know, love, or trust. They show themselves at the edges of ordinary life, like echoes warped through some unseen veil. Sometimes they imitate the living. Sometimes they imitate the dead.

That night in Wray Close was never spoken of again, not really. My mum and dad swore that they didn't see anyone and insisted that I probably just saw Grandad, despite him being on the kitchen at the time. It became one more secret stored away in the attic of my childhood mind. A haunting of a different kind – not a poltergeist, not a whispering voice or cold spot – but something else. Something that wore my cousin's face like a mask.

Was it just my imagination? A trick of the light, or an overexcited boy seeing what he wanted to see?

Maybe.

But I know what I saw. And that makes it just another entry in the growing catalogue of strange, unsettling experiences that coloured my youth.

Another mystery.

Another chapter in the ever-expanding, eerie tale of my life with the unexplained.

The Phantom Motorcyclist

It was the late summer of 1993, and I had just returned to school after the six-week holiday. Despite the ongoing strange disturbances at our house on Serlby Rise, that summer stands out in my memory as one of the happiest of my childhood. I was 10 years old, and life was good – full of family, friends and the kind of carefree adventure that only a child in the early '90s could truly understand.

That summer gave me something else too – something that, in a strange way, would later link back to the supernatural world with which I was slowly becoming familiar. But before I get to that eerie encounter, it's important to understand the warmth and normality that surrounded it. Because, as I've found time and again, the most chilling events often emerge from the most ordinary days.

That summer brought with it one particularly earth-shaking experience – the film *Jurassic Park*. It's no exaggeration to say that the release of Spielberg's blockbuster changed my childhood. I was already a dinosaur obsessive (and I do mean *obsessive*) by that point. Films like *The Land That Time Forgot* and *One Million Years B.C.* had already set my imagination ablaze, but *Jurassic Park* was in a league of its own.

Dad and I went to see it at the cinema the moment it came out, and we were both absolutely blown away. The special effects were jaw-dropping – realistic to the point of disbelief. Even now, in the age of over-polished CGI (hope you're listening, 2025 effects teams), the original animatronics and practical magic of Jurassic Park still hold their ground. For a dinosaur-loving 10-year-old, it was pure wonder.

Dad had always encouraged my interests. I remembered how, two years earlier, he'd taken me to the Birmingham Museum and Art Gallery for a dinosaur exhibition. It was one of the best days of my young life. After we'd marvelled at the skeletons and models, he took me to the gift shop and bought me a T-Rex model. That toy sat proudly on my bedroom shelf for years, a reminder not just of the exhibition, but of the way Dad always supported my curious, adventurous mind.

Later that summer, we went as a family to see *Jurassic Park* again, this time at the old Savoy Cinema. It was a real occasion – Mum, Dad, me, Auntie Diane, Eleri, Nathan and my grandparents, Joan and Frank all came along. I'd already seen the film twice, but I couldn't wait to watch it again and to see the awe on my cousins' faces as the dinosaurs stomped and roared across the big screen. That day is etched in my memory as one of sheer joy and excitement.

It wasn't just films that made that summer special. Every Friday evening, Dad and I had a tradition. We'd drive out to one of the local nature spots – 'the ponds' as Dad called them. Usually it was either the Bottle Pond or the Finger Ponds at Holme Pierrepont. We'd go for long walks, taking in the quiet beauty of the water and woods, Dad enjoying the peace, me letting my imagination run wild with adventure stories in my head. But one Friday evening towards the end of that summer, we took a different route. Dad wanted to explore a new fishing spot he'd heard about. It wasn't part of our usual routine, but he'd gotten a tip and wanted to check it out. My Grandad Don decided to come along too, which was always a bonus. Grandad Don was a big character – funny, sharp, and always good company. The three of us set off toward the village of Shelford, not really knowing what we'd find.

Even now, I couldn't tell you exactly where we ended up. It was somewhere out in the countryside near Shelford, that much I'm sure of. We drove down a narrow country road and eventually came to a large concrete structure, man-made, that seemed to be holding back a sizable body of water. It was peaceful, if a little eerie – one of those places that feels a bit too quiet. We wandered around for a while, taking in the scene, Dad and Grandad pointing out potential fishing spots. But eventually the sky darkened and the temperature dropped. The sun had nearly set, and it was time to head home.

We got back in the car, and Dad reversed out onto the narrow, rural road. The place was entirely unlit, so he switched on the headlights – and that's when we saw him.

A motorcyclist.

He appeared just ahead of us, as if from nowhere. None of us had seen him coming, nor had we heard the familiar growl of an approaching engine. Yet there he was – just a few metres in front, already riding ahead of our car.

Dad was instantly animated. He'd always loved motorbikes, having owned several in his younger days, and seeing one out on a country road brought back a bit of his old excitement. We watched as the motorbike weaved expertly through the bends and curves of the road. His headlight cut through the darkness, the red glow of his tail light blinking rhythmically as he moved.

But there was something … off. There was no fog on the road, yet the motorcyclist seemed to be shrouded in a faint haze, like heat rising from tarmac. And no matter how fast we drove, the distance between us never changed. He remained exactly the same number of metres ahead – never pulling further away, never slowing down. It was as if he was frozen in place yet still moving, like some kind of visual illusion.

Then came a straight stretch of road, lined on both sides by thick woodland.

And just like that – he was gone. No brake lights. No turn-off. No crash. Just gone. One moment he was there, the next he'd vanished completely.

'Where'd he sodding go?!' Grandad Don blurted, twisting in his seat to look behind us.

'I've no idea, Don,' Dad said, frowning. 'That was bloody weird.'

I remember leaning forward from the back seat. 'Maybe he crashed?' I offered, heart thudding.

Dad nodded. 'Yeah … we need to check.' He slowed the car and carefully turned it around on the narrow road, then drove back along the route we'd just taken. We all scanned the roadside, expecting to see a mangled bike, maybe the rider in a ditch or lying on the verge.

But there was nothing.

No bike. No man. No marks on the road. No way out, either – not a single driveway, turnoff or gap in the trees. It was as if the motorcyclist had been absorbed into the night. We searched for a good few minutes, baffled. But eventually we had to accept the impossible: he had simply vanished.

That drive home was a quiet one. Each of us lost in our own thoughts, trying to make sense of what we'd seen. There had been no doubt about it – we had all witnessed the same thing. A motorcyclist, real and moving

… until he wasn't. Later, Dad mentioned the incident to a workmate, describing where we'd been and what we'd seen. His friend looked visibly uncomfortable, then told him something that made our blood run cold, even years later. Years earlier, there had been a fatal motorbike accident on that very stretch of road. A young man had died in the crash … had we seen a ghost? A residual imprint of that tragic moment in time? It's possible. Some paranormal researchers believe in what's known as the Stone Tape Theory – the idea that certain emotional or traumatic events leave a kind of 'recording' on the physical environment, which can then be replayed under the right conditions. Unlike intelligent hauntings, these residual hauntings don't interact with the living. They're simply echoes – moments caught in a loop, destined to replay again and again. This theory would explain the mechanical perfection of the motorcyclist's movements. He didn't seem aware of us. He didn't respond. He simply … replayed. A haunting on tape. That wouldn't be the last time we experienced something like it….

But in 1993, as a 10-year-old boy still riding the high of *Jurassic Park* and summer adventures, it was another true encounter with a ghost outside of our haunted house. And it stayed with me – an indelible moment, another chilling reminder that the strange and supernatural was never far away from us.

Jen's Story

Big Brother

I first heard from Jen in early 2012. It was one of those quiet evenings when I'd been replying to the usual stream of messages on Facebook – people asking about haunted locations, others sharing orb photos they wanted me to analyse, the occasional enthusiastic debate about a ghost show or a YouTube video. But Jen's message was different. There was a weight to it, even in those first few lines. She didn't waste time with small talk. She just told me, plainly and honestly, that something had been happening with her son – something she couldn't explain, and something she thought I might understand.

Jen lived just outside of Oxford, in a little semi-detached house on a quiet cul-de-sac near Abingdon. She told me she wasn't someone who normally reached out to people like me – she wasn't in any paranormal groups, hadn't ever been on a ghost tour, and wasn't into horror films or Ouija boards. But something had changed. Something she couldn't shake off. And it had to do with her boy, Henry.

I asked if she'd be willing to talk more. She agreed almost immediately and said she'd prefer to write things down first. A few days later, she sent me a long, heartfelt message – the kind that reads more like a diary entry than a report. It was raw, emotional, and painfully honest. And that's how I first learned about Thomas.

Jen had been 28 when she got pregnant for the first time. She'd been married to Dan, her childhood sweetheart, for almost three years. They'd bought the house together in 2000, just a little two-bedroom place with a small garden and a converted loft. It was the kind of home you build dreams in – nothing fancy, but full of warmth, photographs on the walls, mugs that didn't match, and a smell of lavender that seemed to live in the carpets. They'd been trying for a baby since their honeymoon. When it finally happened, they were over the moon.

'We were careful,' she told me. 'We did everything right. I took the vitamins, we went to every appointment, we decorated the nursery in pale green before we even knew if it was a boy or girl. It was one of the happiest times of my life. I used to lie on the sofa in the afternoons and just listen to my heartbeat and think: "my baby's in there".'

She found out she was having a boy at the twenty-week scan. They named him Thomas before he was even born. 'We both liked names that felt timeless. Strong. Thomas felt right from the beginning.'

But as is sometimes the cruel way of things, happiness can be fragile.

At thirty-eight weeks, just days before her due date, Jen went in for a routine check-up. She'd noticed that Thomas had been unusually still that morning – no kicks, no rolls, just silence. The midwife's smile faded as she moved the Doppler across Jen's stomach again and again. She called for another nurse. Then a doctor. Jen said she knew. Right then and there. Before anyone said a word.

'They couldn't find a heartbeat,' she wrote. 'I lay there while they scanned me, and I just … knew. My body felt empty even though he was still there. I remember Dan holding my hand so tightly it hurt. And then the doctor said the words.'

Quietly.

Carefully.

But the words still tore through her.

Thomas was stillborn on a grey Tuesday afternoon in October 2001. They held him. Named him. Dressed him in a tiny blue sleepsuit that Jen's mother had bought only a couple weeks earlier. They took photographs – ones that Jen kept in a wooden box in the wardrobe, sealed with a ribbon. They buried him in a small plot under an old sycamore tree at the local cemetery. A single white stone marks the grave, engraved with his name and the words 'Loved before we met.'

Jen told me she barely remembered the weeks that followed. She said her body felt like it had betrayed her. Her arms ached with emptiness. The house felt like a cruel joke – the cot untouched, the mobile spinning gently above it. The green-painted nursery door remained shut for months.

Dan grieved in his own way. He was quiet, stoic, methodical. He went back to work after two weeks. Jen stayed off for much longer. Their love didn't disappear, but it changed – deepened in some ways, cracked in others. 'It's not something you ever really get over,' she told me. 'It's something you carry. You just learn how to walk with it.'

When she found out she was pregnant again, nearly two years later, it was a moment of fear and hope twisted together. She was cautious this time. Protective. Overprotective. She didn't tell many people until the later months. But everything was healthy. The scans were good. The baby was active. And on a bright spring morning in 2003, Henry was born – loud, pink and perfect. Jen said it was the happiest day of her life – and also the most frightening. She couldn't help but watch him constantly, checking he was breathing, terrified something might still go wrong. But Henry grew strong as he grew older. He had his father's calmness and his mother's inquisitive eyes. He laughed easily, loved bedtime stories, and would sit for hours building Lego towers on the living room rug.

They never spoke much about Thomas in front of Henry. Jen told me she wanted to wait until he was older. There was a framed photo of Thomas' hand and footprints in the upstairs hallway, and the little gravestone they visited each October, but nothing more. No ghost stories. No spooky tales. Just life, moving on, as best it could.

But in 2010, when Henry turned 7, things began to change……

Jen first noticed something was different during the summer holidays of 2010. Henry had turned 7 in April, and they'd spent most of that summer enjoying the long, warm days – trips to the park, late bedtimes, sticky fingers from melting lollies. It had been one of those idyllic stretches where the world feels almost suspended in light. But then came August – and something began to shift.

It started, as these things often do, with a single remark. One night, as Jen tucked Henry into bed, he said, 'Mum, who's the boy that sits on the end of my bed?'

Jen told me she smiled at first. She assumed he meant a dream, or perhaps he was talking about a friend from school or a character from a film. But when she asked who he meant, Henry's answer stopped her in her tracks.

'He comes after you say goodnight,' Henry said simply. 'He sits on my bed and he smiles. He doesn't talk, but I think he's nice.'

That night, Jen sat on the landing long after Henry had gone to sleep, listening. Watching the gap under the door. She told herself it was nothing – just a child's imagination running wild. But the words stuck with her. 'The boy that sits on my bed.'

A few nights later, Henry brought it up again – this time unprompted, over breakfast.

'He was back last night,' he said, in between bites of cereal. 'He was wearing pyjamas. They had little moons on them.'

Jen froze. She told me she hadn't seen those pyjamas in over seven years. They hadn't been pyjamas but a pair of baby sleepsuits. They'd belonged to Thomas – a gift from her sister, never worn, folded neatly in a drawer that had since been packed away in a box in the loft. They had had a distinctive pattern, a deep blue with little crescent moons that smiled. There had been no way Henry would have known about them. No photos. No stories. It wasn't just the detail that unsettled her – it was the calmness in Henry's voice. He wasn't scared. He was just describing something that, to him, seemed ordinary.

Over the following weeks, the mentions of 'the boy' became more frequent.

'He stands near the door now,' Henry told her one night. 'He doesn't always sit. Sometimes he looks at the bookshelf.'

'He watches when I do my drawings.'

'He likes the colour blue.'

Each time, Jen would press gently for more. Never wanting to scare Henry, but desperate to understand. One day, she asked, 'Does he tell you his name?'

Henry shrugged. 'No. But I know it anyway. It's Thomas.'

Jen said the moment felt like her whole body turning inside out. She felt cold and hot all at once, like every nerve had been touched. She didn't know what to say. So she didn't say anything. I asked her later if she'd ever told

Henry about Thomas before then. She was adamant she hadn't. 'We were waiting. He was too young. We didn't want to confuse him. We thought maybe when he was 12, we'd sit him down. But not yet. Never before this.'

She and Dan decided not to react too strongly. They agreed to quietly monitor things – see if it was just a phase, or a dream, or something from a book he'd read. But the references continued. And they were always so specific. So eerily accurate.

One evening, Henry came downstairs with a drawing. It was a pencil sketch of two boys standing in a bedroom. One had blue clothing. The other was wearing red, with a faint smile. Above them, Henry had written: Me & Tomas.

Jen still has that drawing.

Around this time, she also began to notice changes in the house – subtle things, but strange nonetheless. A ball that had been left in the garden would turn up in the hallway. Henry's nightlight – one of those plug-in ones shaped like a rocket – would flicker for no reason. Once, she found the bedroom door wide open in the morning, even though she remembered shutting it before she went to bed. Henry never seemed frightened. In fact, he seemed calmer than ever. 'He said the boy made him feel safe,' Jen told me. 'He said it felt like he had someone watching over him.'

There was one night, though, that stayed with her. It was late – maybe close to midnight – and Jen had just got into bed when she heard a sound from Henry's room. Not a thump, not a voice, but music. A lullaby, soft and tinkling, coming from the other side of the wall. She got up quickly and opened his door – but the room was still. Henry was fast asleep. The light from the hallway stretched across the carpet and fell on something that hadn't been there before.

It was a small music box.

One she hadn't seen since Thomas' things had been packed away. She found it originally in a charity shop when she was expecting – an old-fashioned tin box that played Brahms' Lullaby. She could have sworn it had been stored in the loft, inside the box marked T. But now it was here, on Henry's bedside table, ticking faintly in the stillness.

Jen said she didn't sleep at all that night.

Still, nothing ever felt menacing. And that's what made it all the more confusing. This wasn't a haunting in the traditional sense. There were no bangs in the night, no sinister shadows, no cold spots or nausea. There was just … presence. Familiarity. A connection. Henry never seemed disturbed by it. And as the months passed, the visits became less frequent. Jen told me it was like someone slowly stepping away. Like Thomas was letting go.

The last time Henry mentioned seeing him was on the morning of his eighth birthday.

'He came last night,' he said over his cereal. 'He didn't come in the room, though. He just stood at the door and smiled. I think he was saying goodbye…'

Jen's story stayed with me long after I'd finished reading it. Some messages just do that – they settle into you like sediment at the bottom of a pond, subtle but heavy. It wasn't just the detail that struck me, or even the sheer emotional gravity of her experience. It was the tone. The way she wrote about Thomas. The way she spoke about Henry. There was no hysteria, no dramatic claims or sweeping statements. Just quiet grief, deep love, and a mother trying to make sense of something that didn't quite belong to the world we know.

After I'd read her message – and read it again – I wrote back, thanking her. I told her that I believed her. Because I did.

She replied within the hour. 'I'm so relieved to have told someone,' she wrote. 'I've only ever spoken about this with Dan. Not even my mum knows all of it. I still don't know what it means. But sometimes, I wonder if Thomas never really left. What if he's still here, in some way?'

That question – what if he's still here? – became the thread I began pulling at.

Over the years, I've heard a lot of stories from people who have lost someone and later felt their presence in some way. Sometimes it's a voice, a smell, or a dream that's too vivid to dismiss. Other times it's more physical – doors opening on their own, radios switching on, clocks stopping at the time of death. But this – this was different. This wasn't a grieving adult sensing a lost loved one. This was a child who had never met his brother – a child who knew things he couldn't have known.

I knew I had to take a closer look.

My first step was to revisit Jen's timeline. I asked her for permission to speak with her directly – not just through messages, but on a call. She agreed, a little nervously, and we arranged to talk one Saturday morning. I remember the call vividly. She had a gentle voice, soft-spoken, but clear. And she was honest – almost painfully so. No embellishment, no drama. Just a mother reliving the hardest moments of her life, and trying to understand the ones that came after.

I asked her about Thomas' things – where they'd been stored, how accessible they were. She told me the boxes had been sealed and placed in the attic the week after the funeral. She hadn't opened them since.

I asked her if anyone else could have told Henry about Thomas – an overheard conversation, maybe a slip from a relative. She was firm on that. 'No one ever mentioned him by name. And the pyjamas? The music box? He couldn't have known.'

She offered to send me photos – of the music box, the sketch Henry drew, even the photo of the handprint framed in the hallway. I studied each one closely. The sketch in particular was striking – not because of the quality (it was the kind of drawing any 7-year-old might produce), but because of the sureness in it. There was no hesitance in the lines. It showed two boys, standing together, both smiling. One clearly Henry. The other, with different clothes, was labelled 'Tomas'.

There was something about that image that stayed with me.

I also began doing some reading into sibling connections – not just emotional or psychological ones, but stories of siblings separated at birth, children who remembered past lives, siblings who claimed to know details they'd never been told. There are hundreds, if not thousands, of cases recorded over the years. Most are dismissed. Some are too bizarre to ignore.

What stood out most were the stories involving stillbirth. They're rarer, but they exist. I found reports – scattered across blogs, old spiritualist journals, and obscure books – of children speaking to, or seeing, siblings who had never drawn breath. Not imaginary friends, not dream figures, but distinct presences. And they nearly always shared one thing in common: the encounters were peaceful.

Not scary. Not threatening. But connected.

I even came across a few spiritual theories – some from mediums, others from bereavement counsellors – that suggested children are more sensitive to these presences because they haven't yet been conditioned to ignore them. They don't question the impossible. They simply accept it.

Henry hadn't panicked when he saw Thomas. He hadn't run screaming from his room. Instead, he'd smiled, spoken softly, drawn pictures. As far as he was concerned, his older brother was just someone who visited sometimes.

I asked Jen if she'd ever noticed a change in Henry after the visits stopped. She paused before answering. 'Yes,' she said quietly. 'He seemed more settled. More grown up. I think … I think Thomas let him go.'

That phrase haunted me: let him go. Because it suggested something more than memory or imagination. It hinted at intent. Awareness. Love.

Jen and I stayed in touch for several months after that. We spoke a few more times on the phone, and she occasionally sent me updates – little things Henry would say, or moments when she felt Thomas near. One message simply said: 'Sometimes, at night, I stand at the landing and look into his room. And I whisper thank you.'

I've revisited this case more than once since then. Not to debunk it – I believe Jen, completely – but to better understand it. To try and make sense of a phenomenon that defies logic, yet fits perfectly within the raw space of grief and love. Not every ghost story is a horror story. Not every haunting involves fear. Sometimes, what lingers isn't anger or sadness, but something gentler – something protective. Something that doesn't want to leave, not because it's trapped, but because it cares.

Thomas didn't get to take his first breath. But somehow, years later, he still managed to reach out – to connect with the little brother he never met. To sit beside him. To smile. To say goodbye. And in that quiet, flickering way only the spirit world seems to understand, he reminded his mother and father that love never truly dies…

Some stories in this book will unsettle you. Some may make the hairs on the back of your neck stand up. Others might leave you questioning the very nature of the world around us. But this story – Jen's story – does something different.

It stays with you in the quiet moments.

Not because of fear, or shock, or some dramatic, ghostly revelation – but because of its quiet humanity. It's truth. It's ache. It reminds us that the paranormal isn't always about things that go bump in the night. Sometimes, it's about love that refuses to be extinguished – even by death.

I've thought about Thomas and Henry a lot since first hearing their story. I think about them when I see siblings holding hands. When I walk past a child's grave in a cemetery and see a teddy bear resting against the headstone. When I hear a music box playing a lullaby and feel a shiver run down my spine for no reason I can explain. There is something undeniably sacred about the bond between siblings. Even ones who never met in life.

In this case, we're not talking about an angry spirit, or an unfinished message, or a haunted object. We're talking about a boy who died before he could live – and yet found a way, years later, to be part of the life he should have known. A presence that appeared not to frighten, but to comfort. To watch over.

I've often been asked whether I believe children are more in tune with the spirit world than adults. My answer is always yes – not because they're special, but because they haven't yet learned to doubt what they see. They haven't been taught what's 'impossible'. They trust their instincts. They speak plainly. And sometimes, they describe things they couldn't possibly know.

Henry never once seemed afraid of the boy in his room. In fact, he welcomed him. And when the visits ended, he didn't mourn – he accepted it. As if somewhere inside him, he knew the purpose had been served. That whatever that connection was – spirit, memory, energy, love – it had done what it needed to do. I felt a truth that lived in Jen's voice. A sincerity in Henry's words. A sense of peace, not fear. And for me, that is often more compelling than cold evidence. In the world of paranormal research, we're often so focused on the dramatic that we overlook the quiet, powerful experiences – the ones that don't scream, but whisper. The ones that don't scare us, but heal us. I believe that Thomas came back for one reason only: to let Henry know he was never alone, and in doing so he gave grieving parents something she never thought she'd have – one last connection. One moment of grace. A silent promise, made in the stillness of a child's bedroom: I was here. I saw him. I loved him.

There is no greater mystery. And perhaps, no greater comfort.

Vic & Wendy's Story

What's Wrong with Aunt Lynne?

Throughout history, there have been cases that defy medical, psychological and scientific understanding – cases that seem to brush up against something far darker than anything most of us are prepared to believe.

Take George Lukins, for example – the so-called 'Yatton demoniac,' a tailor from Somerset in the late 1700s who was said to speak in strange voices, exhibit unnatural strength, and sing hymns backwards in Latin. Seven clergymen performed an exorcism on him, claiming they cast out no fewer than seven demons from his body. It caused a media frenzy at the time.

Then there is Anneliese Michel – a young woman from 1970s' Germany whose tragic decline is one of the most harrowing and controversial exorcism cases on record. Diagnosed with epilepsy and psychosis, she was nevertheless, subjected to dozens of intense exorcisms over several months. Her behaviour grew increasingly disturbing: violent, contorted, ranting in multiple languages she'd never studied. She died in 1976, malnourished and broken. The case became infamous, raising endless debates about belief, religion and accountability.

Cases like these always divide opinion. Sceptics point to mental illness, misdiagnosis, or spiritual hysteria. Believers argue that something darker – something non-human – had taken root.

And then there are the stories that don't make the headlines. The quiet ones. The ones shared only in whispers. Stories told not to shock, but because the people involved need someone to believe them. To help make sense of what they saw. In 2009, I came across one of those stories myself. It's a case I've never forgotten. One that continues to disturb me to this day. Because whatever happened to Aunt Lynne, it wasn't just heartbreak. It wasn't just loneliness or grief. It was something else.

And once it got in – it wasn't leaving…

I met Vic and Wendy on a rainy October night in 2009, during an organised ghost hunt at Alford Manor in Lincolnshire. My dad and I had booked onto the event after hearing about the manor's reputation for unexplained activity, and as was often the case with these public investigations, the organisers paired guests into small groups for vigils and walkthroughs. That's how we were introduced to Vic and Wendy – a brother and sister from Bridlington, who we instantly got on with. Vic was in his early fifties, broad-shouldered with heavy eyebrows and a thoughtful look behind the eyes. His sister Wendy stood beside him, quieter, thinner, but with a similar weight in her expression – like she was carrying something that had been with her for a very long time. They were friendly, sharp-witted and carried themselves with that down-to-earth warmth you find in people who've seen difficult things and come out stronger. We spent most of the night in their company – conducting vigils, exploring the manor's creaking stairwells and low-lit rooms, sharing whispers in the dark when a tap or knock caught our attention.

But it was during one of the tea breaks – those moments in the base room over polystyrene cups of instant coffee and naff tea – that they told us something that made the hairs on my arms stand on end. Vic mentioned it first. Casually, almost too casually. He said that they hadn't always been interested in ghost hunts or the paranormal – that there had been a very specific reason they'd started attending these kinds of events.

Wendy nodded, then said, 'It was our aunt. Something happened to her in the seventies. Something we've never been able to forget.'

They didn't go into great detail that night – just gave us a rough outline. Enough to send a chill down my spine. They told us that their Aunt Lynne had changed after delving into the occult. That something had taken her over. That the family had tried to help, even brought in a vicar. And that it had ended in such a way that no one ever really talked about it. That experience, they said, is what led them to start seeking answers. Trying to understand the afterlife. Trying to understand what happened to her.

We exchanged details at the end of the night and kept in touch. They were the kind of people who didn't exaggerate. They weren't chasing attention. They had seen something that haunted them, and they were quietly, methodically, still trying to make sense of it.

A year later, in 2010, Vic and Wendy travelled to Nottingham for another organised ghost hunt – this time at the Galleries of Justice. My dad and I weren't attending that night, but we met up with them afterwards. They were ready to talk properly – really talk – and we sat with them for nearly four hours, recording the full story on a Dictaphone.

What they told us that day was truly unnerving. It's a story of grief. Of loneliness. Of something unnatural slipping through the cracks in a person's life. And it all began in a quiet street in Bridlington in 1974…

It all began with a woman named Lynne.

Their mother's sister. Their aunt.

Aunt Lynne had lived three doors down from them in Bridlington, on the same quiet middle-class street. Everyone knew everyone. It was a respectable road, with privet hedges, regular milk deliveries and well-kept gardens. The kind of place where normal middle-class life happened.

In 1974, Vic was 17 and Wendy was 15. They lived at home with their parents, went to school, worked part-time jobs, and occasionally helped their aunt out with little things – taking in shopping, walking her dog, changing the channel on her old TV when the dial got stuck.

'She wasn't mad or strange or anything like that,' Vic told me. 'Not at first.'

Lynne had always been a little different, sure – she was bookish, introverted, a bit eccentric in her tastes. But she was kind. Generous. A quiet presence in the family. She'd always had a nervous smile, the sort that didn't quite reach the eyes, but she was dependable. She'd been married once, briefly, to a man named Anthony, but it hadn't lasted.

'They split up after he had left her for a woman from his office,' Wendy said. 'Lynne was never the same after that.'

The divorce had shattered her. She withdrew, emotionally and physically. Stopped going out. Stopped caring about her appearance. Started drinking a bit more. It wasn't a dramatic spiral – just a slow, sad quietening. The sort of grief that seeps in through the cracks and settles into the wallpaper.

She stopped coming round for Sunday dinner. Her dog, a Yorkshire terrier named Shandy, died suddenly and she didn't replace him. Vic told me she'd sit in the garden sometimes, long after dark, just staring out into the night.

'She looked smaller,' he said. 'Like the light inside her was going out.'

There's a certain type of depression that doesn't make a sound. It doesn't cry, doesn't scream, doesn't even sob quietly into the pillow at night. It just sits there – heavy and invisible – wearing the face of someone who says they're 'fine'. That was the grief that swallowed Aunt Lynne whole. After Anthony left her in 1973, something inside her broke – not loudly, not dramatically, but with the quiet finality of a door shutting in a long, empty corridor. Vic and Wendy both remembered how their mum had rushed over the day Lynne found the letter: just a few scribbled lines left on the kitchen table. 'I can't do this anymore. I've met someone. Don't try to contact me.'

Anthony had packed and gone while Lynne was out shopping. From that moment on, she changed. Not all at once – but like something slowly seeping into her bones. She stopped seeing family, stopped answering the phone. Her garden, once neat and proud, turned ragged. She left the milk out on the step until it curdled. She wore the same housecoat for days at a time. Her eyes – once full of the dry, bookish humour she'd always had – turned flat.

'I think she lost herself,' Wendy said quietly. 'Like there was no meaning to anything anymore. She used to say, 'I must have done something wrong. There must be a reason.'

And that was the crack that let something darker in. Lynne needed an explanation. Some kind of cosmic order to explain why her husband had cheated and left. And when the usual comforts failed – the sympathetic family visits, the vicar's dry reassurances, the watered-down advice from well-meaning neighbours – she went looking elsewhere.

And she found it.

No one ever figured out where the two women came from. They just started appearing one day, on Lynne's doorstep, dressed in long dark coats even in summer, with strange jewellery and too-wide smiles. The family never knew their names. Lynne never volunteered them. She referred to them vaguely as 'the sisters', but Vic, Wendy and their mother were convinced they weren't related. What they were – who they were – remains a mystery.

'She wouldn't tell us where she met them,' Vic told me. 'But she started calling them her guides.'

At first, she seemed to be improving. At least on the surface. She got dressed again. Put on lipstick. Started talking about 'energy' and 'higher understanding'. But it wasn't long before the ideas hardened into something else.

'She told Mum that pain was a gift,' Wendy said. 'That suffering was the way to "wake up". It was like she was parroting someone else's words. It didn't sound like her at all.'

The books arrived next. Heavy, leatherbound things, smelling of dust and mildew. Their mother saw one left open on the coffee table – it had illustrations in it. Dark ones. Circles with slashes through them. Symbols like inverted stars and twisted faces with no eyes. There was no title on the cover.

Next came the rituals.

'She started staying up late,' Vic said. 'Mum would phone her and there would be no answer. She would walk past the house and see candlelight flickering upstairs at one or two in the morning. It felt wrong.'

Wendy recalled the way the living room changed. The curtains were always drawn. There was a blanket nailed over the mirror. The television unplugged. The lights low. And in the centre of the room, always the same three chairs – arranged in a triangle, facing each other.

They didn't know exactly what Lynne and the two women were doing – but it wasn't harmless.

'She stopped being herself,' Wendy said. 'She'd snap at us for nothing. One time I asked her if she wanted help with her shopping, and she just glared at me and said, "You wouldn't understand. Satan understands me." Then she laughed.'

The laughter didn't sound like Lynne.

Vic described it as hollow, humourless, stretched too wide and too long. And it got worse with time. She began swearing at their mother on the phone. Accused her sister of 'feeding poison into her dreams'. She told Wendy that she had a 'dead child's soul stuck in her hair', and refused to let her in the house for weeks.

'She told me I smelled like sanctity,' Wendy said. 'Like that was a bad thing.'

The final turning point came when she admitted what they'd all feared: she was trying to curse her ex-husband.

'She said she'd found a way to "reach him",' Vic told me. 'Said he'd pay for what he did.'

Lynne explained – in cold, practical terms – that Anthony had bound her heart through betrayal, and that pain like hers could be weaponised. The rituals, she said, weren't just to understand – they were to act. She believed that through ritual, focus and the help of the 'other side', she could inflict suffering on the man who had humiliated and discarded her.

'She said pain creates power. That it's a key. And that she'd finally turned it.'

By this point, no one in the family was visiting her alone. The atmosphere in her house had changed entirely. It felt thick, heavy, like the air didn't move. There was a smell to it too – not just incense anymore, but something damp and iron-like. The local vicar – a kindly, ageing man from church – visited once after the family begged him to try and talk sense into her.

He didn't go back.

'She laughed in his face,' Wendy said. 'Told him his God was an old man in the sky who pissed sunlight and wept milk.'

Aunt Lynne, who had once baked Victoria sponges and watched *Coronation Street* with her feet curled under a tartan blanket, had turned into something else entirely.

'There were moments,' Vic told me, 'when I honestly thought – that's not my aunt anymore.'

The family tried everything. But Lynne refused help. Refused doctors. Refused medication. She said they were trying to 'pull her back down'.

She told them, simply, 'I know where I'm going. I've seen the other side. It's beautiful. It's teeth and light. And He's waiting for me.'

They didn't know what that meant.

☽✧✝✧☾

By the autumn of 1974, Aunt Lynne was no longer Lynne. Whatever flicker of her that had remained – the woman with the garden, the tartan blanket, the way she used to hum under her breath while boiling the kettle – had long since gone out. And what was left behind, according to Vic and Wendy, was not simply grief, or madness, or mental illness.

It was something else.

'She just started shutting down,' Wendy told me. 'It was like her body couldn't take it anymore. She wasn't eating, barely drinking. And when she did eat, she'd bring it all up. Not food – not really. It was this thick, black stuff. Like sludge. Like wet earth.'

They took her to the GP. She had blood tests. Referrals. No one could explain it. She didn't have cancer. She didn't have anything physical they could label. The doctor made the assumption that she was mentally ill.

'She was wasting away, and nobody knew why,' Vic said.

Eventually, the family made the only choice they could: Vic, Wendy and their mother moved into Lynne's house to care for her full time. They turned the lounge into a makeshift bedroom – it was easier than getting her up the stairs – and laid her out on a fold-out settee bed, propped up with cushions. Wendy said she could barely look at her at first.

'She didn't look like Auntie Lynne anymore. Her face was … warped.'

Her cheeks had sunk. Her lips looked stretched. The bones beneath her skin had taken on strange angles, like her face had been subtly rearranged. But the eyes were the worst. Vic said they didn't blink normally. They'd stay fixed, wide and glassy, for minutes at a time. Unmoving.

And when she spoke, it wasn't in her voice. It was a low, gravelly rasp that seemed to come from somewhere deeper than the throat – from somewhere behind the body. Sometimes she'd speak in Latin, muttering phrases none of them could understand. Other times, she'd break into a hacking laugh and say things that didn't sound like speech at all – just snarls stitched together with syllables.

'She spat at anyone who came near her,' Wendy said. 'Literally spat. Once she hit the district nurse square in the face. Said she smelled of "false light".'

She told Wendy that she'd see her dead before she was 16. Told Vic that he was already marked. Told their mother she'd be swallowed 'from the inside out'. It didn't feel like threats from a sick relative – it felt like something else was talking through her. Something that hated them.

But things were about to get even more strange, unexplained and disturbing…

One evening, while changing her bedding, their mother found black feathers under the mattress. No one knew where they'd come from. Vic remembered coming down one morning and finding all the cutlery laid out in a spiral on the floor, tips pointed inward, surrounding Lynne's bed like a ritual circle.

Another time, they found her standing upright, stood over them in their beds, at 3.00 am, muttering over and over again, 'I am many. I am the gate. I am many. I am the gate.'

'I don't even know how she got up,' Vic said. 'She'd been too weak to move. But that night she stood there like it was nothing.'

By this point, most of the extended family had stopped visiting. No one wanted to see her. No one could handle it. The house smelled constantly of something foul – not just sweat and illness, but worse. Like rot. Like spoiled meat. And beneath it all, something sharper. Pungent. The kind of smell you never forget.

The smell of death.

Eventually, in desperation, the family reached out to the local vicar again. He was reluctant – he'd been once before, when she'd mocked him – but this time, something in their voices must have changed his mind. He came late in the afternoon. A quiet, serious man, thin-framed with silver-rimmed glasses and shaking hands. He brought with him a small bottle of holy water, a cross, and a Bible so old its spine was cracked.

Vic and Wendy were there for the blessing.

'She was almost asleep when he arrived,' Wendy told me. 'But as soon as he stepped into the room, she opened her eyes. Wide. Like she'd felt him.'

The moment he began the prayer, everything changed.

'She started convulsing,' Vic said. 'The bed was shaking – literally banging against the floorboards. Her mouth opened, and this sound came out. Not a scream. Not a cry. It was like a chorus.'

They described it as laughter – but layered. Not one voice, but many. Male and female. Young and old. All laughing together in a pitch that made your bones itch.

And then came the smell…

'It was like shit,' Wendy said bluntly. 'But stronger. Worse. Like something had died and been buried in it.'

The vicar's hands began to tremble. He kept trying to continue, but his voice broke. The cross slipped from his fingers. A dark patch appeared at the front of his trousers.

'He had wet himself,' Vic said. 'Swear to God, right there in front of us. That was how fucking scared he was.'

He grabbed his things and left without a word. Just stumbled out into the hallway and vanished out the front door. They never saw him again.

Lynne lay still after that. As if she'd won. As if the effort had drained her completely.

'She started saying goodbye,' Wendy said. 'Not in a sad way. In a … satisfied way.'

The next morning, she was calm. Peaceful, even. She asked for toast, which she hadn't eaten in weeks. They began to see some hope. Vic and Wendy went off to school. Sometime during the day their mother had nipped out to fetch something from the shop. When she returned, Lynne had gone; without a coat, without shoes, without saying a word. She had slipped out through the front door and vanished into the grey November morning. They had reported it to the police. They were simply terrified.

The police came to the house later that day. She'd walked over a mile – barefoot, in the freezing cold – to a train line. No one in the family ever found out exactly where. But they were told she stepped onto the tracks as an early train came through, a half-full Class 101 DMU.

There was no suicide note. The coroner's report listed it as 'death by misadventure'. Mental illness. Depression.

But Vic and Wendy knew better.

They'd lived with it. Heard it. Felt it. They knew that Aunt Lynne had taken her own life, or at least something had made her. And even now, all these years later, there's something about that house – even in memory – that makes them flinch.

'She let something in,' Wendy told me. 'And once it was inside, it didn't want to leave.'

☽✧✝✧☾

It's easy to dismiss cases like this as madness. As an illness. As the slow erosion of a mind cracking under the pressure of grief and abandonment. And sometimes, that is exactly what it is.

I've spoken to many people over the years – people who've seen and heard things, felt watched, heard voices, been touched by something they couldn't explain. And I've always said the same thing: we have to be careful. Because real mental illness is just that – real. It's complex. It's tragic. It can twist the mind into terrifying shapes without a single supernatural force involved.

But every now and then, something doesn't fit.

And for me, Aunt Lynne's story is one of those times.

Because this wasn't just a woman spiralling into despair. This wasn't simply depression or psychosis. It started with those things, yes – the loss of her marriage, the heartbreak, the emptiness that followed her husband's betrayal. But it ended with something else entirely. Something cold. Something unknown. Something that moved into her when she was too weak to stop it.

What happened to Lynne was not theatrical. It didn't look like a horror film. It looked like slow possession – the subtle, invasive kind. The kind that rots a person from the inside out. One degree at a time. So slowly that you almost don't notice until it's too late.

She changed. Not just emotionally, but physically. Her personality flipped like a switch. Her eyes, her voice, even her body changed in ways that unsettled trained professionals. Her speech, her strength, the things she said and knew. The language she spoke. The things she predicted. And above all – the effect she had on others.

I keep coming back to that poor vicar – a man of faith so terrified by what he encountered that he wet himself and fled without a word. That's not a panic attack, nor is it anxiety. It's fear at a level few of us ever experience.

And whatever he saw – whatever was in that room with them – it wasn't a delusion.

It was real.

Vic and Wendy didn't want to sensationalise their story. In fact, when they first told me, they were hesitant. Scared, even. Not because they were afraid of being believed or mocked – but because they didn't like thinking about it. Talking about it, they said, was like pulling back a curtain they'd spent years trying to nail shut.

They lived through it. They heard the sounds. Smelled the rot. Watched the woman they loved dissolve into something unrecognisable. They saw the feathers. The cutlery spirals. The mud-black vomit. They remember how cold that house got. How the atmosphere thickened, room by room, like something was waiting.

And maybe that's what frightens me most about this case.

Because if this was a possession – if something truly did crawl inside that vulnerable, grieving woman and take root – then it didn't come with flames and theatrics. It came quietly. Through books. Through whispers. Through awful strangers who smiled too much and spoke too softly.

It came through pain. Through need. And it's that need that terrifies me. Because it makes you vulnerable. It opens the door, and once that door is open – even a crack – something can slip through. Something old. Something cruel. Something that calls itself comfort, but only wants control.

We'll never know exactly what Lynne invited in during that summer of 1974. We'll never know who those women were, or where they came from, or why they chose her. But what we do know – what Vic and Wendy know with absolute certainty – is that by the end, it wasn't Aunt Lynne in that bed. It was something else and when it had finished with her, it left.

Or maybe it didn't…

Maybe it's still out there. Moving from grief to grief. From one hollow heart to the next. Waiting…

But perhaps the most important part of this entire story – the part that must never be lost beneath the fear and the fascination – is that at its heart lies the tragic death of a woman. A real woman. Aunt Lynne wasn't just the centre of a haunting. She was a sister, an aunt, a neighbour. A kind, if fragile, person who was unintentionally let down by those who didn't understand what she was going through – or perhaps couldn't.

No matter what you believe – possession, psychosis, or something in between – what remains undeniable is that a woman in pain was consumed by something she couldn't fight, and in the end, it drove her to take her own life. That is what still haunts her family most. Not the strange voices or the symbols or the stench that filled that room – but the loss of someone they loved, and the terrible helplessness of watching her disappear day by day.

Because when all the theories are stripped away, what's left is a death that didn't have to happen and that, above all else, is what makes this story so heartbreaking.

My Haunted Life

Part Four

Escalation

Despite the normality we tried so hard to preserve, the disturbances in our home never truly left us in peace. Like a damp rising through the walls, the sense of unease soaked into everything – slowly, quietly and with growing intensity. Whatever force lingered within Serlby Rise had begun to press closer, more insistent with each passing week. We'd try to brush it off. Tell ourselves it was nothing. But the feeling never left.

My parents would walk into the living room and find the cushions scattered across the floor, not thrown, but oddly placed – positioned at angles that didn't make sense, almost as if arranged. The curtains, drawn back to let in the watery afternoon light, would be found tightly shut for no reason. And the dog – usually a lively, loving presence – had become jumpy, staring into corners, growling at things that weren't there. Even the air inside the house had changed. There was a weight to it. A pressure. As though something was watching. Waiting.

☽✧†✧☾

Up until my eleventh year, we'd only ever felt the presence. We never saw it. That barrier between suggestion and certainty remained intact, fragile though it was. But that veil didn't hold forever.

And when it tore – it tore completely.

It was an ordinary Tuesday evening, the kind that blurs into all the others. Mum was out working her shift at The Alcester, and I was home with Dad. We'd eaten tea, sat watching TV for a bit – something light, I think. The kind of forgettable evening that offered comfort in its routine.

At one point I got up and headed into the kitchen for a drink of milk. I remember the lino floor was cold under my feet. I didn't put the light on – it wasn't fully dark yet, just that dusky grey that settles in the early evening. Enough light from the hallway to see by. I walked across the room, opened the fridge, poured myself a glass. I wasn't thinking about anything in particular. Just the normal hum of the house. The fridge door. The quiet. The way it always was.

Then I looked up.

Not deliberately. It was just something I did, casually – my gaze lifting slightly as I held the glass, glancing toward the kitchen window above the sink.

And that was when I saw her.

Not outside peering in, but inside the room.

It was her reflection I saw in the window.

She was standing behind me.

My breath caught in my throat. The glass didn't fall. I didn't move. I just stood there – utterly frozen – staring at the window, and at the figure that was now unmistakably there, just a few feet behind me.

She was small, hunched. Her body seemed fragile, like it might collapse in on itself at any moment. She wasn't moving. Just standing there, still as a statue, yet somehow – undeniably alive. Or once alive.

Her hair hung in thin, uneven strands, stringy and dull. Her skin – what little I could make out – looked drained of colour, pallid and greyish, as if whatever blood had once run through her had long since receded. But it was her face that held me. That pinned me.

Even in reflection, it was wrong. The features didn't look fully formed. They were soft, blurred – as if she were a figure from a faded photograph, caught between resolution and decay. The contours of her face wavered slightly, like heat ripples rising from a road.

But the worst thing – the thing that still sits heavy in my chest when I think about it – were her eyes.

Or the absence of them.

Where her eyes should have been were two hollow sockets. Not bloodied or violent, not cartoonish – but blank voids. Empty spaces, utterly devoid of light or emotion or anything remotely human. Looking at them made my stomach twist, like I was being pulled toward something vast and lifeless. The longer I stared, the more I felt like those dark holes were moving, not physically, but internally – like they were reaching, expanding, pulling at me.

I was frozen. Not just in fear, but in something deeper – something primal. My hands didn't tremble. My body didn't run. I just stared, unable to even blink. There was no sound. Not a creak. Not a breath. The silence of the house was total, pressing in around me like water.

I don't know how long I stood there, watching her watch me. It could have been ten seconds. It could have been a full minute. All I know is that eventually – somehow – I forced myself to look away. I turned, slowly, the blood thudding in my ears, my heart in my throat.

But when I turned around, there was nothing there.

The room was empty.

And yet – I knew she'd been there.

She wasn't some strange shape caught in the window, or a trick of the glass. I had seen her. Not just with my eyes, but with something deeper. I felt her, as real as anything I've ever known.

I walked back to the living room in silence. I didn't tell Dad. I don't know why. Maybe I couldn't. Maybe I didn't want to speak it aloud. Because saying it would have made it more real. And I wasn't ready for that. But that night, something changed forever.

I had seen her.

And from that moment on, I knew the haunting wasn't just noise or shadows or objects moved when no one was looking.

It had a face.

When I finally stumbled back into the living room, Dad was still perched comfortably on the sofa, utterly unaware. The light from the television flickered softly across his face, the colours of the film playing out in shifting bursts – warm oranges, icy blues – oblivious to what had just occurred only steps away.

I sat down beside him, rigid with terror, the glass of milk still clutched in my hand. It trembled slightly, the surface rippling, though whether from the chill in my fingers or the sheer force of what I'd just experienced, I couldn't say. I wanted to speak. Needed to speak. The words burned at the back of my throat, but I couldn't form them. My jaw was clenched tight, my chest locked. I sat there, in silence, every nerve on fire, as my mind replayed the image again and again. Each time it looped, the memory distorted slightly. Her face grew dimmer, then clearer. The sockets of her eyes seemed deeper. Her outline more insubstantial. More real. Like a nightmare that wouldn't fade with waking.

The minutes dragged by.

The shadows in the corners of the room seemed to stretch, pulling toward us. Every tiny sound – the creak of the floorboards, the faint tick of the radiator cooling – was suddenly louder, closer. My senses were heightened to the point of exhaustion. It felt like the house itself had become conscious. Like it was listening.

Eventually, I couldn't keep it in. The pressure became too much. The fear had nowhere left to go.

I broke down.

I don't remember the exact moment the tears started – only the heat of them on my cheeks and the way my shoulders shook as the dam inside me collapsed. Through stuttered breaths and a voice thick with panic, I told Dad everything. Every word felt raw. I described the figure, the way she stood, the blank hollows where her eyes should have been. How I'd seen her reflected behind me. How I knew she had been there in the room.

At first, Dad just looked puzzled. Concern flickered across his face, but it was the concern of someone trying to make sense of a frightened child's outburst. His first thought, naturally, was that someone – an intruder, maybe – had been outside the house, looking in. A prowler. A practical explanation.

But the moment he began to think it through, I saw his expression shift.

He knew the layout of our home better than anyone. And the angle of that kitchen window made one thing undeniably clear: if someone had been outside, visible from that position, they would have had to be at least eight feet tall. It just didn't make sense. No one could have stood outside that window and appeared the way I described.

He went quiet then.

His eyes didn't leave mine, and in that silence, something passed between us. A realisation. A surrender. His face changed – subtly, but unmistakably. The protective rationality drained from it, and what remained was something rawer. A grim, haunted understanding. Like a truth he'd been trying to bury had just clawed its way back to the surface.

Neither of us spoke much after that.

We didn't need to.

That night, I couldn't face being alone. The thought of going up to my room – of lying there in the dark, surrounded by silence – was unbearable. I was terrified she would come back. That I would wake in the night and see her standing at the end of the bed. Or worse, feel her breath against my neck before I even opened my eyes.

I begged Dad to let me sleep in their bed, and he didn't hesitate. I curled up beside him under the covers, clinging to his warmth like it was the only barrier between me and something unfathomable. He spoke quietly, trying to calm me. Soft reassurances. Familiar phrases. But they didn't land. I nodded, but I didn't believe them.

Because I knew better.

I lay awake the entire night, staring at the bedroom door. Every time I blinked, I saw her face. Every shadow became her form. Every twitch of the curtain, every shifting pattern in the darkness – it all seemed alive. It all seemed to watch.

Sleep never came.

That moment marked something irreversible. A threshold had been crossed. Whatever had been haunting us had now made itself known. It had stepped into the light. The poltergeist had shown its face.

And the worst part – the part that stayed with me, long after that night – was the realisation that it hadn't just 'appeared'.

It had seen me too.

☽✧✝✧☾

After my sighting of the ghostly old lady in the window, fear attached itself to me like a second skin, a dark and heavy presence that refused to be shaken off. It clung to me through every hour of the day, but it was at night when it became almost unbearable. As darkness fell over our house on Serlby Rise, it brought with it a dread that pressed against my chest like a weight. No longer did night-time offer rest or comfort; now it was a long stretch of silent waiting, where every shadow seemed a little too deep, every sound a little too sharp. The image of her would replay over and over in my mind whenever I tried to close my eyes. I would see her again, that frail, unsteady form hovering just behind the glass, staring at me without seeing, her blurred outline a grotesque smear against the night. My bedroom, once a place of refuge, transformed into a claustrophobic prison after dark, and the mere thought of sleeping alone filled me with a paralysing kind of fear. Even the simple act of needing the toilet became something I dreaded. To reach the bathroom, I would have to climb the stairs – a journey that now felt like ascending into a place where something unseen might be waiting. Every step up creaked under my weight, and my imagination tortured me with thoughts of something crawling just behind me, reaching out a hand that would brush the back of my leg. I would fling open the bathroom door with shaking hands, heart hammering against my ribs, eyes darting immediately to the mirror. I dreaded that glass surface, half-expecting to catch a glimpse of her standing behind me, closer this time, or perhaps lurking in the corner, waiting for me to notice her. The thought made my blood turn to ice in my veins.

Once I had finished, getting back downstairs was no easier. The landing seemed wider, the shadows thicker. Every creak of the floorboards sounded like a footstep that wasn't mine. I would rush down the stairs, feeling as though something was following just behind, breathing down my neck. I would crash into the living room, gasping for breath, desperate to feel the normality of Mum and Dad sitting there, the telly murmuring in the background, anything to drown out the lingering terror that threatened to consume me……

Patricia's Story

Mary

I've always been fascinated by Jack the Ripper.

From a young age, long before most kids had ever heard the name, I was poring over books about Victorian London, the cobbled streets of Whitechapel, and the dark figure who haunted them. While other kids were collecting football stickers or watching Saturday morning cartoons, I was studying the murders of 1888 – the clinical brutality, the eerie taunting letters, the thick fog that never seemed to lift from the gaslit alleys. Something about the case got under my skin. It still does. It's not just the violence that disturbed me – it was the silence that followed it. The absence of a solution. The sheer emptiness left behind. A mystery that defied time.

Over the years, I'd read everything I could get my hands on. Books, autopsy reports, crime scene photos, crackpot theories, you name it. I knew the names of the victims by heart. I knew the geography of the East End in the 1880s better than some parts of Nottingham. I knew the suspects – the real ones, and the laughable ones. And I never grew tired of it. There was something about the Ripper case that demanded attention. That whispered, always, that you were almost about to understand something ... only for it to slip away again.

I even started to write a book about it in 2007. In fact, I've spent the last eighteen years trying. I've started it more times than I can count. I'd get so far – outlines, opening chapters, long evenings of momentum – and then something would break the flow. Life. Doubt. The overwhelming feeling that everything's already been said. That nothing I could add would be enough. But the pull of the case never left me.

It was that obsession, that need to connect with others who felt the same, that led me to join a few online forums and groups when I first gained access to the Internet. This would have been the mid-2000s, back when people still used desktop computers to discuss the subject on Ripperology forums, pages and group chats, looking for others like me – other armchair detectives, historians and insomniac thinkers who couldn't stop scratching at that same old wound. That's how I met Patricia.

She was a regular in one of the more serious Ripper forums – an East Ender with a head full of knowledge and very little patience for conspiracy theories. Her posts always stood out. She didn't speculate wildly. She didn't fall into the traps of aliens or royal cover-ups. She knew her stuff, and she had a sense of humour that cut like a razor when someone posted something daft. A proper Cockney – opinionated, spirited and proudly born and bred in the East End.

We got chatting over time. Swapped messages. Became friends. She told me about her upbringing in Stepney, her work, her theories on the case. It was only after several weeks of back and forth that she asked what else I was into. When I mentioned that I was a paranormal investigator, there was a brief pause in our chat history. Then, late that same evening, she sent me a message that simply read:

'I've got a story you might want to hear. A real one. It happened to me.'

I didn't press her straight away. I'd had enough people over the years tell me vague stories about strange shadows or spooky feelings in old pubs. But Patricia insisted. And over the next few nights, she began to share something far stranger than anything I'd expected.

A few months later, in 2009, Dad and I finally took a long-overdue trip down to Whitechapel. It had been years in the making. A chance to walk the actual Ripper sites, to feel the geography of it beneath our feet. We visited the locations of the five canonical murders, took a walking tour, and wandered into the surviving alleyways, now caught between old worldly grit and gentrified blandness.

While we were down there I arranged to meet Patricia in person. I'll be honest – I was nervous. Meeting someone you've only spoken to online is always a bit strange. But she was exactly as I imagined. Short, slightly hunched, with thinning grey-brown hair pulled back into a bun that didn't quite hold. She was 48 at the time, though she looked a little older – years of working in dim light and sitting over needlework had left her with fine lines around her eyes and a faint squint. She had a slight overbite, which gave her a permanently quizzical expression, and she wore long cardigans, sensible skirts, and house slippers.

There was something undeniably old-fashioned about her – not in a performative way, but in the very fabric of who she was. She was, in every sense of the word, a spinster. Not the bitter or mocking stereotype the word sometimes conjures, but a quiet woman who had lived most of her life alone, working hard, keeping to herself. She was private, proud and possessed of a quiet dignity that made you feel like you were intruding if you asked too many personal questions.

We met her at her flat in Stepney – a little place, narrow and overstuffed with things. China cats, sewing patterns, teacups, Ripper books, faded newspaper clippings, little ornaments on every flat surface. Her front room smelled faintly of lavender and old thread. A boxy electric fire sat flickering under the mantel, even though it was warm out. She'd made a pot of tea and had laid out Rich Teas on a plate without asking if we were hungry.

And that's where she told us her story.

She told it like someone recalling something they still couldn't quite believe. Like they had seen it and still couldn't grasp it – something that still confused and unsettled them. It had happened in 1994, she said. She was 34 at the time, working in a family-run tailor's shop in the East End. She'd worked there since 1990, sewing garments for private clients. She was good at what she did – steady hands, sharp eyes, meticulous detail.

But it wasn't the tailoring she remembered most about that place.

It was the mannequin.

And the feeling that, somehow, it had never stopped watching her.

☽✧☨✧☾

Patricia described the shop so vividly that I could almost see it. It was unlike anywhere I'd ever been – and that's saying something, considering the places I've visited as a paranormal investigator. As she spoke, I could hear the wooden stairs creak beneath her shoes, smell the faint scent of dust and fabric glue, feel the thick stillness in the air. It was more than just a workplace. It was a place caught between centuries.

The tailor's shop sat tucked down a narrow lane just off one of the busier East End roads – a place you could easily walk past without noticing. There was no flashy sign, no display window filled with sleek modern suits. Just a small, square window and a brass bell above the door. The building had stood for generations – originally a Victorian lodging house, converted into a family-run tailoring business in 1902. And very little had changed since then.

Even in the 1990s, it looked and felt like it belonged to a bygone era, according to Patricia. The exterior was aged but dignified – old brick, soot-stained from decades of London grime, and a wooden door with peeling paint the colour of dried oxblood. Inside, the entire place was panelled in dark, heavy wood – walls, banisters, floors. It drank in the daylight and gave very little back. Even on the brightest days, the interior remained dim and warm, lit mostly by tall lamps and old-fashioned sconces that cast long shadows. It was like stepping into the past – not in a charming, nostalgic way, but in a way that felt heavy. Pressed down. Every room held echoes of the building's previous life. The narrow corridor to the back room was once a hallway of sleeping quarters. The upper level still had doors with old peeling wood – remnants of the time when it had housed transients, drunks and working men during the age of gaslight and smog.

The tailoring area itself was cramped but beautifully kept. Wooden workbenches lined the walls, covered in reels of thread, pin cushions, paper patterns and half-finished garments. The owner at the time, Michael, had made a conscious decision not to modernise. He wanted to retain the character of the place, to honour its legacy. All the tools were vintage. The iron sewing machines – big, black Singer models with brass inlays – still functioned, still groaned rhythmically as the pedals were pumped. A tailor's dummy stood in each corner, draped in various stages of suits and coats. All of them were vintage – early twentieth century, made of canvas and wood, with curved hips and faded measurements still scrawled across the fabric in black ink.

The air inside the shop had a stillness to it – a kind of enclosed quiet that you don't notice at first but that settles into your bones after a while. Even when the machines were whirring and the scissors snipping, there was something subdued about the space. Patricia said it always felt like the building was watching. Not hostile, not even menacing – just present. Listening.

And yet, there was love in the walls too. The business was a family one, passed down through generations. In the early '90s, the shop was owned and run by Michael – stern, traditional, and deeply proud of his craft. His adult son, James, worked there too, tall and good-natured, with a knack for cutting patterns. And then there was Paige, Michael's daughter, who managed the books and handled clients with a no-nonsense efficiency that kept the wheels turning. The family had a rhythm, an ease with each other that Patricia found comforting. They were kind to her, treated her like one of their own despite her being the only employee who wasn't blood. Back then, she said, she was just grateful to have the work. She kept her head down, did her job, didn't ask questions. And for the first few years, there were no questions. Nothing that couldn't be explained. If a pair of shears had gone missing, someone had misplaced them. If a coat had shifted slightly on the hanger, it was the draught from the door. It was an old building. It made old-building noises. Wood creaked. Pipes clanged. She never gave it a second thought.

Still, the family had their stories.

According to them, the building had been haunted for decades – not by a malicious entity, but by a familiar one. They referred to the ghost, quite casually, as 'Bob'. Supposedly, 'Bob' was the spirit of Michael's uncle – Robert – who had worked in the shop after the war. He'd been a quiet, hard-working man who preferred solitude and, one evening in 1953, while finishing a suit alone after hours, he suffered a fatal heart attack right there on the workbench. He had been found the next morning, slumped across the cutting table with the chalk still in his hand.

After that, things began to happen. Little things. Footsteps upstairs when no one was up there. The doorbell chiming when nobody was there. Objects vanishing, only to reappear hours later in plain sight. Once, a freshly pressed suit was found turned inside out on its hanger. No one ever saw it happen. But it became a running joke in the family. 'That'll be Bob,' they'd say. 'Bob's at it again.'

It was harmless stuff. Playful, even. Over time, the stories became folklore within the family – something to chuckle about over lunch or mention to new clients for a bit of colour. And Patricia, ever the sceptic, paid no mind. She'd never experienced anything herself, and she had no reason to believe otherwise. As far as she was concerned, Bob was just a name they gave to creaks and forgetfulness. She liked the routine, the quiet industry of it all. Her work was steady, her hands busy, and the atmosphere – though old – was never unpleasant. The shop was strange, yes, and filled with shadows. But not frightening.

Not yet…

It wouldn't be until 1994, four years into her employment, that Patricia would begin to question everything she thought she understood.

That was the year the mannequin moved.

☽✧✝✧☾

By 1994, Patricia had settled fully into her role at the tailor's shop. She worked five days a week, sometimes six if there was a backlog. She'd grown close to the family – especially Paige, who shared her dry sense of humour – and she'd found a rhythm she liked. It was honest work. Quiet. Repetitive in the best way. There was comfort in the needle and thread, in chalking lines on fabric, in the soft thump-thump of the iron being pressed onto wool. She didn't have much of a social life, and she didn't mind. The shop gave her purpose. It gave her somewhere to be.

That's why she said it hit her so hard when the atmosphere began to change.

At first, it was just a feeling. She'd be bent over a hem, her back aching, eyes straining against the dim light, and she'd suddenly feel like someone was standing behind her. Not just the passing sense of presence that old buildings sometimes give off – but a specific sense. The unmistakable weight of being watched. Studied. She'd straighten up, glance behind her – and of course, no one was there. It happened once or twice in late spring. Then again in June. She didn't say anything to the others. Not because she was scared – Patricia was far too practical for that – but because she didn't want to be laughed at. She was the outsider. The only one not tied by blood. If she started piping up about feeling watched, it'd just feed into their silly ghost stories. She wasn't about to give them that satisfaction.

Then came the voices.

She never heard them clearly. Just low murmurs, indistinct, like someone whispering two rooms away. Sometimes it was a single sound. Other times it was a faint string of words she couldn't quite catch. But it always came when she was alone. The sound would drift through the walls or down the stairs or rise from the back fitting room, and she'd stop what she was doing and listen, her needle frozen mid-air.

Then silence.

She tried telling herself it was just the old pipework, or the shop settling. Maybe even voices from outside echoing through the brickwork.

'Did you tell the others about what was happening?' I ask.

She shakes her head. 'No. I didn't want them to think I was mad,'.

But then there were the mannequins.

The shop had six of them – four male torsos and two females. All were vintage. Their cloth coverings had yellowed with age, and the bases were made of heavy cast iron. Most of them had no heads, or just smooth wooden domes. But one – just one – had a head. It was a full-sized female mannequin, pale and old-fashioned, made of painted plaster and wood, with a featureless white, smiling face. Expressionless.

The staff called her Mary.

She'd stood in the back fitting room for decades, dressed in a dark Edwardian-style dress with high collar and pleated bodice. Paige would occasionally redecorate her with different shawls or lace trims, depending on what they were working on. But mostly, she just stood there. Lifeless. Forgotten.

Until she wasn't.

The first time Patricia noticed anything odd was during a quiet Tuesday afternoon. She was pinning the cuff of a blazer on the workbench, her back to the fitting room. The shop was empty except for her and Michael, who was upstairs going through invoices. The air was still. Dust hung in the sunbeams. All was normal.

And then she heard it.

Three taps.

Not loud, not sharp. Just a slow, deliberate tapping – tap … tap … tap – like a knuckle against wood.

She froze. Looked up. Listened.

Nothing.

She waited, her ears straining in the silence, then cautiously turned around and peered toward the fitting room. It was empty. The mannequin stood exactly where it always had. One arm slightly bent. Head tilted downwards. Blank face forward. She shook it off.

A few days later, it happened again. This time, she thought she saw something out of the corner of her eye – a flicker of motion where there shouldn't have been any. She turned, heart hammering. Mary hadn't moved. But she looked … different. Her head was tilted just slightly more to the side than Patricia remembered. Her torso angled ever so slightly toward the workroom.

Patricia told herself she was imagining it. That she hadn't been paying attention to how she was positioned earlier. That the light was playing tricks on her.

But once you notice something like that, it's impossible to unnotice it.

The days that followed became a slow, quiet nightmare. Patricia began to convince herself she was going nuts. She started marking her position with tailors' chalk on the floor. Just little dots. Barely visible. No one else knew she was doing it. But each time she came in the next morning, the marks didn't quite line up. The mannequin had moved. Never much. A few inches to the left. A shift of the shoulders. A slight turn of the base.

Then came the day she found her facing the door. In the shop front itself…

Completely turned around.

Patricia stood in the doorway, keys still in her hand, staring at the figure. Mary had been facing the fitting mirror the night before, in the back. Now, she faced the front of the shop, as though watching for her arrival. She didn't scream. Patricia wasn't the screaming type. But she did lock the door behind her, walk slowly past her without looking, and spent the rest of the morning trying not to think about it.

That afternoon, she casually asked Michael if anyone had been in early.

He had shook his head. 'No one's touched her,' he said, glancing toward the back. 'Except maybe Bob, eh?'

She didn't laugh.

Unfortunately, that night she had to stay late. Sometimes she did this, and Michael never objected. She was working on a bespoke three-piece for a difficult client and the deadline was tight. The others had long gone home. The shop was quiet, just her and the low hum of the iron, the occasional distant clang from the old pipes. She worked steadily, trying not to think about the figure in the fitting room behind her.

But then – just after eight – she heard it again.

The tap.

But this time, it wasn't three. It was more. Fast. Rhythmic.

Tap-tap-tap-tap-tap-tap-tap…

She turned, goosebumps rising, her stomach knotted tight.

And Mary was gone.

☽✧✝✧☾

Patricia stood in the doorway, staring at the empty space where Mary had always stood.

The mannequin was gone.

Not shifted slightly. Not angled differently. Gone. The floorboards beneath her were bare. The corner she'd always occupied – a place so familiar it barely registered in Patricia's mind until now – was empty. The silence of the shop seemed suddenly louder. She felt it pressing against her eardrums.

She stepped forward slowly, scanning the darkened fitting room. No one else was in the building. The front door was still bolted, the lights at the front of the shop were off, and she'd been working alone all evening.

She checked the front anyway – just to be sure. She walked past the workbenches and bolts of fabric, past the scattered threads and paper patterns. The main showroom was in total darkness, just the faint yellow glow spilling from the back room casting warped shadows across the walls.

No mannequin.

Her heart thudded harder now – not with fear exactly, but confusion. Disorientation. She stood still for a moment, thinking.

And then, on impulse, she turned and climbed the stairs. The upper rooms weren't used much anymore. A few storage spaces, the office, and the old upstairs workroom with a wide oak table and moth-eaten curtains. She pushed the door open and flicked on the switch.

And there she was.

Mary.

Standing beside the desk. Her clothes weren't there. Arms still slightly bent. Shoulders squared. Head dipped just faintly, as though studying the grain of the floorboards beneath her. Patricia stared at her for a full minute, lips parted, breath shallow.

She wasn't afraid. She was baffled.

The sheer impossibility of it sat heavy in her stomach – but rather than entertain the notion of the supernatural, her mind did what most minds do: it reached for a rational answer.

James. Or Paige. One of them had moved her. It was a prank. A silly little joke at her expense. Maybe they'd seen her checking the chalk marks. Maybe they'd overheard her muttering about the mannequin. They were childish sometimes, weren't they? Grown adults, yes – but still brother and sister, still capable of the kind of stupid, mischievous tricks siblings never quite grow out of.

She laughed out loud.

It wasn't fear. Not yet. Just the nervous energy of someone who'd started to feel the edges of the rug slipping beneath their feet. She went back downstairs, finished her work, and left the shop in good spirits.

The next morning, Patricia arrived early, humming to herself, coat unbuttoned and gloves in her pocket. She opened the door and stepped into the familiar gloom, calling out a cheerful 'Morning!' as she walked in. Paige was already there, sat at the back workbench, sipping tea from her favourite chipped mug. James was just coming in through the rear entrance, box of supplies under one arm. Patricia grinned.

'All right, you lot,' she said, tossing her scarf onto the hook. 'Nice try, by the way. Very funny. Got me good.'

Paige raised an eyebrow. 'What are you on about?'

'You know exactly what I'm on about,' Patricia said, trying to hide her smirk. 'Mary. Upstairs. Don't play innocent.'

Both James and Paige exchanged a glance. Michael wandered in moments later, shrugging off his coat, and Patricia wasted no time.

'Tell your kids to keep their jokes to themselves,' she said, still half-laughing. 'Woke me up a bit last night, they did. Moving that bloody mannequin around like we're in some old Hammer Horror film.'

Michael stopped, looking from one child to the other. 'What are you talking about?'

She explained. Told them everything. That she'd come in the night before, found Mary gone, searched the shop and found her upstairs. The lot.

By the end of it, she wasn't laughing.

Because they weren't smiling.

James looked confused. Paige looked uneasy. Michael just stood there, quiet.

'Patricia,' he said slowly, 'nobody's touched Mary. We've not moved her. I've been in the office all week. And they haven't even been up those stairs in days.'

The lightness in her chest evaporated.

Paige spoke, her voice unusually small. 'Are you sure she wasn't just … moved before? Maybe you didn't notice?'

But Patricia shook her head. She was sure. Still, she didn't press the point. She shrugged it off, mumbled something about being tired, and got on with her work. But the seed had been planted. And as the day wore on, she kept catching herself glancing toward the fitting room.

Just to check.

☽✧☨✧☾

That night, Patricia stayed late again. She was back to working on the bespoke suit – the deadline was looming, and she needed the hours. She wasn't afraid. Not really. The moment with Mary still unsettled her, but her mind was determined to stay logical. She put it down to stress. Lack of sleep. A long day making her misremember details.

At around 10 pm, she carried her fabric bolts and sewing kit upstairs to use the larger worktable. The room was dimly lit, the bulb overhead humming faintly. Mary stood where she'd found her before, beside the desk, arms still and rigid. Patricia sat down and got to work. For the first half hour, she made great progress. Her hands moved automatically – pinning, trimming, folding. She was back in the flow.

But then came that feeling again. The weight. Like something pressing down on the back of her neck. Watching. She paused, hands still, and looked up.

Mary hadn't moved.

But her position in the room now felt … intrusive. As though she were too close … too near to where Patricia was working.

She shook her head, forcing a breath out through her nose. 'Get a grip,' she muttered to herself. 'You're making yourself daft.'

She went back to work. Ten minutes passed. Then fifteen.

And then – just at the edge of her vision – she saw it.

Mary's head turned. Ever so slightly. Just a flick. The barest tilt. The motion of someone shifting their gaze.

Patricia gasped, recoiling from her chair, heart hammering. But when she turned to look – really look – Mary's head was still.

Straightforward. Blank.

Had it moved? Had she imagined it? She stood there for a full minute, staring at the mannequin, willing it to twitch again. But nothing happened. Eventually, unnerved but clinging desperately to her rationality, she packed up and went home early.

☽✧✝✧☾

The following day, Patricia arrived with a fresh mindset. She was determined to put it all behind her. No ghost stories. No silly games with mannequins. Just work. Focus. And it worked. She had a brilliant day. The final fittings on a coat came together beautifully. Michael even complimented her on the lining. Paige brought in cream cakes at lunchtime. Everything was normal.

When the others left for the evening, she offered to lock up. 'I'll stay a bit longer,' she said, with a smile. 'Might as well keep working on that suit while I'm on a roll.'

By 11.30 pm, she was nearly done. The last buttons were sewn, the seams pressed. The shop was silent but comforting. She didn't even notice the time – until she heard it.

Tap.

She stopped mid-stitch.

Tap… tap…

It came from the corner. From where Mary stood. Patricia closed her eyes for a moment. Breathed in. Then carried on.

Tap… tap-tap…

She gritted her teeth. 'Ignore it,' she whispered.

And then – laughter. A sharp, twisted chuckle. Female. Ragged and malicious. A sound filled with delight and menace, rising from the shadows.

Then the voice. 'Patricia…'

It drew the name out, sing-song and horrible. 'Paaaaa… tricia…'

She froze. Her blood turned cold. The voice was right there. In the room. She turned her head slowly – terrified of what she would see.

Mary was looking at her. Not just the mannequin. Not her usual blank expression.

A face. A real face.

Leathery, wrinkled skin twisted into a grotesque grin. A long, hooked nose. One eye slightly larger than the other, both glinting with wet malevolence. The mouth was stretched, thin-lipped, cracked – smiling in a way that radiated pure insanity.

The figure didn't move. It didn't need to. The face did all the damage. Patricia yelped – a dry, strangled sound – and ran. She didn't gather her things. She didn't switch off the lights. She didn't even lock the door. She just fled, the tapping echoing behind her. The voice still in her ears.

Laughing.

☽✧✝✧☾

After she left, Patricia didn't go home. She didn't feel safe there. Instead, she walked the short distance through the East End streets to the house of Sarah, her mum's best friend since childhood. Sarah had always been like a second mother. The two women were close in that quiet, unspoken way – never needing to say much, just being there. And at that moment, that was exactly what Patricia needed.

She knocked on Sarah's door just after midnight, her hands trembling, her eyes wide and bloodshot. Her breath came in sharp little gasps. When the door opened, Sarah stared at her in alarm.

I remember asking her, during our conversation in 2009, 'What did Sarah say when she saw you like that?'

Patricia gave a little shake of the head, the memory flashing behind her eyes.

'She didn't say anything at first,' she told me. 'She just pulled me inside and held me like I was a kid again. I could barely speak. I didn't know how to explain it. I didn't know if I should explain it.'

Even now, in her small Stepney flat, she looked shaken recalling it. Her fingers twitched slightly as she told me. Her voice was soft. Measured. But there was a tension beneath it – like she was still trying to keep something inside. She eventually found her voice, and Sarah listened. Calm. Unflinching. That was Sarah. The type of woman who'd make you a cup of tea before calling an ambulance. Steady in a storm.

Sarah's daughter Marie was also there that night. Patricia had grown up seeing Marie as something between a cousin and a big sister. She made them all a tea and sat with them, holding Patricia's hand gently under the table as she spoke.

I asked her what Marie and Sarah meant to her.

'They're my safe place,' she said simply. 'I've never had a big family, but those two… I could go to them with anything. Even something like this.'

Patricia poured out her story. Every terrifying detail. And the fear she'd felt wasn't just about the mannequin anymore. It was about herself. Was she losing her mind? Was something unravelling inside her?

But Sarah was firm.

She listened, nodded slowly, and said, 'If you were really going loopy, love, why is it only happening in one place?' She reminded Patricia that whatever she was seeing – hearing – feeling, it was contained to the shop. That made it likely that Patricia wasn't losing her mind. That mattered.

It calmed her. A little.

Patricia left just after 3 am. She didn't sleep much when she got in. The next day, she called in sick. Her voice was hoarse from crying. Michael, the owner, was furious. Not because she was off work – but because the shop had been left unlocked overnight. Patricia had feared that would be the end of her job.

But it wasn't. He accepted it. Chalked it up to a mistake. There was no mention of it again.

Patricia took three days off, claiming it was a stomach bug. She spent that time alone, resting, thinking, trying to rationalise. Trying to believe Sarah's logic. In her own home, with the curtains drawn and the telly playing quietly in the background, she felt normal. Safe. She didn't see anything out of place. She didn't hear any voices. There were no cold spots, no tapping, no mannequin.

She told me in that moment: 'That was the part that gave me peace. I wasn't mad. I could feel that I wasn't. Whatever happened, it wasn't in my head – it was in that shop.'

I asked her, gently, what she did next.

Patricia looked down at her hands for a long moment. Then up at me, her face unreadable. 'I went back,' she said. 'And what happened next was worse.'

Patricia returned to work the following week, determined to take back control of her life. To her surprise, Michael was in good spirits. There was no mention of her absence. No stern looks. Just a nod, and back to business. She finished the VIP suit for the client by the end of that week. It turned out beautifully. The customer was delighted. For the next two weeks, everything was fine. The shop felt … normal again. Patricia worked her usual hours, stayed behind a couple of nights, and walked past Mary without so much as a second glance. Nothing moved. Nothing whispered. Mary stayed put and Patricia began to believe it was over.

Until a Thursday. It was a wet, miserable night. The rain tapped against the windows and ran down the glass like nervous fingers. Patricia was upstairs working late – just her, her needles and the gentle rumble of the storm outside. The others had left at six. She had the whole place to herself and had been working solid for about two hours. She was about to trim the lining of a jacket when the lights suddenly went out.

Total darkness. Just like that.

She groaned. Not in fear, but frustration. It had happened before. The electrics in the shop were ancient. She already knew the drill. She told me this part with a shrug. I asked her if she was scared when that happened.

'No, I wasn't – not at first. It was bloody annoying, but that was it. I just assumed it was a blown fuse.'

She had stood, stretching her back, and started to look for a torch.

Then she heard it.

The soft shuffling. From the landing outside. The corridor that ran along the upper floor was long, narrow, lined with old doors to rooms no one really used anymore. And someone – something – was dragging their feet across the wood. Slowly … Deliberately.

Patricia froze. She crept to the door and gently pulled it open. What she saw stole the breath from her chest.

A figure… tall; distorted. Backlit by the faint glow of a streetlamp filtering through the far window. Its limbs were crooked.

Wrong.

The head twitched slightly as it moved forward. The sound of its feet brushing the wood echoed softly in the silence.

Then came the voice.

That same voice from before. The chuckle. The word…

'Patricia…' A sing-song whisper of cruel delight. Then the laughter. Sharp. Female. Familiar.

At this point in telling us her story, Patricia began to tremble. Her voice quivered. My dad, watching from across the room, raised a hand gently.

'Let's take a moment,' he said softly.

We paused. She wiped her eyes. Took a long breath. After a few minutes, I asked her, 'Are you okay to go on?'

She nodded. 'Yes,' she whispered.

☽✧✝✧☾

Patricia snapped into action. Her paralysis broke and she turned, scrambling for the torch. She finally found it and flicked it on – and shone it down the corridor.

The figure stood still now. Unmoving. It was Mary. But she wasn't dressed. No coat. No scarf. Just the bare mannequin. Arms by her sides. Blank face staring forward. The torchlight made her seem oddly real. Real skin. Real presence.

Patricia couldn't breathe. She turned off the torch … And the moment the darkness swallowed the landing – Mary moved!

Patricia screamed. She fumbled wildly with the torch, hands slick with sweat.

I couldn't help myself. I leaned in, my stomach clenched tight.

'What was going through your head at that moment, Pat?' I asked.

Patricia looked right at me. 'I thought I was going to die.'

She had found the switch on the torch. The light snapped on. Mary stopped. Instantly. But this time she was closer. A couple of feet from the door.

And now, her mouth … was different.

There was a smile. Barely there. Just the faintest curl of the lips. Patricia edged forward, the beam fixed on the mannequin's face. She passed her, inch by inch. Heart pounding. Hands trembling. She never took her eyes off Mary. The mannequin didn't move. She made it past, bolted down the stairs, grabbed her things and left.

Patricia never returned to the shop. She handed in her notice a few days later, and never gave the family a reason why. Didn't explain. She simply vanished from that part of her life.

☽✧†✧☾

Patricia's story is, without question, one of the most disturbing I've ever been told. It reads like something from a horror film; a creeping tale of madness and impossible things. A haunted mannequin. A voice in the dark.

On the surface, it's ridiculous.

And yet, as she told it – there was no laughter in her eyes. No sign of performance. Just trembling hands, pale skin, and a memory she'd been carrying for fifteen years.

I don't believe Patricia is lying. I don't believe she made it up. But somehow, I can't quite believe it, because it sounds impossible.

Could it have been some kind of mental break? Maybe. I'm not a psychiatrist. But Patricia had no history of mental illness before this. No history since. And if it was a breakdown – why did it only happen inside that shop? Why did it feel so targeted?

1994 was the same year I had my first major sighting at Serlby Rise. When the veil between what's real and what isn't first lifted for me. Who am I to say her truth is any less valid than mine? Whether you believe in ghosts or not, one thing is certain: Patricia believes she met something evil in that tailor's shop.

And she's still running from it.

☽✧☥✧☾

Steven's Story

The House That Remembered

Not every story in this book came to me directly. Every now and then, one arrives by another path entirely – quietly, like something passed under a door.

This one came from the files of an old friend.

Derek was a well-respected paranormal investigator based in Nottingham, with a reputation for being methodical, honest and unshakably curious. When he passed away in 2018, he left behind a collection of case files, handwritten notes and transcripts – some unfinished, some barely more than scribbled thoughts. Among them was a folder marked Derby: 2005 – written in Derek's neat, unmistakable handwriting. I remember the feeling I had when I first read through this particular file. It wasn't fear. It was fascination. There was something different about this one. It wasn't poltergeist activity or a haunting in the traditional sense. There were no flying plates, no screams in the night. It was something else entirely – something quieter and harder to define.

A man named Steven Calder, 44 years old at the time, living in a Georgian townhouse on the edge of Derby's historic quarter, had begun to experience what he believed were time slips inside his own home. According to Derek's notes, Steven was a successful man. He wasn't prone to fantasy or superstition. Quite the opposite. He was a heritage architect by trade, the founder of a well-established consultancy firm that specialised in restoring listed buildings to their former glory. His projects included stately homes, chapels, and even a few National Trust properties. He knew the past intimately, but always through stone and timber – not through dreams.

Steven had lived in the Peak District for most of his adult life, but after a divorce in his late thirties he relocated to Derby to be closer to his teenage son, Eric. It was there that he met Marcia – a bright, sharp-witted art curator – and within a year, they were married. She was fifteen years his junior, stylish and driven, with a calm but aloof manner that didn't always sit well with everyone. Still, to Steven, she brought a renewed energy to his life. A chance to start again.

In 2004, they bought the house.

It was a three-storey Georgian townhouse built around 1815, just after the Regency period. The brickwork was soft red, weathered from years of Derbyshire rain. Sash windows framed the front, each with original glazing that shimmered oddly in certain lights. An iron railing bordered the small front path, and ivy crept modestly up the right-hand side, stopping just below the master bedroom window. It had once been the residence of a prominent surgeon in the mid-nineteenth century, later divided into boarding rooms during the war years, and eventually returned to a private dwelling in the 1970s. Steven had fallen for it instantly. To him, it was a living thing. A beautiful, breathing artefact. He poured money into its restoration – not to modernise it, but to revive it. Everything was done properly. Lime plaster, period-appropriate wallpaper, even antique light switches. Where other owners might have installed spotlights and laminate flooring, Steven worked with artisans and historians to retain the house's soul.

And the house did have a soul.

It creaked at odd times. It groaned in the wind. It had peculiar acoustics, the kind that made your own footsteps sound like someone else's, one room over. It wasn't frightening – just old. A place with memory in its bones.

Steven moved in with Marcia and Eric in early 2005. They'd been there just over a year when the dreams began.

They were always the same.

In the dream, Steven would find himself standing in his own home – but it wasn't his anymore. The furniture was different. The lighting was softer, more golden. Candles lit alcoves that no longer existed. He'd hear voices – sometimes hushed, sometimes full of laughter. A woman in a muslin gown would walk briskly through the hallway, carrying a folded letter. Children's laughter would echo faintly from upstairs. On more than one occasion, there was music – a high, tinkling melody played delicately on what he later believed was a pianoforte.

Nothing dramatic ever happened in the dreams. No danger. No jump scares. Just scenes from another time. Lives unfolding quietly in the same space his own life now occupied.

He began writing them down, curious to see if they would change. But they never did. The same events, the same lighting, the same feeling. It was as though he was revisiting a memory that wasn't his.

Marcia didn't think much of it. She told him he was probably just absorbing too much from his work – that all the reading about period architecture was bound to seep into his subconscious eventually. Eric, then 16, was less diplomatic. He rolled his eyes and made jokes about his dad losing it.

But Steven wasn't so sure.

He'd had vivid dreams before, sure – but not like these. Not dreams that lingered well into the morning. Not dreams that left him with the sensation of having actually been somewhere. He tried to ignore them. Put them down to stress. New marriage, new house, teenage son going through a difficult patch. It was all explainable.

Until the day he walked into the drawing room – and saw the dream while awake.

☽✧✝✧☾

The first time it happened, Steven was entirely awake.

It was a quiet Sunday afternoon, the sort of grey, overcast day Derby is known for – where the sky feels low and heavy, and the rain hangs in the air but never quite falls. Marcia had gone out to meet a friend for lunch. Eric was upstairs in his bedroom, lost in headphones and whatever teenage world he occupied that week. The house was still…

Steven had spent the morning rearranging some books in the drawing room. The bottom shelves of the tall bookcases had started to bow slightly under the weight, and he'd been meaning to reorganise them for weeks. It was mundane, slow work – the kind that allowed the mind to wander. He stacked paperbacks, grouped old architectural volumes by century, and paused occasionally to flip through some of his older, dustier titles.

It was around three o'clock when it happened.

He had just stood up from a sofa, pressing one hand to his back, when a strange stillness came over the room. Not silence exactly – the usual distant hum of the street was still there, the faint creak of the staircase as Eric shifted his weight upstairs – but something else had changed. The quality of the light, perhaps. Or the air itself.

It was cooler.

Sharper.

He glanced toward the window and stopped. The sash curtains were no longer the ones Marcia had chosen last spring. Gone was the heavy velvet in deep emerald. In its place were lighter, patterned drapes – a pale cream with tiny blue flowers – and they were tied back with twisted rope cords.

He turned fully and looked around the room.

The wallpaper had changed. The framed etchings they'd hung were gone. In their place were three oval portraits in gilded frames, hanging in a perfectly symmetrical row. The rug beneath his feet was no longer the Persian one he'd purchased in a gallery in Norwich, but something more muted – hand-woven, with a faded floral pattern in rose and ochre.

The furniture too – rearranged. Replaced.

A smaller table now sat beneath the window, its legs thin and tapered. Two ladies' hats sat upon it. Beside them, a leather-gloved hand rested against the edge of a wooden chair.

Steven blinked.

The hand was still there. Attached to a woman seated calmly at the table. She wore a bonnet and a long muslin dress, her profile only half-visible. Her features were soft, her skin pale, and her hands were folded neatly in her lap. Opposite her sat a man – bearded, with a narrow face and waistcoat. He was pouring tea.

There was no sound from them. The room remained filled only with the ambient hush of the day. But they were there. Clearly there.

Steven didn't move. He didn't dare. He watched, heart pounding but his feet rooted to the floor. The couple sat together for what felt like several minutes, going about their silent routine – pouring tea, gesturing as though in conversation, the woman dabbing her mouth with a handkerchief.

And then –

A blink.

A shift.

The room was back. The velvet curtains. The Persian rug. The etchings. The bookcase he'd just rearranged. For several seconds Steven remained perfectly still, staring at the space where the woman had sat, his breath barely audible. He wasn't sure if he'd moved. Wasn't sure if he'd breathed at all during the entire event.

There had been no fade-in, no swirl of light or distortion. The room had changed as seamlessly as a slide in a projector – click, and it was different. He sat down slowly on the arm of the chair and looked at his hands. They were shaking. Not violently, but enough to notice. Enough to worry him.

It wasn't like the dreams.

It wasn't a feeling. It wasn't a daydream or some imagined overlay. He had seen them…

Really seen them.

☽✧†✧☾

He didn't tell Marcia that evening. She was in a snappy mood when she came home, frustrated with her friend for being late, and irritated that Eric had left his muddy trainers in the hall. There was already a row brewing between her and the boy by the time Steven had opened his mouth. He'd let it go.

That night, lying in bed with his eyes wide open, Steven began to question everything. Had he fallen asleep without realising? Had he stood too fast, triggered some sort of head rush that brought on a hallucination? Was he overworked? He didn't feel unwell. His mind felt clearer than it had in days.

And that, in itself, was more unsettling than anything.

The next morning, he stood in the same spot in the drawing room. The light was different now – brighter, colder – but the room remained as they had decorated it. No echo of his vision remained. No trace. But something had happened. Something real.

And he wasn't ready to dismiss it.

☽✧†✧☾

After that first experience in the drawing room, something in Steven shifted. He tried not to dwell on it, but it was like trying not to think about blinking. The more he tried to push it aside, the more his mind circled back. Had he really seen them? Was it a trick of the light? A momentary lapse? A fragment of a dream slipping through the cracks?

But within days, it happened again.

This time, in the upstairs hallway.

He'd been heading to his study – mid-morning, coffee in hand – when the corridor seemed to darken slightly. Not dramatically. Just enough to make him pause. The light from the window at the end of the landing had a warmer hue to it, more golden. Dust particles hung in the air like falling ash. The wallpaper had changed again – more patterned, floral, the kind he'd seen in National Trust houses. A thick runner stretched the length of the floorboards, its tasselled edges brushing against his shoes.

At the far end of the corridor, just for a second, he saw movement. A figure slipping through one of the bedroom doors. A swish of skirts. A pale hand pulling the door closed.

Then gone.

No sound. No trace.

He stood there a long time, heartbeat in his ears. By the time Marcia returned from her errands that afternoon, he had talked himself back down. He didn't mention it. He didn't want to sound paranoid. Didn't want to admit – even to her – that he was beginning to anticipate them. Wait for them. Like catching glimpses of a memory that didn't belong to him, unfolding in slivers.

The days that followed brought more of these mysterious visions:

- A toddler crawling across the flagstone kitchen floor, chasing a toy horse on wheels.
- A woman beating a rug with a wicker paddle in the back courtyard.
- A man in a red waistcoat lighting a candle at the hallway sconce.
- A black spaniel curled at the foot of the stairs, looking up at him with bored, sleepy eyes before fading like smoke.

They never lasted long. Never more than thirty seconds. Sometimes only five. But they were always full. Full of atmosphere. Full of life.

And they were never threatening.

Just … other.

Steven began to document them. He bought a leather-bound notebook and began writing down what he saw. Dates, times, weather conditions, what room he was in, what he'd eaten, how he'd slept. He even noted the mood of the house. Was it unusually still? Did he feel cold beforehand? Was there a smell – parchment, polish, tobacco?

Patterns began to form. Most of the visions occurred between three and five in the afternoon. Most often when he was alone. Always in the older parts of the house – drawing room, hallway, kitchen. Never in the newer extension. He began to suspect that the house itself was playing a role. That it wasn't something happening to him, but rather something the building was showing him.

The most vivid event came in late April. It was a Thursday, around 4.30 pm. Steven was in the dining room, tidying up some plans for a restoration project in Matlock. The room was bright and still smelled faintly of polish from earlier that morning. He stepped into the hall to fetch a glass of water.

And there it was.

As he turned back into the dining room, everything shifted. The light dimmed to a golden amber. The scent in the air changed – something older, richer, the smell of pipe smoke and beeswax. The furniture had changed again. The heavy dining table was smaller, square and surrounded by four people.

They sat, chairs slightly angled inward, all mid-conversation. Three men and one woman. All dressed in period clothing – high collars, cravats, tailored bodices. One of the men was older, bearded and wore spectacles. Another was clearly military – dark jacket with brass buttons, a faded red sash. The third was younger, animated, hands gesturing as he spoke. The woman, quiet and poised, held a teacup and gave a small nod of amusement.

Steven could hear them. Not just muffled sounds – actual words.

'…Keene says the rail will pass just north, but I told him – no, not with that bank in place…'

'Keene,' the older man interrupted gently, 'is a surgeon, not a land surveyor.'

'I'd trust his judgement more than half the men in Parliament,' the younger one replied with a grin.

The woman laughed softly.

'August fourteenth, then,' the military man said. 'If the weather holds.'

Steven's breath caught. He was in the room with them. Standing silently at the threshold. They didn't see him. Didn't respond to him. But they were vivid. Real. The colour of their skin. The way the lace at the woman's wrist trembled when she lifted her cup. The nick on the edge of the bearded man's chin where he'd recently cut himself shaving.

And then –

It faded.

No warning. No blink. Just … gone. The dining room was his again. His furniture. His light. His silence. But the name – Keene – and the date – August 14th – lodged themselves in his mind like a hook.

That night, Steven sat on the edge of the bath while Marcia brushed her teeth. He wanted to tell her. To say, 'I think I'm seeing the past.' But she'd had a difficult day – there had been another argument with Eric. Something about phone bills. She was tired and short-tempered. He didn't want to add more to her mood.

So he said nothing.

Instead, he went downstairs, poured himself a Scotch, and opened his notebook. He wrote down everything. The faces. The clothes. The names. The date.

Then, without quite knowing why, he wrote:

'I don't think I'm imagining this. And I don't think I'm ill. I think I'm witnessing something.'

And in the quiet of the house, Steven began to believe it.

☽✧✝✧☾

As spring turned into summer, the house seemed to breathe in a rhythm all its own. Some days were quiet – normal, even. Steven would go about his work, Marcia would potter around the house, and Eric would stay mostly confined to his bedroom, the muffled bassline of his music pulsing faintly through the floorboards.

But then there were days when the air seemed different. Thick, expectant. On those days, Steven almost knew something was going to happen. And sure enough, the visions would come.

He would step into the kitchen to make tea and find himself standing in a room that no longer belonged to him: the stone-flagged floor wet from a recent mopping, the hearth blackened with soot. He'd see a woman in a plain muslin apron tending a pot on the stove, humming softly under her breath. There would be a moment – a heartbeat – where he almost wanted to speak to her. To ask who she was. What year it was.

But it never lasted long enough. The scenes were like breathing in smoke. They filled him briefly, then left nothing but the faintest trace.

Steven told no one. It wasn't that he didn't want to. It was that the moments he might have shared it – the quiet pauses over dinner, or the rare, peaceful afternoons – were never quite right. The tension in the house was a weight pressing down on everything. It was in the air when Eric and Marcia passed each other in the hall without speaking, or when Eric muttered under his breath at the dinner table and Marcia responded with clipped sarcasm. It was in the way Steven felt himself stretched thin between them, trying to hold two worlds together – his family, and whatever strange echoes the house kept revealing.

He didn't have the energy for both. The arguments between Eric and Marcia grew sharper. Sometimes over little things – dirty plates left out, the washing machine left unemptied. Other times, it was bigger. Eric's resentment simmered just beneath the surface. He didn't like Marcia. He didn't trust her. And he didn't hide it.

'Why do I have to listen to her?' he snapped one evening after she told him to turn his music down. Steven tried to mediate, but it always left him feeling hollow. He would sit at the dinner table, fork in hand, while the words flew back and forth. He felt like a ghost himself sometimes, invisible in his own home. Like he was watching his family through the same lens as the figures from the past.

One evening, after a particularly heated argument between Marcia and Eric about his schoolwork, Steven stood in the kitchen, staring at the sink, the voices rising behind him like a distant storm. He felt the pressure building in his chest – the weight of it all – and he turned his head slightly…

And there she was.

The woman from the dining room. The one with the pale hands and the delicate lace at her wrists. Standing just behind him. Her face soft in profile, eyes downcast, as though waiting for someone.

The kitchen around her was different again – darker, simpler, with a large wooden table and a flickering oil lamp in the corner. The smell of bread baking hung faintly in the air. And the sound of the argument – Marcia's sharp voice, Eric's clipped replies – faded away, replaced by the crackle of a hearth fire and the creak of the floorboards underfoot.

For a moment, Steven let himself stand in it. Let the past settle around him like dust… Then it was gone. The kitchen was his again. The harsh electric lights, the chrome kettle, the hum of the fridge.

And the sound of a door slamming upstairs.

It was during these weeks that Steven began to question his own mind.

He told Derek, in the files, that he began to fear there was something wrong with him. Was it stress? A breakdown brought on by the pressures of home life? The new marriage, the teenage son, the demands of his career – was it all too much?

He decided to seek help. Quietly. Without telling Marcia. He booked an appointment with a private psychiatrist. He told her everything. The dreams. The visions. The sounds. The names. The doctor listened carefully. Took notes. Asked thoughtful questions.

After several sessions, she told him gently that there was no evidence of psychosis. No signs of delusion or hallucination. His mind, she said, was healthy.

He wasn't sure whether to feel relieved or disappointed. If it wasn't mental illness – then what was it? It was at this point that Steven began to believe he wasn't imagining it. That these weren't just tricks of the brain, but something the house itself was showing him. A kind of memory pressed into the walls, like an old painting beneath layers of wallpaper.

He started to wonder if the house was trying to teach him something. Or maybe just let him witness something he wasn't meant to see.

Whatever it was, he was beginning to accept it.

And yet, in the background – the arguments continued. The house wasn't just Steven's private gallery of the past. It was still a home. Still filled with the complicated, messy lives of the living.

And that tension – between then and now – was beginning to take its toll.

☽✧☨✧☾

Steven wasn't the kind of man to sit with questions for long. He'd built a career on knowing where to look, how to research, how to dig into the past and pull the bones of history into the light. The house, in its quiet, unspoken way, had given him clues – a name, a date, a face – and now it was up to him to see if they meant anything.

He began his search at a local study library in Derby. It felt almost normal at first – this was his world, after all. Stacks of bound parish records, yellowed newspapers on microfilm, property deeds scrawled in old handwriting. A dusty, familiar landscape of the past. He focused on what he knew.

Keene. August 14th.

A name and a date. That was all.

He started with the census records. It was slow going – page after page of cramped, faded lists of names, occupations, and ages. But there it was: an entry for Dr [name withheld] Keene, age 47, residing at the address that matched his own house in the 1841 census. Occupation: surgeon.

It was like a switch flicking in his brain. The man was real. He had lived in the house. A tangible, breathing person who had once walked the same floors Steven now paced.

From there, Steven's research became more focused. He cross-referenced directories, probate records, local archives. He found a mention of Dr Keene in a small article from 1842, printed in the *Derby Mercury*. It was a passing note about a gathering hosted at the residence of Dr Keene, attended by several local figures – names Steven recognised from the voices in his visions.

The tea party had been real!

The conversation he'd overheard in the dining room – the lighthearted dispute about the railway line, the mention of the date – had taken place. The article confirmed it. August 14th.

Steven sat in the library that afternoon, a quiet pulse of adrenaline running through him. It wasn't just imagination. It wasn't a trick of his mind. The names, the conversations, the fragments he had witnessed – they had happened.

He copied the article, folded it neatly, and slipped it into his notebook alongside his own accounts. He didn't tell Marcia. She had enough on her plate – she and Eric were still barely speaking, the air between them brittle and sharp. The house felt divided into islands: Eric upstairs in his room, Marcia in the living room scrolling through her PC, Steven at the kitchen table, notebook open, piecing together the past.

One evening, as the rain drummed softly against the window panes, Steven sat with a glass of wine, staring at the lines he'd written.

'I think I am seeing the past.'

It was the only explanation that made sense.

☽✧✝✧☾

Steven returned to the library again the following week, chasing smaller details. He found a baptism record for a child born to Keene and his wife. He learned the doctor had died in 1853, of 'congestion of the lungs'. A sad, unremarkable death, noted in a small obituary. But no dramatic stories. No scandals. No murders. No dark history.

It was just life; a quiet, ordinary life.

And that, in a strange way, made it feel more real. These weren't spirits trapped in a cycle of torment. They were people. And for a few fleeting moments, Steven had shared a space with them. Had seen them, as they were. It unsettled him – not in a fearful way, but in a way that made him feel small. Like he'd brushed against the thin fabric that separates now from then.

He told Derek that this discovery left him feeling both reassured and disoriented. It was comforting, in a way, to know that the house's past was real. That he wasn't losing his mind. But it also left him with a new question – why was he seeing it? And why only him? Why not Marcia? Why not Eric? Had the house chosen him, or was it simply that he was open to it?

There were no answers. Just the quiet ticking of the clock, the rustle of leaves outside the window, and the weight of lives long gone pressing faintly against the present.

After a little while, the visions grew less frequent. The house seemed to settle.

☽✧✝✧☾

The visions didn't continue forever. For all the strangeness, the quiet awe and the sense of standing at the edge of something inexplicable, the episodes grew less frequent over time – until, quite suddenly, they stopped altogether. No grand finale. No final message or farewell. Just a slow, quiet fading, like the last ripples on a pond smoothing out into stillness.

Steven never saw the figures again. The rooms stayed as they were – fixed in the present, no longer shifting into half-glimpsed scenes from the past. The names, the faces, the subtle sounds – gone. It was as though the house had shared its story with him, then simply… closed the door.

He told Derek: 'It left me with a feeling I can't quite describe. It wasn't fear. It wasn't relief. It was more like … standing in an empty theatre after the curtain falls. The show's over, but you know something important happened here. You just don't know why it happened to you.'

Life in the house continued, but the atmosphere remained strained. The arguments between Marcia and Eric never truly settled. The sharp words, the quiet silences – they lingered long after the time slips had ended. Steven did his best to keep the peace, but it was like trying to smooth out a crease in fabric that wouldn't lie flat.

A couple of years after the experiences, Steven and Marcia divorced. It wasn't dramatic. No explosive fights. Just a quiet understanding that whatever had brought them together had faded. They parted ways amicably enough, but Steven later admitted to Derek that the house – and everything that had happened there – had left a mark on him, in ways he hadn't fully understood at the time.

Eric, now older, moved out not long after. Life moved on. The house became just a house again. The past, it seemed, had retreated into the walls.

When I first read through Derek's file on Steven's case, I was struck by how quiet the story was. No screaming ghosts. No poltergeist chaos. Just the gentle, inexplicable bleed-through of other lives – moments long gone, imprinted somehow on the walls of a house in Derby.

I began researching time slips in earnest. It's a phenomenon I've come across before – rare, but not unheard of. One of the most famous cases is the 1979 incident involving two couples holidaying together, Len and Cynthia Gisby and Geoff and Pauline Simpson. They were travelling through France when they claimed to have experienced a sudden shift – finding themselves in what appeared to be an old-fashioned inn staffed by people in period clothing. Later, when they tried to return to the same location, the inn had vanished. Their story has been debated for years, and while it sounds incredible, it's not unique.

Could Steven's experiences have been something similar? Was he somehow seeing through time – catching echoes of the past, moments that still lingered in the fabric of the house?

Or was it something else entirely? Another theory is that of a residual haunting – where events from the past imprint themselves on a place and play back under certain conditions, like a recording stuck on a loop. There's no interaction, no awareness – just the repetition of life long gone.

Steven's story seems to fit that idea, too.

I can't say for certain what happened to him. But I believe him. I believe he saw something – something that wasn't a dream, or a trick of the mind, or a simple case of overwork.

Whether it was a time slip or a haunting – or perhaps something we don't even have the words for – I don't know. But I do know this:

Some places remember.

And sometimes, if you're standing in just the right spot, at just the right moment, they let you see.

☽✧☨✧☾

My Haunted Life

Part Five

Seeking Help

Steven's story certainly leaves you thinking a lot about the nature of time – about how certain places seem to hold on to the past, refusing to let it fade completely. His case wasn't frightening in the traditional sense, but it had a way of making you question the fabric of reality itself. Was it a haunting? A time slip? Or something else entirely? I didn't have the answers. I still don't.

But as I think about his case now, one thought keeps coming back to me.

If Steven's house could echo with the lives of those who had come before… could the same be true of the place I grew up? Because just like Steven, my own family was living through something that we just didn't understand.

And those shadows were growing thicker by the day…

Seeking Help at Serlby

At that point in our lives, Dad was a man consumed by his faith. A devoted Christian, he attended church services diligently every Thursday and Sunday. His Christian faith actually stemmed back to April 1973, when he was making a name for himself on the local football scene at the age of 19. He was a decent goalkeeper, despite only being 5ft 9in – he was agile, fearless and quick to dive for the ball. But one match in particular would mark a strange turning point in his life. During a Sunday league game, he went for a save and smacked his head hard against the goalpost. From everything he later described, it was likely a concussion – dazed, nauseous, seeing stars – but instead of heading to A&E to get checked out, he did something that, in hindsight, was a big mistake. It was something that was very typical of my dad. That evening, with his head still throbbing, he went to the cinema with his then-girlfriend to see *The Exorcist*!

The film had only just been released and was causing a stir across the country – people fainting, walking out, claiming it was evil. For my dad, already vulnerable from the knock to the head, it proved to be too much. The imagery, the themes, the sheer intensity of it all – something about it got under his skin in a way nothing else had. It disturbed him deeply, left a mark that he couldn't quite shake.

In the weeks that followed, his outlook changed dramatically. He started having trouble sleeping, felt anxious all the time, and became fixated on the idea of evil – not in a metaphorical sense, but real, tangible evil. It was as though the film had cracked something open inside him. Eventually, he turned to religion. He started going to church, reading the Bible, and trying to make sense of what he'd seen – and maybe what he'd felt. For the first time in his life, he said he 'found God'. Whether it was the head injury, the film, or something deeper, I don't know. But from that point on, his faith became a central part of who he was.

Now, over twenty years later, his faith remained strong and his conviction was resolute – our home, he believed, was haunted, likely by something evil. He believed because he knew himself that ghosts existed. Dad knew this because he had encountered them years before.

Moffat Street, 1968

It was in 1968 when my dad had what he always described as his first real brush with the paranormal. He was just 14 at the time, living on Moffat Street in St Ann's with his parents – my nana and grandad, Joan and Frank – and his little sister, my Auntie Diane. Back then, ghosts weren't something that really crossed his mind. He was a down-to-earth kid, more interested in football and music than anything supernatural. But that day changed all of that.

It was one of those grim, grey Nottingham days – rain hammering at the windows, the streets outside slick and miserable. Dad had come down with a bad cold. Nothing dramatic, just one of those annoying, lingering illnesses: blocked nose, sore throat, low temperature. He felt rough enough that Nana decided to keep him off school. She and Grandad both had to go to work, and since Dad was old enough to be trusted on his own, they left him at home to rest. It was just him, the telly, a bottle of dandelion and burdock, and a heavy quilt to keep him warm.

He told me this story years later, and I'll never forget the look on his face. Even then, long after the event, you could see it still unsettled him. This wasn't a tale told for effect – this had happened, and it had stayed with him.

He was lying on the settee in the front room, watching whatever was on the box, trying to ride out the worst of the cold. Everything was quiet, ordinary.

Until it wasn't.

From out in the hallway, something caught his attention. A sound – soft at first, but distinct. Footsteps on the staircase. At first, he thought it might have been his imagination, or maybe a sound from next door. But no; these were definite footsteps. Slow, deliberate, descending the stairs one by one. And they were getting louder. He froze. Completely rigid. His whole body tensed as the footsteps came closer. Louder. Heavier. There was nobody else in the house. That he knew for certain. For a brief moment he thought someone had broken in. The steps continued – pounding now – making their way down towards the hall.

Dad turned his head and looked through the open living room door. From that angle, he had a clear view of the bottom of the staircase.

There was no one there.

But the footsteps carried on, coming down, as plain and as physical as if someone invisible was walking right past the banister. And then – just as suddenly as they had started – they stopped. Dead. Like the sound had been cut off mid-step.

No more noise. No figure. Nothing.

The house was silent again, but the atmosphere had shifted completely. The warmth of the room, the comfort of the quilt – it all vanished under a wave of creeping dread. All that day, my dad said he couldn't shake the feeling that something was watching him. That it hadn't just been footsteps, but a presence. Something that had come down those stairs and lingered just out of sight, at the very bottom, watching him from the shadows.

The footsteps never returned. In fact, nothing ghostly ever occurred in the house again. But something had changed in my dad from that moment on. That was the day he discovered that ghosts were real.

Back at Serlby Rise, despite everything that had happened, the idea that our house might actually be haunted seemed absurd to my mum. She dismissed it outright, waving away any talk of the supernatural with a scoff or a sharp look. To her, these things were nonsense, fairy stories. But Dad – Dad had seen the fear in my eyes, had heard the crack in my voice when I tried to explain what I had seen. He knew something wasn't right. He decided to act. One Sunday after the church service, Dad approached our vicar, Darryl, a soft-spoken man with a kind face but an edge of firmness to him. He told Darryl everything – the strange atmosphere, the unexplained disturbances, the sighting of the old woman. And to Dad's relief, Darryl listened. He didn't laugh or shake his head. He simply nodded and promised that he would come to our home and help.

The Blessing

The weeks dragged by. Each day seemed to stretch longer than the last, steeped in the same tense, uneasy atmosphere that had begun to define life inside our house. The nights were the worst. It wasn't just fear anymore – it was dread. The kind that sat in your stomach and made your skin crawl the moment the sun dipped below the rooftops. Every evening, as darkness crept in, I'd feel it – that weight pressing down on me, the sense of being watched from the corners of empty rooms. Even when the house was silent, it didn't feel still. Something had changed in the air. Something subtle, but undeniable.

I found myself thinking constantly about that faceless figure in the kitchen. I couldn't explain it, no matter how many times I went over it in my head. What I'd seen hadn't just scared me – it had shifted something inside me. It had confirmed what I think I'd already begun to suspect deep down. This wasn't just a house. It wasn't just a bad dream. Something was living here with us. The house had a pulse of its own now, and we were living inside it.

Mum had gone back to working more shifts at The Alcester, often in the evenings. It was her way of earning extra money. She wasn't one to dwell on the unknown. To her, if it couldn't be fixed or explained, it was better ignored. But that didn't work for the rest of us – not anymore.

Then one chilly evening, as the daylight faded early and the streetlights cast long shadows across the living room carpet, Darryl arrived. He didn't come alone. There were three or four other people with him. All from his church. They weren't what I expected. No robes, no incense, no drama. Just normal-looking people, all dressed in everyday clothes. But they carried with them something else – a seriousness, a quiet determination that made the atmosphere shift the moment they walked through the front door. I remember watching them as they entered, noticing how none of them smiled or made small talk. They were there for a purpose.

Dad answered the door and greeted them with a kind of nervous relief. He kept glancing behind him to check where I was, making sure I wasn't too close. But I was already listening. Already watching. Before anything began, Dad pulled me aside and knelt down beside me. He looked me square in the eyes – serious, but kind.

'You mustn't tell Mam about this,' he said gently. 'She won't understand. You know what she's like.'

I did know. If Mum had been there, she would have rolled her eyes and called us 'daft boggas' – her way of saying we were being stupid or gullible. She'd have chalked everything up to overactive imaginations or the stress of daily life. And maybe, in some ways, I wished I could believe that too.

I nodded and promised I wouldn't say a word. Then I stood quietly in the background as Darryl and the others moved through the house, a silent procession of intent. They didn't speak much. Just murmured quietly to one another as they began the blessing. I followed them at a distance, always a few steps behind, trying to understand what they were doing. Every room they entered seemed to grow colder, more still. It was strange – the house somehow felt larger, as though the walls had shifted when I wasn't looking. The familiar spaces of our home – the kitchen, the living room, the hallway – suddenly felt foreign, stretched out and eerie. Even the furniture looked different. The sofa, the dining table, the cabinets … everything felt harder, more angular. It was like the house itself was holding its breath.

Darryl led the way. He held a small glass vial in one hand and used the oil inside it to mark the sign of the cross on every window, every doorframe, every mirror. I still don't know what that oil was. I didn't ask. I just remember watching those little glistening crosses appear on the glass and feeling deeply, uncomfortably unsettled. There was something about those marks that made it all feel so real. This wasn't just a story any more, something we were imagining. We were doing battle with an invisible entity, something we couldn't see but could all feel. And those little oil crosses – wet and shimmering in the dim light – felt like lines drawn in a war.

As they moved through the house, Darryl spoke softly. He never raised his voice, never shouted or performed. He just moved steadily from room to room, murmuring prayers under his breath, crossing himself, sprinkling oil. At one point, I remember him pausing by the stairs and placing a hand on the bannister, closing his eyes.

'There is something here,' he said quietly. 'It's been here for a while.'

He didn't look scared, but there was a seriousness in his voice that made the hairs on my arms stand up. He talked a little about what he believed it was – a dark spirit, something evil. He said it wasn't just a ghost. It was something that wanted to twist things, to terrorise, to feed off fear. That it had attached itself to our home somehow.

That stuck with me – attached. Like a parasite.

For what felt like hours, they went through every part of the house. The bedrooms, the bathroom, the kitchen. No corner was left untouched. And all the while, I stood by and watched. Not fully understanding what was being done, but knowing – deep down – that it had to be done.

Eventually, they gathered back in the living room. Darryl looked exhausted. There was a sheen of sweat on his forehead, despite the chill in the air. The others looked tired too – drained, like they'd each carried a weight for the last hour and were only now being allowed to put it down.

'It's done,' Darryl said, looking at me and Dad. 'The spirit was something evil. But it has been cast out. You don't need to be afraid anymore.'

I looked at my dad. His shoulders had relaxed, his eyes softer than they'd been in weeks. I could tell he believed it. He wanted to believe it. And standing there, surrounded by the people who had come to help us, I wanted to believe it too. I smiled, trying to mirror my dad's relief. Trying to feel the peace he seemed to feel.

But inside, something twisted. A small knot of doubt lodged itself in my stomach. It wasn't that I didn't trust Darryl or what he'd done. It wasn't even that I thought he was wrong. It was just … a feeling. A sensation I couldn't shake. Like something had been covered up, rather than removed. Like we'd patched a crack in the wall, but the damage behind it was still there. I didn't say anything. Not to Dad, not to Darryl, not to anyone.

But that night, after they'd all gone, I lay in bed and stared at the ceiling for hours.

Listening.

Waiting.

Hoping that silence would be just silence again.

But the fear didn't leave me. It lingered like a shadow at the back of my mind, whispering that it wasn't over.

And I was right.

☽✧✝✧☾

Melanie's Story

Curse of the Crying Boy

This next story came to me not through a case I investigated directly, nor from an old friend like Derek, but from a simple email I received out of the blue in 2017.

It was a damp Thursday afternoon, and I remember the moment clearly – sitting at my desk with a beer, catching up on messages. Among the usual pile of junk mail and social media notifications, there was one that stood out. The subject line was short, simple:

My parents' story

It was from a woman named Melanie, and her email was brief – just a few lines, really – but it gripped me instantly. She said her parents, Christine and John, had experienced something strange in the early 1980s. It was something she felt I might be interested in. She described a painting, a house fire and a series of unsettling events that had left her family shaken and, in her words, 'haunted for years afterwards'.

Melanie had found my 'Nottingham Ghost Investigations' page on Facebook. She told me both her parents had died – her mother in 2013, and her father a couple of years later. Melanie had always wanted to tell this story but she hadn't felt comfortable to share until her parents had passed away. I emailed her back straight away, thanking her for sharing the story and asking if she'd be willing to talk more. A week later, we set up a Zoom call.

I still remember seeing Melanie's face on the screen for the first time. She was in her late forties by then, with short dark hair and kind, intelligent eyes that seemed to carry the weight of what she was about to tell me. Behind her, I could see shelves lined with family photographs – snapshots of holidays, birthdays, everyday life.

After the usual introductions, I asked her gently. 'Tell me about your parents, Melanie. What were they like?'

She smiled, but there was sadness in it.

'They were ... normal people, you know? Working class. My dad worked in a factory all his life, the old Guy Motors factory. My mum was a housewife. Nothing fancy. Just ... a family. They loved each other, but times were hard sometimes. And the house ... well, it wasn't always easy.'

I nodded, letting her speak at her own pace.

'And the painting?' I asked.

'That's what I wanted to tell you about,' she said. 'The Crying Boy. That bloody painting. That's where it all started.'

☽✧†✧☾

Christine and John had moved into their house – a semi-detached in a working-class Wolverhampton neighbourhood – in 1979. Melanie would have been about 6 then. It was the kind of place you could walk past a dozen times without noticing. The front garden was small, just a patch of grass and a cracked concrete path leading to the door. Inside, it was cosy but cramped – three bedrooms, a narrow staircase that creaked underfoot, a small galley kitchen where the smell of cooking always seemed to linger. The wallpaper was dated, the kitchen tiny, but it was theirs. It was a fresh start.

'Mum was always house-proud,' Melanie told me. 'She liked things neat, you know? She didn't have much, but she kept it nice. Dad wasn't fussy, but he liked a tidy living room.'

The family weren't well-off, but they made it work. There was food on the table, clothes on their backs, and the telly in the corner for when the day was done.

Life was ordinary for those first few years – quiet, working-class routine. John worked long hours at the local Guy Motors factory, Christine kept the house running, and Melanie and her younger brother Stephen played in the back garden, went to school, and argued over the telly in the evenings.

That changed in 1982, when John's mother – Melanie's grandmother – gave them a gift.

Christine hadn't been close to her mother-in-law. The relationship had been strained for years – polite on the surface, but with an edge that could cut if you weren't careful. John's mum was an old-fashioned woman. Sharp-tongued. The sort who'd make pointed comments about your cooking, or the way you kept your house, or how the children were dressed. Christine, quiet by nature, didn't argue. She smiled, nodded, and kept her feelings tucked away like loose change at the bottom of a handbag.

John's mother had popped round, clutching a black plaid bag from the flea market. She handed it over with a little smile – half-pleased, half-superior – and told Christine it was 'something to brighten the place up a bi'.

Christine opened it, and her heart sank. It was a print of *The Crying Boy* – one of those cheap, mass-produced images that seemed to haunt the walls of working-class homes up and down the country in the '70s and '80s. A little boy, maybe 7 or 8 years old, dark blonde hair, a tear trickling down his cheek. His eyes were wide, blue, and so sad it almost hurt to look at them. The background was a strange, washed-out black-brown, like old varnish, and the frame was thin, plastic, the kind that bends if you press too hard.

Christine hated it.

Melanie's face darkened slightly as she spoke. 'Mum didn't like it. She told me that years later. She said it gave her the creeps from the moment she saw it. But it was a gift from Dad's mum, and she didn't want to cause any trouble, so she put it up in the living room. Above the fireplace. Right in the centre, like it was meant to be there. Me and Stephen even had a photo taken where you can see it.'

From that day on, the painting seemed to settle into the room like it had always been there. The family tried to ignore it. Life carried on – taking the children to school, packed lunches, tea on the table at five.

But the painting's presence grew, in that quiet, insidious way that creeps into a home without anyone really noticing at first. Neighbours came by – Liz and Pete from next door. They were regulars, often popping in for a drink and a chat. Liz was a bit different, though. She had a reputation for being sensitive. Not psychic, not a medium, but the kind of person who'd stop in a doorway and say, 'Oh, there's something not right in here.'

The first time Liz saw the painting, she froze. Stood dead still in the middle of the living room, her eyes fixed on the boy's face. Christine noticed it immediately and asked if she was alright.

Liz had hesitated, then spoke – low, careful. 'Chris … that picture. It's not good. There's something off about it. I don't like the feel of it.'

Christine laughed it off, awkwardly. John dismissed it outright – said Liz was imagining things, always had been a bit of a funny one.

But Liz didn't let it go. Every time she came round after that, she'd glance at the painting, her mouth tightening, her tea growing cold in her hands. Christine tried not to look at it, but it was there. Always there. Watching.

And the house…

Well.

The house began to change.

☽✧✝✧☾

It wasn't a single moment. It wasn't a bang or a crash or a sudden cold gust in the dark. It was slower than that – more malignant. Like a fog seeping through cracks in the brickwork, finding its way into the smallest spaces of the house, the edges of things.

It began with a feeling.

Christine noticed it first in the afternoons, when the kids were at school, John at work, the house settling into its usual quiet hum. It was in the living room, mainly – the front room, where the painting hung above the fireplace, its frame catching the faint, greyish light from the window.

The fire would be on, the little gas flame flickering behind the glass, but the warmth didn't seem to spread. The heat sat in a thin layer around the hearth, but beyond that – nothing. The room felt … cold. Not in the way of a draught, not the sharp bite of winter air coming in through a cracked seal, but a deeper, more stagnant kind of cold.

The kind of cold that made the air feel heavy.

Christine would sit in the armchair by the window, folding clothes or flicking through the radio stations, and find herself pulling her cardigan tighter around her shoulders without thinking. There was a weight to the room now, like the walls had thickened, the ceiling dropped an inch lower, the air pressed in just a little more than it had before.

She tried to ignore it, at first. Tried to tell herself it was nothing. The damp. The season. A cold snap. She even checked the windows, the seals, the fire itself. Everything seemed fine.

But the feeling lingered.

It was worse in the evenings, when the curtains were drawn and the streetlights outside threw long, distorted shadows across the walls. Christine would sit there, smoothing the wrinkles from a tea towel or writing a shopping list at the little side table, and she'd feel it. A faint pressure behind her eyes, a subtle tightening in her chest. It wasn't enough to make her panic – just enough to make her pause, to glance up from her notepad and feel the prickle of awareness running down her spine.

And always, the painting was there. The boy's eyes seemed darker now, or perhaps it was just the low light. The tears on his cheeks seemed shinier, as though the paint had never fully dried. His gaze, though static, seemed to lean toward her, the way a door left ajar might feel like it's waiting to swing open.

Buster, their little Yorkshire Terrier, noticed it too. He'd always been a bold, nosy little thing – always underfoot, always sniffing at shoes or curling up in the warm patch by the gas fire. But since the painting had gone up, he refused to go into the living room at all. Christine tried coaxing him in the first few days, tapping her knee, calling him over with that soft, affectionate tone she always used. But Buster would stop dead at the doorway, his paws rigid against the carpet, his eyes fixed squarely on the painting. His body would lower, almost a crouch, his tail tucked tight beneath him, ears flat.

Then came the soft whimpering. Low, barely audible, but constant when he was near the room. Christine watched him one afternoon as she sat on the settee, a basket of washing on her lap. Buster stood at the threshold, just a little thing silhouetted by the pale light from the hallway. He let out a low, rattling whine, barely more than a breath, and backed away slowly, as though there were an invisible barrier keeping him out.

She told John that evening, as he sat at the table reading the paper, his glasses perched low on his nose.

'John, I don't know what's wrong with him. He won't come into the room anymore.'

John didn't look up. Just licked his thumb, turned a page. 'Probably just picked up a funny smell or something. He's a daft little thing, that dog.'

Christine wanted to believe him. She needed to. But there was something about the way Buster kept looking at that painting – staring at it, ears back, body low – that made her stomach twist in a way she couldn't shake.

The feeling in the room deepened. It was as though the walls had absorbed the damp, the oldness, the quiet. The smell of the room changed too, though Christine could never quite describe it. It wasn't musty, not like damp clothes or a blocked vent. It was more like … varnish, she thought. Or old floorboards heated too long in the sun. A dry, sharp smell that seemed to come and go without reason.

Melanie, during our Zoom call, told me quietly. 'Mum said it smelled like the house was holding its breath. That's how she put it. Like it was waiting for something.'

Christine started noticing the stillness in the evenings. The front room had always been the cosy part of the house – where the kids would play with their toys, where the radio played in the background, where the dog would snooze under John's chair. But now, when the house settled and the hum of the day faded, there was a quietness that felt … off.

The radio seemed quieter in that room, the tick of the clock louder. The light from the gas fire didn't flicker the way it used to. It sat still, flat, as though the flame had been trapped behind glass and couldn't breathe.

Christine started taking her tea in the kitchen instead.

She didn't say anything to John. Not yet. What could she say? That the room felt wrong? That the dog was afraid of a painting? That the air itself seemed to press on her skin? No, she kept it to herself. But each day, she found more reasons to leave the room. She'd fold the laundry in the kitchen, even though the table in the front room was bigger. She'd turn the radio off when she walked in, even though she liked the company of the music. She stopped sitting in her usual chair by the window.

And always, always, her eyes were drawn back to the painting. The boy, with his wide, tearful eyes. His face pale, his expression hollow.

It never changed.

But it never looked quite the same either.

Christine had always been a woman of routine. The kind of woman who kept her days ordered, her tasks precise. Monday mornings were for washing, Tuesday afternoons for ironing, Wednesdays she'd polish – steady, predictable, the shape of her life carved into the rhythm of the week.

But after the painting arrived, her routines started to slip. It wasn't deliberate, not at first. It was more that she'd find herself pausing.

One night, she was alone downstairs. John was working a night shift and she was in the kitchen folding the washing when she stopped, mid-fold, her hands hovering over the pile.

The house was quiet.

Too quiet.

The sort of quiet that made your ears strain for something – anything. The distant rumble of traffic, the clatter of a pan in the kitchen, the muffled footsteps from upstairs. But there was nothing. Just the ticking of the clock from the living room.

And then she realised the sound wasn't even. It was slightly out of time, like the second hand was hesitating on each tick, dragging itself forward. A small thing – tiny, really – but once she heard it, she couldn't un-hear it.

But that was just the beginning.

The strange stillness settled over the house. It was the sort of stillness that makes you pause, spoon in hand, as though your own heartbeat is suddenly too loud.

That's when she heard it.

The first time, she thought she'd imagined it. A faint, soft sound – thin, distant, fragile, like a child's whimpering, barely there, yet distinct enough to catch the breath in her throat. She turned off the radio, and strained to listen. There it was again.

A quiet, shivering crying.

Low and broken, the kind that scrapes at the edges of your nerves. Christine stood frozen, the washing still in her hand, her mind racing through the logical explanations.

It must be Melanie or Stephen, she thought, creeping to the stairs, the sound seeming to drift from the hallway, from the living room. But when she checked upstairs, both children were fast asleep, their soft, even breathing filling the dark.

Back downstairs, the sound lingered.

It came from the living room.

Christine edged toward the doorway, her breath catching in her throat, and the crying seemed to retreat – fainter now, almost teasing, like it was slipping just beyond reach.

She flicked on the light. Nothing.

The painting sat above the fireplace, the boy's tear-streaked face shimmering faintly in the yellow glow. His eyes seemed deeper now, the darkness within them heavier, the glint of painted tears more vivid, almost wet. Christine felt her stomach twist, the hairs rising on the back of her neck.

Melanie, years later, would tell me quietly: 'Mum said she thought the crying was coming from the painting. She never said it out loud then, but she told me years later – she was sure of it.'

Christine tried to tell John, her voice tight with nerves, but he just waved it away.

'You're overtired, Chris. You've been up too late, that's all.'

But Christine felt watched. It was in the way the boy's eyes seemed to follow her around the room, the way the air seemed to grow denser when she sat alone at night, the way her skin would prickle as though she were being observed.

One night, a week later, Christine was tidying the living room, smoothing the fabric of the armchair in absent, fidgeting movements. Christine had always been a bit of a night owl. She wasn't a heavy sleeper, not really. Even before the painting arrived, she'd often find herself awake into the small hours, tidying up, sipping a cup of tea in the soft hush of the house. But after the painting arrived, sleep became a stranger to her. It wasn't just restlessness – it was a heavy, prickling dread that seemed to settle over the house as soon as the sun dipped low, a feeling that if she closed her eyes, something might creep closer in the dark. Night after night, she sat in the kitchen long after the clock had ticked past midnight, her hands wrapped around a cooling cup of tea, her ears straining for the smallest sound. This particular night, the radio was off, the house hushed in that late-night stillness that felt like it could swallow you whole. The kids were in bed, John snoring faintly upstairs, and the gas fire ticked softly in the hearth.

The weight of the day hung heavy on her shoulders, and her hands moved without thought – straightening a cushion, tucking a stray corner of the rug beneath the coffee table.

It was as she leaned down to smooth the fabric of the armchair that she saw it – just a flicker, the barest suggestion of movement. She straightened slowly, her breath catching in her throat. The room seemed to tilt for a moment, as though the air had shifted, thickening, slowing. The shadows deepened in the corners, and the soft glow from the fire seemed to dim, like a film had settled over her eyes. Her gaze fell on the painting…

And her blood turned cold.

For a fraction of a second – a heartbeat, no more – the boy's face shifted. The tear-streaked cheeks, the soft, sad mouth, the wide, sorrowful eyes … they moved.

His right eye – the one closest to her – winked.

It wasn't playful. It wasn't innocent. It was slow, deliberate, a sickly, knowing contraction of the lid, like a private signal between them. Christine felt her heart stutter in her chest, a hot rush of blood flooding her face, then draining just as quickly, leaving her ice-cold. Her mouth fell open, a dry, breathless sound escaping her lips, but no scream came. The boy's expression settled back into place as if nothing had happened – eyes wide, glistening, eternally sorrowful. The tears on his cheeks gleamed softly in the fire light.

Christine staggered back, her pulse racing, a thin sheen of sweat breaking out across her skin. Her hands trembled, fingers twitching, as though the fear itself had crawled beneath her skin and taken root. She stood there, frozen, unable to look away, every instinct in her screaming to flee.

It had happened.

She knew it had happened. She could still feel the aftershock of it, like a low vibration in her bones, as if something unseen had touched her, crossed some boundary that shouldn't have been crossed.

And in that moment, Christine knew she was no longer imagining things. This wasn't tiredness, or stress, or the tricks of a tired mind. The painting had moved.

It had seen her.

And it had winked.

☽✧✝✧☾

Over the next few weeks, the crying still came – soft, distant, like a child sobbing in the night. It seemed to seep from the walls, from the edges of the room, and though Christine told herself it must be the neighbours' kids, deep down, she knew better.

Then came the bad luck.

It started with the washing machine. Christine had loaded it as usual – school uniforms, tea towels, John's overalls – but halfway through the cycle, she heard a gurgling, a strange, shuddering noise that made her pause. The machine gave a loud, sudden bang – a deep, metallic thud that rattled the floorboards – then a spluttering hiss. Water poured across the kitchen floor in a sudden rush, soaking the lino, slipping under the units. Christine froze, her heart racing, before she scrambled to turn it off. The washing was ruined, the machine dead, the room a mess of water and soap bubbles.

A week later, it was the gas cooker.

She was in the middle of making tea, standing by the stove stirring, when there was a sharp pop, a bright spark, and the cooker cut out with a heavy, final click. The kitchen fell into a cold hush. The cooker was done for – John tried fiddling with it, but it was no good. They'd only had it a year.

Buster the dog grew thinner, his ribs showing beneath his scruffy coat, his eyes dull, his tail limp. Buster moved. He sat by the kitchen door most days, staring into the hallway with a fixed, glassy gaze, as if waiting for something.

John brushed it all off, at first. 'It's just bad luck, Chris,' he'd say, waving it away as he sipped his tea. But even he started to feel it – the little things going wrong, the atmosphere that seemed to cling to the air like a fog. One afternoon he came home from work pale and quiet, a small white bandage wrapped around his left hand.

He'd been at the factory, same as every day, when a piece of machinery had slipped – just a sudden, sharp slip – and caught him across the knuckles. The cut wasn't deep, but it bled, and it shook him.

'Could've been worse,' he muttered that night, as he flexed his fingers awkwardly.

Christine said nothing, but the thought circled in her mind: What next?

The children weren't spared either. Melanie fell ill – feverish, listless, her skin hot to the touch. Her little brother Stephen soon followed, coughing at night, dark circles under his eyes, restless in his sleep. Christine sat by their beds, stroking their damp hair, a knot of fear twisting tight in her chest.

The house felt wrong.

Melanie, years later, told me:

'Mum said it was like the house had turned on her. Like it was feeding off us.'

The arguments grew sharper, too. Christine and John found themselves snapping over the smallest things. The toast burnt. The washing left too long. The noise of the telly. Their words cut quicker, voices rising in that tight, sharp way that feels dangerous even when it's quiet.

One evening, Linda came by again. She stood in the kitchen doorway, arms folded tight across her chest, her eyes narrowed, her expression tense.

'Chris,' she said, her voice low, urgent, 'you have to get rid of that painting. It's not right. I can feel it. There's something bad in it.'

Christine felt her stomach twist, a cold sweat rising on her skin. But what could she do? 'It was a gift,' she said weakly. 'From John's mum. He won't let me throw it out.'

Linda shook her head, her lips pressed into a thin, tight line.

Melanie, during our call, said it quietly, almost whispering:

'Mum told me she felt like it was laughing at her. Like it knew she couldn't get rid of it.'

Christine felt trapped. The house held its breath.

And Christine … she began to fear that it was only a matter of time. The tension in the house thickened. Christine began to dread being alone in it. She'd find herself going out for pointless reasons, just to avoid being home. But *The Crying Boy* remained.

Watching.

Waiting. The painting sat above the fireplace, unmoving, unblinking and Christine knew, deep in her bones, that it was alive.

☽✧✝✧☾

Buster had been part of the family for years. He wasn't just a dog; he was a little shadow who followed Christine from room to room, a scrappy, loyal thing who'd curl up by the fire or on the worn patch of carpet at the bottom of the stairs. As the months wore on, he began to fade.

It was subtle at first. Christine noticed now that he wasn't finishing his meals – would nose at his bowl, take a bite or two, then wander away to sit in the kitchen doorway, staring into the gloom of the living room. His tail, once a constant wagging blur, lay still and limp. His coat lost its shine, thinning in places, the skin beneath looking too pale, too dry.

Christine tried everything – changing his food, tempting him with bits of leftover roast or sausage, sitting with him and stroking his ears, pleading softly, 'Come on, Buster, love. You've got to eat.'

But it was like he wasn't there anymore. No matter how much they fed him, no matter how carefully they measured out his meals, Buster wasted away.

It was the children who found him.

One grey morning, Christine heard Melanie's voice – sharp, panicked – floating down the stairs. 'Mum! Mum! Something's wrong with Buster!'

She ran, heart racing, and found the kids standing in the doorway of the kitchen, Melanie's hands clutched over her mouth, Stephen pale and silent beside her.

Buster lay curled in his bed by the back door, his body still. Too still.

Christine's breath caught. He looked impossibly small – shrunken, as if the life had been drained out of him, leaving behind skin stretched tight over sharp little bones. His ribs jutted out starkly, his fur patchy and dull. His eyes were half-lidded, clouded, his body cold to the touch. Christine sank to her knees, her hands trembling as she reached out to touch him, but she knew – before she even laid a finger on him – she knew he was gone.

The kids cried. Christine felt the weight of it settle deep in her chest, a grief laced with a sick, gnawing fear. He had been fed. They had cared for him, watched over him – but still, he had wasted away, as though something had been feeding off him.

John came home from work that evening looking worn, his face drawn tight, a tension in his shoulders that Christine hadn't seen before.

'Factory's shutting down,' he muttered, sitting down heavily in the kitchen chair. 'Everyone has lost their jobs. I'm out.'

Just like that.

Laid off.

A string of bad luck – or so it seemed.

But Christine felt it in her bones.

It wasn't bad luck.

It was the painting.

☽✧✝✧☾

The weeks dragged on, each day heavier than the last. The house had grown oppressive – like it was holding its breath, waiting. Autumn grew deeper and the dark nights set in. Melanie and Stephen were pale and quiet now, both of them still coughing in the night, dark circles smudging their young faces. John, short-tempered and worn down, snapped at the smallest things. And Christine – she barely slept at all. When she did, she'd wake with a start, her heart hammering in her chest, sure she'd heard it: a faint, distant crying, coming from the living room.

It was a Saturday afternoon when it happened. They had gone to visit John's sister – just a routine visit, nothing unusual. The house had been left as it always was: the gas fire off, the windows closed, everything in its place. Christine glanced back once as they left, a strange unease prickling at the back of her neck. She felt an urge to check something – but the kids were tugging at her sleeve, John was locking the door, and the moment passed.

It was early evening when they returned home. They had picked up some fish and chips on their way home for tea. The sky hung low and heavy, threatening rain, the air cool and damp. The kids bickered quietly in the backseat, John humming tunelessly under his breath, and Christine sat in the passenger seat, her mind elsewhere – half on the visit, half on the house they'd be returning to.

As they turned the corner onto their street, Christine felt it first – a tightening in her chest, an instinctive clench deep in her gut.

Something was wrong.

The smoke hit them before they even saw the flames – a thick, black plume rising above the rooftops, billowing into the grey sky like a dark, choking bruise.

Christine's breath caught in her throat. 'John – stop the car!' she cried, her voice raw, panicked, but John was already slamming on the brakes, pulling up haphazardly by the kerb.

Chaos met them as they flung the doors open and stumbled out.

Their house – their home – was ablaze.

The fire roared, a living, breathing thing, devouring the front of the house in a fury of orange and red. The living room windows had shattered, jagged shards catching the light like teeth, and the flames licked greedily at the brickwork, smoke curling and choking the air.

The sound was like nothing Christine had ever heard – an angry, crackling roar beneath the shriek of sirens. The heat hit her in the face like an open oven, forcing her to stumble back, coughing, eyes stinging.

Neighbours were gathered in clutches on the pavement, watching in helpless horror, some with hands clamped over their mouths, others murmuring in disbelief.

John stood frozen, his face pale, his mouth slack. The children clung to Christine's legs, both of them crying, voices thin and lost beneath the noise. Christine's legs felt weak beneath her, a sick wave rising in her stomach. Her home – the place where they were supposed to feel safe, where they had eaten, laughed, fought, and loved – was burning.

Everything was gone.

She wanted to run forward, to push past the firefighters, to do something, but a firm hand stopped her – one of the firemen, his face grim beneath his helmet.

'It's too dangerous. You can't go in.'

They stood there, helpless, as the flames consumed the front of the house – the curtains, the settee, chairs, the pictures on the walls. The memories. The life they had built. It felt like the fire went on forever, but eventually, the flames died back, smothered by jets of water, leaving behind a wet, blackened ruin that smoked and hissed in the damp air.

Hours later, when it was safe to approach, they stepped into what was left. The house was unrecognisable – walls blackened, furniture charred, the ceiling sagging in places. The smell was thick and bitter – burnt wood, melted plastic, scorched fabric – and something else beneath it, something sour, like old varnish mixed with damp ash.

Christine, silent now, her face pale and streaked with tears, moved slowly through the house. John moved numbly, kicking through the wreckage, his boots crunching over fragments of their lives – half-melted photo frames, warped cutlery, a child's shoe blackened at the edges. Christine's eyes scanned the living room, barely able to process the destruction.

And then she saw it.

The painting.

It lay in the wreckage of the living room, propped awkwardly against the scorched bricks of the fireplace. The frame was intact, unbroken. The boy's face stared out, pale and perfect, his dark, hollow eyes glistening as if they had just been wiped clean. Untouched.

Christine felt a wave of nausea rise in her throat, bile burning the back of her tongue. Her hands trembled at her sides.

Melanie, during our call, spoke in a hushed voice, as if still trying to make sense of it herself. 'Mum said it was like the painting had just sat there and watched everything burn. Like it wanted to survive.'

John had said nothing. His face was hard, set in a grim line, but his eyes darted toward the painting with a look of something close to fear before he quickly looked away.

Christine couldn't bear to go near it. She left it where it was, sitting like a silent witness among the ashes. The fire had taken everything. The photographs, the clothes, the children's toys, the wedding album – gone.

But the painting had survived.

Christine could feel it, heavy and dark, watching her still.

☽✧✝✧☾

The house was a ruin, but the family carried on – because they had to. They moved in with John's sister for a few months, cramped in a small terrace house with too many people and not enough space. Christine tried to smile for the children, tried to keep the rhythm of normal life going – school bags packed, uniforms washed, meals on the table – but she wasn't the same. None of them were.

Something had shifted.

Christine grew quieter, withdrawn. She moved like a woman in a fog, her eyes dull, her hands trembling when she thought no one was watching. Her hair thinned, her face grew pale, and there were dark smudges beneath her eyes that no amount of sleep – or what little sleep she got – could soften.

She never bought another painting. Not one. Not even a cheerful landscape or a still life of flowers. The space above the fireplace in their new house, when they finally got it, stayed empty. Christine wouldn't even hang a clock there.

Melanie, during our chat, told me: 'Mum blamed that painting for everything. She said it was like a curse. She used to say, "It wanted us to suffer, Mel. It wanted to ruin us." She never stopped believing that.'

John, for his part, refused to talk about it. He threw himself into work when he eventually found a new job. The long hours and shifts kept him out of the house. The fracture in the family never fully healed. The arguments continued, sharper now, laced with an edge they couldn't quite name. It was like the tension had rooted itself in their lives, even after the painting was gone.

And then there was Buster's absence – an empty space in the corner of the kitchen where his bed should be. The family carried on, because what else could they do? But the memory of the fire, of that untouched painting, lingered like smoke in their lungs.

It wasn't until a few years later – 1985, to be precise – that the story of *The Crying Boy* curse exploded across the newspapers. It was *The Sun* that first broke the story, in an article that ran under a bold, tabloid headline: 'Blazing Curse of the Crying Boy!'

The story told of other families who, like Christine's, had suffered devastating fires in their homes – fires that destroyed everything ... except for the same eerie, mass-produced painting of a tearful young boy. The article was full of sensational language – talk of curses, bad luck, strange coincidences – and it captured the public imagination in a way few stories had.

Suddenly, *The Crying Boy* was everywhere.

Other papers picked it up, and soon the story had taken on a life of its own. People began coming forward with tales of fires, accidents, and strange occurrences, all tied back to the same sorrowful face. Radio stations debated it, phone-ins buzzed with callers eager to share their own strange experiences.

The newspapers published letters – pages of them – from readers who had once owned the painting, many describing how they'd rushed to throw it out, terrified it might bring misfortune into their homes.

It became a media phenomenon, a modern urban legend born from soot and ash, and when Christine saw those headlines, she felt an odd, sharp relief.

It was as though someone had thrown open a window in a room she'd been trapped in for years.

She wasn't mad.

It wasn't just her.

There were others. Families across the country – ordinary people, just like them – who had suffered the same inexplicable disasters, who had watched their homes burn while that same tearful face stared out from the wreckage, untouched.

For a brief moment, Christine felt vindicated.

'Mum said it was the first time she felt like she could breathe again. Like she wasn't alone in it. Like it wasn't all in her head.' Melanie told me.

But that relief was fleeting.

Because knowing you're not alone doesn't undo the damage. It doesn't rebuild a house, or erase the nights spent awake, listening for the soft sounds of crying, or the memories of watching a dog waste away, helpless. It doesn't mend the cracks that had split through their family. The headlines faded, as headlines do, replaced by the next scandal, the next story.

But for Christine – for all of them – the damage was done. The painting had left its mark, and no tabloid exposé could ever wash it away.

Christine never fully recovered. Her health faded – aches and pains, restless nights, a creeping anxiety that gnawed at her. She grew thin, worn down by the years, and in the end, she passed away quietly in her sleep. Melanie, holding back tears, said to me in that quiet, almost reverent tone. 'Until the day she died, Mum believed that painting had cursed us. She really did.'

☽✧☨✧☾

I've thought about that story a lot since Melanie first contacted me. It's not the only story I've heard about *The Crying Boy* – far from it. There have been dozens, hundreds, of accounts over the years: homes destroyed by fire, always with the same detail – somehow, impossibly, the painting survives.

It's a pattern too consistent to ignore.

Is it a residual haunting? A moment of trauma, trapped in the fibres of the canvas, playing over and over like a recording? Or is it something darker – a curse, an object infused with the weight of sorrow and loss, reaching out across generations?

There are simply too many instances of this happening for it to be dismissed as coincidence. Too many homes reduced to ash, too many families torn apart by loss, and always – always – that same sorrowful boy staring out from the wreckage, untouched by flame.

For whatever reason, this particular set of paintings – whether original prints, mass-produced copies, or cheap knock-offs – seems to act as a kind of catalyst. A trigger that, in certain homes, under certain circumstances, sets off a chain of events that leads inexorably to the same, devastating conclusion: fire.

A fire that destroys lives, takes lives, and leaves families shattered in its wake.

And yet…

There are hundreds, if not thousands, of homes across the country where these paintings still hang – dusty on the walls of old council houses, tucked in the corners of charity shops, forgotten in attics – and those families have never experienced anything.

So, what does that mean? Does the curse require specific, mysterious conditions to be triggered? Is there a threshold – an alignment of energy, of mood, of fate – that ignites it?

Or is it simply a roll of the dice, a question of who gets chosen?

I don't have the answers. But I do know this: after speaking to Melanie, after looking into her eyes as she shared her family's story – seeing the weight of those memories pressing down on her even now – I have no choice but to accept her truth.

And in accepting her story, I find myself facing a frightening conclusion: I believe the curse is real. Whether you believe it or not, *The Crying Boy* has left a trail of ruin behind it.

And for Christine and her family, it left a mark that never healed.

☽✧✝✧☾

My Haunted Life

Part Six

Rupert

As we settled back into the rhythm of life at Serlby Rise, I tried my best to push away the lingering unease that clung to me like a second skin. After Darryl's blessing of the house, the mood within our home lightened considerably. My dad, in particular, wore a mask of contentment, utterly convinced that the apparition that had haunted us had departed for good. He was completely satisfied that whatever was haunting us had left. And for a time, all was quiet.

Yet, as the months passed by, those feelings began to slowly creep back into my awareness. As the sun dipped below the horizon each evening, a chill began to crawl back into my room, and I found myself increasingly agitated, unable to escape the feeling that I was being watched. In the dead of night, while the world outside was blanketed in darkness, I would lie huddled beneath my duvet, my heart racing as I felt those unseen eyes boring into my vulnerable form. My imagination conjured up all sorts of terrors lurking just out of sight, waiting for the moment when I was most defenseless. It was not that I hadn't believed Dad's assurances; it was more that, deep down, I sensed there was something much more insidious that still clutched the edges of our lives, something that Darryl's incantations hadn't quite exorcised. Sharing my fears with my parents felt out of the question; I didn't want to burden Dad, who had just found a semblance of peace after weeks of haunting uncertainty.

As the weeks rolled by, and in a bid to bring life and vibrance back into our house, Mum brought home a bright splash of colour in the form of Rupert, a rare orange canary. His brilliant plumage glinted like a small flame flickering against the grey backdrop of the winter. Immediately, we all fell for his charm: the way he fluttered about his cage, chirping little melodies, brought a warmth to me that had long been absent. Even Harry, our gentle dog, who would slink around Rupert's cage as if he were guarding a treasure, seemed to find joy in watching the lively little creature. Yet, the atmosphere in our house could be deceptive; beneath its new-found cheer, the shadows still lurked, weaving through the corners and hiding beneath the furniture. I couldn't shake the feeling that something was still lurking just out of sight. Despite being a happy little bird, I noticed that sometimes Rupert would suddenly screech, a sharp, horrendous cry that sliced through the tranquility of our day. He would flap his wings violently, careening around his cage as if trying to escape from something unseen. Harry would perk up at these moments, his curious head cocked to one side, as though he, too, could sense that something was amiss. Mum would rush over to comfort and soothe Rupert, convinced it was merely a case of startled nerves, but I couldn't shake the unsettling thought that perhaps he was responding to something far more sinister than a mere fright.

And then, one dreadful morning, we stepped into the living room to a scene that froze the very air we breathed. There, at the bottom of his cage, lay Rupert, lifeless and still. I felt my stomach lurch, a devastating weight pressing against my chest as I took in the sight. One moment, he had been the epitome of life, flitting about happily, and in the next, he had vanished into the cold embrace of death. We had no explanation for it; Rupert had shown no signs of illness or distress, at least none we had noticed. Mum was heartbroken. Dad tried to console her, yet I was struck by a deep discomfort, an instinctual dread that gnawed at me. Something had frightened Rupert so terribly that it had ultimately led to his death. Afterwards, the atmosphere shifted in our home, replacing the sense of buoyancy that Rupert had brought with a dense silence.

As I lay in bed that night, my mind swirling with the events of the day, the weight of the invisible eyes bore down on me again, and I was acutely aware that it was back. Whatever had haunted us may have shifted its focus, but as I lay in the hush of the night, I couldn't shake the feeling that it had simply bided its time.

New Neighbours

Just before my sighting of the ghostly old woman in the kitchen window, a new family had moved into the house next door. That house had always carried a bit of a reputation in the neighbourhood – an unspoken, half-joking kind of notoriety. It was privately rented out by an absentee landlord, the sort who seemed to have little concern over who he let it to. Over the years, the tenants had usually been a ragtag bunch – mostly grungy students with long hair, battered acoustic guitars slung over their shoulders, and a heavy preference for smoking marijuana at all hours of the day and night. The disruption they caused had been a thorn in my parents' side for years. There had been no end of quarrels, usually my dad banging on the wall or shouting over the fence while Mum muttered under her breath about the 'bloody druggies'. It wasn't just the noise, although that was bad enough; it was the feeling that the house attracted chaos, like some sort of magnet for trouble.

An interesting little twist came from Warren, who would often tell me in hushed tones that the house next door was supposed to be haunted. As a kid already wrapped up in my own unnerving experiences inside our home, this rumour fascinated me. I would stand in the garden sometimes, staring at the house's battered windows and imagining the kind of spirits that might be lurking within those walls.

When the old tenants finally moved out, there was a short spell of quiet. The house sat empty for a while, its curtains hanging limp and grey with dust. And then, one day, a new family appeared. Their arrival was low-key. No loud moving vans, no fuss – they just seemed to quietly slide into the street, blending in with the winter greyness.

For a long time, they kept themselves to themselves. It was as though the house had swallowed them up whole. Rarely were they seen out front, and when they were, they didn't linger. Of course, the neighbours, as neighbours do, began to gossip. Who were these people? What were they doing moving into that house of all places? We, kids included, took to calling them the 'Addams Family' – half in jest, half because there was something genuinely odd about the situation. It made us laugh all the more when we later learned, to our amazement, that their real surname actually was Adams.

They had previously been from the travelling community. There was mum Caroline, her husband John, and their two daughters: 16-year-old Christine and 11-year-old Dana. As it turned out, Dana was the same age as me and my friends, and in time, she drifted into our little gang, fitting in fairly naturally despite her family's strange reputation.

The Adams were, to put it bluntly, a peculiar bunch. They were all pale looking and had heads of jet-black hair. Caroline had a strong Celtic feel about her – everything from the way she spoke to her mannerisms. She was massively overweight, always struggling with swollen feet and legs, often visible under the long, flowing dresses she seemed to favour no matter the weather. Something about her always seemed weary, burdened and yet fiercely proud. The most striking – and, frankly, bizarre – thing about Caroline was that she kept her late mother's gravestone propped up against the front wall of the house. There it sat for months on end, an eerie monument that none of the neighbours dared ask about, but everyone noticed. It became one of those unspoken things – you'd glance at it, feel a shiver, and then quickly pretend you hadn't seen it at all.

John, her husband, was a character in his own right. He was wiry and always seemed to have the air of someone involved in slightly dodgy dealings. His old battered van would clatter down the street at all hours, loaded with random odds and ends. He always had a wink and a nod ready for my dad, often joking that the latest load was 'knocked-off gear'. Whether he was serious or not, nobody knew for sure – but there was a certain sly charm to John that made it hard to dislike him.

And then there was Christine. Christine was, by far, the most unsettling of them all. She was painfully thin – not just slim, but gaunt, with hollow cheeks and an almost sickly pallor to her skin. Her eyes were dark, heavy-lidded, and she seemed to move through the world with a detached, almost ethereal quality, as though she wasn't entirely there. She dressed exclusively in black, long skirts and oversized jumpers that hung off her thin frame, giving her a gothic appearance. There was a certain fragility to her, but also something harder to define – a sense that she was tuned into a different frequency to the rest of us.

Her obsession with the boyband East 17 was another thing that made her stand out. I mean, it's normal for teenagers to have crushes on pop stars, but this was something different. She didn't just like them – she lived for them. Posters covered her bedroom window to the point that you couldn't even see inside, and she would often be spotted walking down the street wearing one of their tour shirts, her face distant, lost in some internal world that nobody else could reach.

Despite all this, the Adams family were, on the whole, good neighbours. There were no loud parties, no late-night rows spilling into the street. After years of battling noise from the previous tenants, my parents breathed a cautious sigh of relief. For a while, life seemed relatively calm on our little stretch of Serlby Rise.

But the Adams family were destined to become more than just passing characters in the story of our lives. In ways none of us could have imagined, they would soon become woven deeply into the strange and often chilling tapestry of events that defined our time there.

The Strange Day on Serlby Rise

It was one of those perfect summer days. July 1994, and the sun was blazing – easily one of the hottest days of that summer. Everything about the morning felt right. Serlby Rise looked beautiful in that kind of golden early light that only seems to appear during the school holidays. The street shimmered slightly with heat, the tarmac soft underfoot, and the birds were in full song, darting between hedges and rooftops as if they had the whole world to themselves. There wasn't a single cloud in the sky. It was a proper Nottingham summer's morning, and all seemed well.

Being the six-week holidays, I was off school, and the usual plan was for me to spend the weekdays at Nana and Grandad's while Mum and Dad were at work. They'd drop me off in the morning and collect me again at teatime. But on this particular week, Don and Audrey were away on their holiday to the Isle of Wight. That ruled them out. My other grandparents weren't available either, so Mum had asked Warren's mum, Sandy, if I could spend the day at theirs. Luckily, Warren was off too, and Sandy was more than happy to have me.

Mum dropped me off around 9 am. The moment I stepped through the door, Sandy welcomed me like I was one of the family, ushering me into the kitchen for breakfast. The house felt homely – cool compared to the heat outside, with the sound of birdsong drifting in through the open windows. Sasha and Claire were both away for the day, off to Drayton Manor Park, so it was just me and Warren. That suited us just fine.

We spent most of the morning in Warren's bedroom, sat cross-legged on the floor in front of his telly, playing on his Nintendo. The fan buzzed gently from the corner of the room, trying to keep us cool as we took turns on *Super Mario Bros. 3* and *Battletoads*. We were proper engrossed, heads tilted slightly to the side, eyes wide, thumbs flying over the buttons. Those kind of mornings – no school, no responsibilities, just pure escapism – were some of the best.

Around lunchtime, with our stomachs grumbling, we headed down to Lou's shop. It was part of the routine – getting snacks, a can of Coke, a few penny sweets. I remember the pavement being hot beneath my trainers, the smell of sun-warmed tarmac and distant cut grass hanging in the air. We stocked up on crisps, cola bottles, Wham bars, and a big bag of fizzy cola laces, then strolled back home, chatting away about school, horror films, and the kind of nonsense kids talk about when they're killing time.

When we got back, we hovered outside Warren's front gate, eating our sweets and leaning against the warm brickwork. I remember squinting up at the brightness of the day, lulled into a kind of relaxed daze.

Then something changed.

I glanced up the road, towards the top end of Serlby Rise – the part that meets Ranby Walk, where the street curves round and opens up slightly. Right next to the distinctive red post box, there was a man standing there.

An old man.

He wasn't moving, just … standing there. Still. Dressed in a cardigan – beige or grey, I can't remember exactly – and navy trousers. He was almost bald, wispy bits of white hair. He looked like someone's grandad, the kind of bloke you'd see waiting at a bus stop. But something about him didn't sit right. Even from a couple of hundred yards away, I could make out the look on his face. He was grinning. A huge, toothy grin that stretched his face unnaturally wide. It wasn't a friendly smile. It was wrong. There was something sinister about it, something deeply unpleasant.

He was looking at us sideways, his head slightly tilted, as though he was half-hunched and peering at us from an angle. His eyes were too wide, too focused. He wasn't just glancing – he was watching. Staring.

I felt my stomach twist. Something about him just looked out of place. Not just in a 'he doesn't belong here' kind of way, but in a 'he doesn't belong at all' kind of way – as if he wasn't part of the same world we were standing in. I couldn't put it into words at the time, but everything about him felt ... wrong.

I nudged Warren and nodded towards the corner. 'Look at him,' I said.

Warren turned his head and stared. His expression quickly changed from curiosity to concern.

'He's really strange,' Warren said after a long pause.

'Yeah,' I said, barely able to speak.

The man hadn't moved. Not a step. Just stood there grinning, hunched over slightly, like he was about to topple forward.

And then, in the silence, I heard something.

It was low. Guttural. A horrible, gravelly sniggering sound that seemed to vibrate at the edge of hearing. It wasn't loud – it was distant – but somehow it reached me clearly. A dry, awful laugh that didn't belong in the sunlight. I thought I was imagining it. I didn't say anything. But then I looked at Warren, and I knew from his face that he'd heard it too.

'Why is he staring and laughing like that?' Warren asked, voice small.

I didn't answer. I didn't have an answer. A wave of fear washed over me – not the kind that jolts you, but the slow, creeping kind that builds from deep inside. I didn't want to stand there anymore. I didn't want to be outside. I wanted to be away from that man, away from his horrible smile and his impossible laugh.

We turned to each other, both of us pale, both searching each other's faces for some kind of explanation – but there was none. Just confusion. Just dread.

We looked back up the road.

And he was gone. Just like that.

He hadn't walked away. There had been no sound of footsteps. No turning, no leaving. One moment he was there, the next he wasn't. The spot where he'd stood was empty. No doorways nearby, no garden gates. Nothing. He had vanished.

A chill ran through both of us, completely at odds with the heat of the day. Without a word, we went back inside. Neither of us said much for a while. We just slumped back onto the carpet in front of the Nintendo, hoping the pixelated worlds would distract us from what we'd just seen. But the atmosphere had changed. That feeling stuck with us. We both knew something strange had happened. We sat in silence for a while, the buzz of the game humming in the background, but neither of us could focus on the screen. Eventually, Warren broke the quiet. 'Maybe he was just some weird old bloke,' he said, though his voice lacked any real conviction. I could tell he was shaken. He was trying to reason it out, trying to find a normal explanation to cling to – but it was written all over his face. He was scared, just like I was. We both knew, deep down, that what we'd seen didn't feel normal. Not in the slightest.

Mid-afternoon came, and Sandy came into the room with a smile. 'Right, you two. Enough of that bloody computer – go and get some fresh air. You've been sat there for hours!'

Warren and I exchanged a glance. Neither of us felt like going outside. Not now.

Not after him....

Eventually, after much grumbling and a few half-hearted protests, Warren and I gave in to Sandy's insistence. We put the controllers down, stretched out stiff legs, and made our way reluctantly back outside. The afternoon heat was still clinging to the pavements as we wandered down Warren's front path toward the little wooden gate that opened onto Serlby Rise. We hesitated there for a moment, our hands resting on the latch, neither of us speaking.

Then we both instinctively glanced up toward the top of the Rise, to the place where that strange old man had stood earlier.

Nothing.

The junction where Ranby Walk met Serlby Rise was empty now. No hunched figure, no chilling grin. Just the hazy shimmer of the heat rising off the road and the sound of a distant lawnmower buzzing away in some neighbour's garden.

We were relieved, silently thankful. For a few seconds, we stood there, still cautious, before finally stepping outside into the afternoon light. Once again, everything was normal again. We shuffled around, kicking bits of gravel with our trainers, making small talk about football and computer games, pretending as best we could that nothing had happened earlier.

The longer we lingered, the easier it became to relax. Warren eventually suggested we wander two doors down to my house and hang about in the front garden there for a bit. I agreed. It felt safer somehow – my home, my turf. We ambled along, football tucked under Warren's arm, and soon found ourselves in the familiar patch of grass outside my house. We passed the time the way we always did – kicking the ball lazily between us, daring each other to see how many keepy-uppies we could manage, laughing when one of us booted it too hard and sent it bouncing into the hedge. For the first time since that incident, the world felt normal again. The sun was still blazing, the sky an endless stretch of blue, and a gentle hum of insects floated through the thick, warm air.

We started to believe, just a little, that the weirdness of earlier was over.

Then it happened.

That feeling.

It wasn't subtle. It wasn't gradual.

It swept over us like a tidal wave, swallowing the easy mood we'd built and replacing it with a dense, choking unease.

We both felt it at the same time. It was so immediate, so physical, that we actually froze mid-kick, the football bouncing away and rolling to a stop by the curb.

'What's happening?' I asked, my voice unnaturally loud against the sudden, eerie stillness. Warren only shook his head, wide-eyed and pale, just as clueless and unnerved as I was. The sun, still high and strong only moments earlier, seemed to dull somehow.

But not as though it was hidden by clouds – there were no clouds – but as if something invisible had smothered it, draining the colour from everything around us. The vibrant greens of the hedges and lawns turned a sickly greyish hue. The blue sky turned a flat, lifeless shade. Shadows lengthened and deepened in impossible ways, despite the fact that the light hadn't changed.

The world around us didn't just look different – it felt different.

And then the wind came. One moment, the air was sunny and still, the next it was howling, battering the trees and whipping at our clothes. It wasn't a natural wind. It didn't feel like it came from any direction – it seemed to press in on us from all sides at once, pushing against our skin with invisible, clawing fingers. The hedges along Serlby Rise thrashed violently, branches cracking, leaves scattering across the street like confetti from some unseen explosion.

It felt wrong.

It felt evil.

The air thickened, each breath harder to draw than the last, as if the atmosphere itself had grown denser, heavier. There was a sharp, electric tang to it – the kind of charged feeling you get before a thunderstorm – but there was no storm brewing. The sky was clear.

This wasn't nature.

This wasn't normal.

Warren and I stood there, rooted to the spot, our eyes darting around helplessly, trying to make sense of what was happening.

I could feel it – this invisible force – crawling over my skin, whispering against my ears without making a sound. The hairs on the back of my neck stood on end. Every instinct screamed at me to run, but I couldn't move.

It was like we had stepped into another world.

Honestly, the only way I can describe it is that it felt as though we had slipped into some twisted alternate reality. One second we were in our familiar, safe street – the next, we were somewhere else entirely.

Like the bloody Twilight Zone!

And even though the old man didn't reappear, even though we never saw anything tangible, we both felt it – that deep, gut-wrenching certainty that something else was there with us.

Watching.

Waiting.

The entire street, every house, every blade of grass, seemed to vibrate with an invisible tension, as though reality itself was holding its breath. I honestly believe, even now, that some kind of portal had opened that day.

Some door had been cracked ajar.

And for those few minutes, something from somewhere else leaked into our world.

Then, just as suddenly as it had begun – it ended. The wind stopped dead, like someone had flicked a switch.

The air cleared.

The colours returned.

The hot summer day snapped back into place, as bright and ordinary as if nothing had ever happened. The birdsong returned, faint but growing stronger by the second, as if the world itself was trying to erase what had just occurred. Warren and I looked at each other, both of us pale and shaken.

Neither of us spoke. There wasn't anything to say. We just picked up the football silently and went back to kicking it about, trying – and failing – to pretend that we hadn't just witnessed something neither of us would ever be able to explain.

Over the years that followed, Warren and I spoke about that day often. We'd bring it up now and again, usually late at night, when conversation turned to the strange and the unexplained. But no matter how many times we went over it, we could never make sense of it.

Because deep down, we both knew… It wasn't just a weird weather event. It wasn't our imaginations.

That day on Serlby Rise, something paranormal – something other – had touched our world. And we had been right there in the middle of it.

Looking back now, I often wonder whether that day was more than just a random, isolated event. At the time, it felt like a strange one-off – an afternoon where something weird and frightening pushed its way into our world, then slipped back again just as quickly.

But as the years passed, and as more strange events unfolded around me on Serlby Rise, and beyond, I began to question whether it was part of something bigger. Maybe it wasn't just a freak occurrence. Maybe that overwhelming shift in atmosphere, that unnatural flatness, that thick, choking energy we felt, was somehow connected to the other things that had been happening – the hauntings in our own home, the old woman in the window, the endless uneasy feeling that clung to the street.

Maybe that day, Warren and I hadn't just stumbled into a bad patch of weather or a coincidence. Maybe we had brushed up against something we were never meant to see – a crack in the fabric of reality that had opened, just for a moment, to let something through.

And even though the old man didn't reappear that day … in my heart, I've never been able to shake the feeling that he was still there.

Watching.

Waiting.

Hidden just beyond the veil.

Amanda's Story

Near Death Experience

I first heard about Amanda's story through my friend and fellow paranormal researcher, Rick.

Rick and I had been friends for years – one of those online friendships that grows quietly over time. We'd first crossed paths on Facebook, swapping theories and sharing stories in paranormal groups. He was a down-to-earth bloke from Manchester, no ego, no nonsense – just a genuine passion for the paranormal, the kind of person who kept digging at cases long after most people would have given up. We'd spent a lot of time on calls, talking through investigations, sharing ideas, helping each other make sense of the things we couldn't quite explain.

It was during 2022 that Rick first told me about Amanda. He'd been investigating her case for a while by then – checking in with her, trying to help her make sense of what she'd been through. I remember him calling me on more than one occasion, just to talk it through, to bounce ideas off me, to ask what I thought. It was clear it had gotten under his skin. There was something about Amanda's story that had unsettled him, something he couldn't quite shake off. When the case eventually reached its end, Rick asked Amanda if she'd be willing to share her story with me. He knew I was working on this book, looking for real cases that spoke to the darker side of human experience. And he thought her story deserved to be told.

Rick had explained that he'd been trying to help Amanda, a nurse in her early fifties who'd had a close brush with death. She claimed to have seen something while she was clinically dead. Not just a white light, not a loved one waiting for her – but something else. Something dark. Something that wasn't done with her.

When Rick would ring and give me updates, I could feel that cold prickle of intrigue spreading across my skin, the same one I get every time I come across a case that feels off. Not just your standard 'bumps in the night' story

– this had weight to it. And the way Rick was describing it, the urgency in his tone, I could tell it had rattled him too.

I agreed straight away to speak with Amanda. We set up a video call later that week. When the time came, I sat in my bedroom, the screen flickering to life – and there she was.

Amanda.

She struck me as a woman you wouldn't mess with lightly. Short and plump, with that unmistakable Salford accent – sharp, no-nonsense, the kind of woman you could imagine standing her ground in a pub argument or telling off a disrespectful patient at the hospital. But there was kindness in her eyes too, a warmth that shone through despite the strain written across her face.

She was fashionable, in a way that felt effortless – her hair cut into a neat bob, makeup just right, big silver hoop earrings, a chunky cardigan draped over her shoulders. She had that look about her: someone who cared about herself, who took pride in her appearance. But there was something else too. A weariness in her eyes, like the world had chewed her up and spat her back out.

'I've been through hell, Adam,' she told me, straight off the bat. 'I'm not the same since it happened. I feel like … like there's something changed in me. I don't know. But I beat it, Adam.'

I listened. I let her talk. I watched the way her hands moved as she spoke – fluttering, fidgeting with her sleeve, tapping her fingers against the desk. There was a nervous energy about her, like she was holding back more than she was letting on. Amanda wasn't the kind of person who frightened easily. I could tell that straight away. She had that grit, that Northern resilience that comes from years of hard work, raising a family, looking after everyone else first. But whatever had happened to her – whatever she'd seen, or felt – it had left a mark.

She spoke with a fierce determination, like she was going to get her story out no matter what. And as I listened to her, I started to get that feeling in my gut – that slow, creeping sense that this wasn't just another case of sleep paralysis, or anxiety or someone spooking themselves in the dark. This was something else.

Something that had started when Amanda's heart stopped beating.

Something that had come back with her.

Amanda wasted no time getting into her story. From the moment we started the call, she sat forward, elbows on the table, hands clasped together. Her voice was steady, but I could hear the weight behind every word, like she'd been waiting for this chance – to get it out, to make someone really listen.

'I'll tell you exactly how it happened, Adam,' she said, her eyes narrowing, almost daring me to doubt her. 'Because I remember everything.'

It was 4 March 2022, a damp, grey afternoon in Salford. Amanda had been at home, a cosy little semi-detached she'd lived in for years. It was a house that reflected her – stylish, well-kept, with thoughtful touches: candles on the windowsill, a knitted throw folded neatly on the sofa, framed photos of her family in the hallway. That day, she'd been in the living room, sipping tea, the TV on in the background. Nothing out of the ordinary.

Her brother, Paul, had popped round to check in on her, as he often did. Amanda had always been the glue that held the family together – one of those women who never asked for help, always the one giving it. So when Paul noticed she looked a bit off that day – pale, tired, a little out of breath – he mentioned it, but Amanda, in true fashion, brushed it off.

'I'm fine, Paul,' she'd said. 'It's just the weather. I'm just tired.'

But then, out of nowhere, it hit. A crushing pain in her chest, like an iron fist clamping down, stealing her breath. Her vision blurred, and she felt a wave of nausea rise up, hot and choking. She clutched at her chest and collapsed back into the sofa, gasping, her hands trembling.

Paul leapt into action, thank God. He dialled 999, his voice rising in panic as he told the operator his sister was having a heart attack. The operator guided him through what to do, and Paul, bless him, didn't waste a second. He helped her to the floor, checking her breathing, feeling her pulse – Amanda was going grey, her lips turning blue. He started chest compressions right there in the living room, counting out loud in a shaking voice, his hands pressing down hard and fast, trying to keep her alive.

By the time the paramedics arrived – blue lights flashing, sirens wailing down the street – Amanda was barely hanging on. The paramedics took over, working quickly, efficiently, like a well-oiled machine. One of them started an oxygen mask while the other attached defibrillator pads to her chest. The jolt lifted Amanda's body slightly off the floor. The second shock came moments later. Her heart had stopped – they were in a race against time now.

Amanda said it felt like watching it happen from somewhere far away – like she was floating above the scene, looking down at her own body on the floor, Paul stood to the side, the paramedics moving fast. She said she remembered the coldness, the sudden, terrifying sense of being pulled.

At the hospital, they rushed her straight into resus – code blue. The doctors worked on her for what felt like forever. Adrenaline injected, another round of shocks, an emergency ECG showing a severe blockage in her left anterior descending artery – the so-called 'widow-maker'.

They had no choice. Amanda was taken into emergency coronary angioplasty – a life-saving procedure where they thread a catheter into the artery and inflate a tiny balloon to push the blockage aside, inserting a stent to keep the artery open. Time was critical; her heart had already stopped once.

Amanda's life hung in the balance on that operating table, every second a fight between life and death.

And in those moments – those terrifying, fragile moments between the beats of her own heart – something else began.

☽✧†✧☾

Amanda was lucky to survive that day. The doctors told her that bluntly – no sugar-coating it, no soft words. She'd suffered a massive heart attack, one that could have killed her outright if her brother hadn't been there, if the paramedics had arrived just a minute later. They said the blockage in her left anterior descending artery was severe.

The emergency angioplasty and stent placement had saved her life, but it had left her battered – both physically and mentally. The next few days passed in a blur of beeping monitors, whispered conversations in the hospital corridors, and the smell of antiseptic hanging thick in the air. Amanda drifted in and out of consciousness, her body pumped full of medication, her chest aching from the compressions and the shocks, her arms bruised from cannulas and blood draws.

But the part Amanda remembered most wasn't the hospital, or the surgery, or the panic on her brother's face as she lay on the floor.

It was the part in-between.

It was the place she went to when her heart stopped.

☽✧†✧☾

She described it to me in chilling detail. Her voice dropped to a low, measured tone when she spoke about it, like she was reliving it as she told me.

'It wasn't like the stories you hear, Adam,' she said. 'It wasn't just some warm, glowing light and a feeling of peace. It started like that, but then… it changed.'

She said the first thing she noticed was the silence. Not a peaceful silence, but a dead silence, the kind that seemed to swallow up every sound, like her ears had been stuffed with cotton wool. Then came the weightlessness – a feeling of floating, as if she were no longer bound by her body. She found herself in a vast, endless grey space. It wasn't fully dark, nor was it light – it was a strange, shifting twilight that seemed to go on forever. There was no floor beneath her, no ceiling above. Just an emptiness that seemed to stretch on and on, like being adrift in the middle of a foggy ocean.

And then she saw the light.

It was far away at first, a soft white glow that seemed to pulse gently, almost like it was breathing. It felt warm, inviting. As she focused on it, Amanda said she felt a pull – like a current dragging her forward, guiding her toward it. She could hear whispers, too. Faint at first, like the sound of a radio tuned between stations. Then they grew clearer, more insistent. Voices she couldn't quite place, but they seemed to know her name.

'Amanda,' they called. 'Amanda, come with us. It's safe here.'

Her body – or whatever part of her she was now – felt lighter, almost like she was shedding layers of herself as she drifted closer to the light. The pain she'd felt moments before, the crushing weight in her chest, the panic – it all seemed to melt away. For a moment, Amanda thought that was it. That she'd died. That this was where she was meant to go.

But then, just as she was about to let herself drift fully toward the light, something else appeared.

Something dark.

It was off to her left, lurking just beyond the edge of the light's glow. She said it looked like a hole in the world – a jagged, black void that seemed to pulse with a sickly energy, almost like it was alive. And from that hole, something stepped forward.

A figure.

It wasn't human. At least, not anymore.

It was hunched, its body thin and twisted, wrapped in what Amanda could only describe as shadows – not a cloak or fabric, but a darkness that clung to it. Its arms were long and spindly, ending in clawed hands, fingers too long, too sharp. The skin – what little she could see of it – was grey and withered, stretched tight over bones that jutted out at odd angles.

The head was the worst.

It was bald, the skin cracked and mottled like old leather. Its eyes were hollow, dark pits that seemed to suck in the surrounding light. And its mouth … Amanda struggled to describe it.

'It was like a bony hole, Adam. A maw … stretched too wide. The teeth – if you could even call them that – were long, yellowed, rotting. And it was grinning at me. That's the only way I can put it. It was grinning.'

As she spoke, Amanda's voice faltered for the first time. Her hands trembled slightly, and she gripped her mug of tea tighter.

The thing beckoned to her with one clawed hand, its fingers curling in a slow, deliberate motion. And she heard the whispers again – but this time, they came from the darkness.

'Amanda. Come here. Come to me. Come … with me.'

She felt herself being pulled – away from the light, towards the dark figure. Her whole body seemed to go heavy, like she was sinking into a pit. She could feel a coldness seeping into her, filling her lungs, her veins. A deep, gnawing chill that seemed to reach right into her bones.

Amanda said she fought. She didn't know how, but she fought. She told herself, over and over in her mind, No. No. No. She thought of her daughter, Kirsty. She thought of her family. She thought of everything she hadn't done yet, everything she didn't want to leave behind.

But the thing kept pulling. It whispered to her, its voice low and oily, almost seductive in its promises: 'There's no more pain here, Amanda. No more struggle. Just let go. Come with me. Let me in.'

And then – just as she felt herself starting to give in, starting to drift toward that darkness – she heard a shout. A distant, urgent voice, calling her name.

It was Paul.

It was as if his voice reached through the veil, snapping her back, anchoring her to the world of the living. She felt a sudden, sharp jolt – the shock of the defibrillator paddles – and then she was back in her body, gasping, choking, tears running down her face.

Amanda said it was like being slammed back into a freezing, wet sack of flesh. The pain, the weight, the terror – it all came rushing back in an instant.

And she knew, without a doubt, that whatever had been in that darkness – it wasn't gone.

It had seen her.

And it wasn't finished with her yet.

☽✧✝✧☾

Amanda's recovery was slow. The doctors told her she was lucky to be alive, that the procedure had gone well, that the stent would help prevent further damage. But physically wasn't the problem. It was the aftermath.

She felt … changed; weaker. Shaken in a way that didn't make sense for a woman as strong as she was. There were days she barely got out of bed, staring at the ceiling for hours, the same whispering voice echoing in her mind.

Kirsty, her daughter, was extremely worried. Amanda tried to put on a brave face, to act like everything was fine – but Kirsty could see it. The fear in her mother's eyes. Amanda's physical recovery surprised the doctors. They told her she was healing remarkably well. Her blood pressure stabilised. The pain in her chest eased with the medication. The bruising on her ribs slowly faded. On paper, she was fine. When she was eventually allowed to go home, Kirsty decided to move back home to care for her. But as the days wore on, Kirsty could see it in her mother's face – the way she smiled, yes, but it didn't quite reach her eyes. The way she sat in bed, staring into the middle distance, lost in thought for hours. The way she'd startle at small sounds: a knock on the door, the creak of the stairs, even the central heating ticking as it cooled down in the evening.

Kirsty had always seen her mum as this unshakable figure – a woman who could handle anything, who held the family together. Amanda wasn't the type to let life knock her down. But now … now there was something brittle in her, like she was holding herself together with the sheer force of will.

And it wasn't just the mood changes.

Kirsty started to notice little things. The way Amanda would mutter to herself when she thought she was alone – soft, whispering words, almost like a conversation. The way she'd sometimes freeze in the middle of a sentence, her eyes glazing over, her lips moving silently as if mouthing words to someone unseen. Once, Kirsty walked past her mum's bedroom and heard her talking. It was late – after midnight – and Amanda's voice was low, soft, almost affectionate. Like she was talking to a loved one in the dark. Kirsty paused outside the door, her heart racing. She listened carefully – but there was no reply. Just Amanda's voice, murmuring in that same slow, hypnotic rhythm.

It wasn't right.

Kirsty pushed the door open quietly, holding her breath – and saw Amanda sat up in bed, the bedside lamp off, the room dimly lit by the glow of the streetlamp outside. She was sitting perfectly still, her eyes wide open, staring at the far corner of the room. Her hands were folded in her lap, but her fingers were twitching, curling inwards like she was holding something invisible.

'Mum?' Kirsty whispered.

Amanda didn't respond.

Kirsty stepped into the room, her skin crawling, the air thick with a cold, heavy feeling – like the oxygen had been sucked out of it.

'Mum?'

Amanda finally blinked, turning her head slowly toward her. There was a strange look in her eyes – dark, almost glassy, like someone else was looking out from behind them.

'Oh, darling,' Amanda said softly, smiling faintly. 'It's nothing. Just a dream.'

But Kirsty knew that wasn't true.

☽✧✝✧☾

Over the next few days, it got worse. Amanda would stop mid-conversation, tilting her head slightly, as if listening to something only she could hear. Kirsty caught her standing at the bedroom window more than once, staring out at the darkened garden, her lips moving silently, her eyes darting from shadow to shadow.

The house itself seemed to change too. Kirsty felt it when she was alone – this oppressive, heavy atmosphere that seemed to press down on her, making her chest feel tight, her skin prickle. She'd catch a movement in the corner of her eye – a shadow that wasn't there when she turned, a fleeting shape that seemed to melt back into the dark.

Sometimes, at night, she'd hear whispering.

It was faint, almost like the wind, but it was there. Words she couldn't quite make out – low, guttural, urgent. It sounded like her mother's voice, but there was something wrong with it – something strained, like it wasn't really Amanda at all.

And the smell.

A faint, rotting smell that seemed to cling to certain spots in the house. Amanda's bedroom, mostly, but sometimes in the hallway too, or the corner of the lounge where she liked to sit. It was subtle at first – like damp wood or mould. But over time it grew stronger, more distinct – a sour, decaying odour, like meat left to rot in the heat.

Kirsty tried to tell herself it was her imagination, the stress of looking after her mum, the weight of it all – but she couldn't shake the feeling that something had followed Amanda home.

Something that was still here.

Something that was waiting.

☽✧✝✧☾

It was a cold, still night when it finally broke. Kirsty had been tiptoeing around her mum for weeks, trying to hold everything together – making cups of tea, tidying up, checking on Amanda in the evenings – but all the while, the fear gnawed at her like a rat in the dark.

And Amanda … she just got worse.

Her skin looked grey and papery, her eyes sunk into dark hollows. The sparkle – the fierce, no-nonsense woman Kirsty had always known – was fading away, replaced by someone pale, shrunken, almost fragile. But the thing that unsettled Kirsty the most was the way Amanda's eyes would sometimes lock onto her. Like she wasn't quite sure who Kirsty was. Like she was seeing something else.

Kirsty couldn't take it anymore.

It was late, the house silent except for the creaks and groans that seemed louder now, more insistent. Kirsty had been lying in bed, staring at the ceiling, when she heard it again – murmuring from her mum's room. Her heart hammered in her chest as she got up, bare feet cold against the floorboards. She crept to Amanda's door, the hallway light throwing long shadows on the walls. The murmuring grew louder – Amanda's voice, soft but steady, as if speaking to someone who wasn't there.

Kirsty opened the door. Her mum was sitting in the armchair by the window, the curtains half-closed, the orange glow from the streetlamp casting strange shapes across her face. Amanda was whispering. Her hands rested on the arms of the chair, fingers twitching slightly, her gaze fixed on the far corner of the room – the darkest part, where the shadows pooled.

'Mum?' Kirsty's voice cracked.

Amanda stopped. Slowly, she turned to her daughter. Her face looked wrong. Not monstrous, not twisted into something inhuman – but just off. Her eyes too wide, her lips stretched in a faint, strained smile. Like she was forcing herself to look normal.

'I didn't want to scare you, love,' she said softly. Her voice trembled.

Kirsty stepped into the room, the air thick and heavy. 'Mum, what's going on? Please … tell me.'

Amanda stared at her for a long time, her eyes glistening in the half-light. Then, finally, she exhaled a long, shuddering breath – like she'd been holding it in for weeks. She looked down at her hands, twisting her fingers together.

'It's here, Kirsty,' she whispered. 'It followed me back.'

Kirsty's breath caught in her throat. Amanda's voice dropped, barely audible.

'When I was in that … that place … after my heart stopped … I saw it. The thing in the dark.'

Kirsty felt a chill ripple through her, cold and sharp, as if someone had run an icy fingertip down her spine.

Amanda looked up at her, tears welling in her eyes. 'It's been coming to me,' she said, her voice breaking. 'Every night, in the dark. Standing in the corner of the room. It watches me, Kirsty. It waits.'

Her hands trembled as she spoke, her knuckles white.

'It's … it's like a man, but not. Twisted. Hunched. Its skin is black, but not like a shadow – like burnt flesh. Its fingers are long, bony, ending in claws. Its face …'

She stopped, shivering. Her eyes flicked to the dark corner, as if expecting to see it standing there.

'Its face is a skull. A … bony maw, with yellow, rotted teeth. It's always grinning. And its eyes – Jesus, Kirsty, its eyes are like holes, black and endless. When it looks at me, I feel like it's … peeling me apart. Like it's waiting for me to let go.'

Kirsty's stomach lurched, a cold, sick feeling blooming in her chest. Amanda's breathing quickened, her voice a desperate whisper now.

'It whispers to me, Kirsty. It tells me to leave. To come with it. It says my time here is done, that I don't belong anymore.'

Kirsty felt tears prick her eyes. She reached for her mum's hand – but Amanda recoiled, pulling back sharply, her eyes wide with terror.

'No,' she gasped. 'Don't … don't touch me. It doesn't like it when you're near.'

Kirsty froze, her hand halfway out, a lump rising in her throat. 'Mum, it's not real,' she said weakly, her voice barely above a whisper. 'It's just … it's just in your head.'

But even as she said it, she felt the words crumble. Because deep down, she knew it wasn't just in her head. She had felt it too.

The cold. The heaviness in the air. The way the shadows seemed to move when you weren't looking directly at them.

Kirsty swallowed hard, her voice shaking. 'What does it want?'

Amanda's face crumpled. Tears spilled down her cheeks as she whispered, 'My soul.'

The word hung in the air like a stone dropped into a still pond and in that moment, Kirsty realised the terrible truth.

Her mum wasn't getting better.

She was slipping away.

And whatever had followed her back from the darkness wasn't finished with her yet.

☽✧✝✧☾

Kirsty couldn't take it anymore. The fear had wrapped itself around the house like ivy – creeping into every room, every shadow, every dark corner. She felt it when she was lying in bed at night, her heart thudding in her ears, listening to her mum whispering in the next room. She felt it when she walked down the stairs and caught a glimpse of Amanda sitting in her chair, staring at nothing, lips moving in silent conversation.

She knew she couldn't handle it alone, so she reached out to Rick. She'd been scrolling through Facebook late at night, desperate for answers, when she stumbled across a group dedicated to paranormal investigations in the North West. Rick was one of the admins, his name popping up again and again in the comments – offering advice, asking questions, always calm and measured. She clicked on his profile, read through some of his posts, and thought: This is someone who might understand.

She sent him a long, rambling message. Poured her heart out. Told him everything – about her mum's heart attack, the whispers in the dark, the thing she'd seen in Amanda's eyes. She described the cold spots, the smell of rot, the way Amanda would talk to herself in the dead of night.

Rick had messaged back quickly. He could hear the panic in her words, the desperation. He didn't brush her off or offer empty reassurances. Instead, he asked questions – good, sensible ones – and told her, simply: 'I'm going to help you.'

Over the next few weeks, Rick visited the house himself. Not just once, but multiple times – bringing with him a small team of investigators, people he trusted. They spent several nights there, setting up equipment in every room: EMF meters, temperature sensors, digital voice recorders. They even left motion sensors and trigger objects on the stairs.

And the house did not disappoint.

Rick told me the EMF meters spiked repeatedly in Amanda's bedroom – especially in the corner where she said the figure stood. The temperature in that spot dropped by several degrees, a sudden, sharp chill that didn't match the rest of the room.

They captured EVPs too – faint voices on playback, whispering in the static. Words like 'come back', 'let go', and a chilling, drawn-out 'Amanda…' that made the hair on the back of Rick's neck stand up.

Rick told me that during the investigation, when he first started picking up on the strange readings, he knew this wasn't just a typical case. He'd ring me up late at night, sometimes while sitting in his car parked outside Amanda's house.

'I don't know what the hell's going on here, Adam,' he said to me once, his voice low and tense. 'I'm getting EMF spikes in places where there's no electrics, cold spots that don't make sense… but it's the feeling, mate. It's heavy. Dark. Like it's waiting for something. You know what it's like with demonic cases. You've experienced them'

I nodded. I didn't envy him. I certainly knew what it felt like to deal with this kind of case. I listened to him. I tried to help him piece it together –

gave him advice on cleansing techniques, things to look for, how to protect himself and the others in the house. It was clear Rick wasn't taking this lightly. He knew they were dealing with something serious – and he wasn't about to let Amanda face it alone.

One night, Rick sat alone in the lounge, listening in the dark, and he heard it with his own ears – whispering. Soft, low, just beyond the range of normal hearing – but it was there. He knew, without a doubt, that there was something in that house. Something that wasn't finished with Amanda.

And that's when Rick decided to call in Roz.

☽✧✝✧☾

Roz was a sensitive Rick had worked with many times before – someone who could read the energy in a space like a book. He trusted her instincts. If anyone could get to the bottom of what was happening to Amanda, it was her.

Kirsty didn't know what to expect when she arrived, but the moment Roz stepped into the house, she stopped dead in the hallway, her face going pale.

'There's something here,' she whispered, her eyes narrowing as she scanned the air. 'It's strong. Heavy. And it's not just in the house – it's attached to her.' she had pointed at Amanda.

Amanda sat on the sofa, her hands folded tightly in her lap, her eyes darting between Roz and Rick like a cornered animal. Roz approached her slowly, her voice calm but firm.

'I'm going to help you, Amanda. I need you to trust me.'

Amanda nodded, tears glistening in her eyes.

Roz set to work that night. The ritual was simple on the surface, but it felt anything but. She lit white candles in each room, tracing symbols in the air with sage smoke. She recited prayers of protection, her voice low and steady, the words filling the house like a heartbeat. In Amanda's bedroom – the epicentre – she placed bowls of salt water in the corners, burning frankincense until the air shimmered with heat.

As Roz worked, Amanda sat rigid in her chair, her breathing shallow, her eyes wide and glassy. Kirsty hovered in the doorway, arms crossed tight over her chest, feeling the cold prickle of goosebumps rise up her arms.

At one point, Roz paused, her hand hovering over Amanda's head. 'It's here,' she whispered. 'Right now. It's … waiting. Watching.'

The room seemed to darken. The shadows in the corners stretched longer, the air turning heavy, oppressive. Roz began speaking louder, firmer now, commanding the entity to leave. She called it by name – 'the dark thing', 'the parasite', 'the shadow that feeds on fear' – and told it to release Amanda, to leave her in peace.

Amanda began to cry. Deep, wracking sobs that seemed to shake her whole body. And then, suddenly, she let out a sharp gasp and slumped forward, as if something had been torn out of her. Roz kept going, not stopping until the room seemed to lighten, the air easing, the pressure lifting.

And when it was done – when the candles had burned low and the smoke had cleared – Amanda looked up at her daughter.

Her eyes were clearer.

The tension in her face had eased.

And for the first time in weeks, Kirsty saw a glimpse of the real Amanda again.

The days that followed were like the first warm days after a long, hard winter. The house felt different – lighter, safer, almost like it could breathe again. Amanda's energy returned. The fear in her eyes faded. She started to eat properly, to sit in the garden, to laugh with Kirsty and her friends and family. It was like she'd come back from the edge of something terrible.

She told Rick and Roz she didn't know how to thank them. It was Rick, in the end, who suggested she tell her story to me.

'You need to speak to Adam,' he'd said. 'This is one of those stories people need to hear.'

And so she did.

After hearing Amanda's account, I have no doubt in my mind that what she experienced was real. Her story isn't unique – not really. Because when I was a child, growing up in that strange, haunted house on Serlby Rise, I experienced something exactly like this too.

Something dark.

Something that watched from the corners of the room, waiting.

Something that whispered to me in the night, just like it whispered to Amanda. Back then, I didn't have the words for it. I didn't understand it. But hearing Amanda's story – it sent a cold shiver through me, because I recognised it instantly. A similar thing to that which followed Amanda back from the brink of death…

It had been with me, too, in that summer of 1994.

☽✧†✧☾

My Haunted Life

Part Seven

A Malevolent Encounter

The Thing by the Window

After that strange day that Warren and I had outside, my fear-filled nights inside continued. Despite being 11 years old, I found myself continually heading to sleep in my parents' bed, squeezing in between them or having one of them come to my room while I slept with the other. Their bedroom was even colder than mine, and I could see my breath misting in the air like tiny ghosts escaping my lips. The chill clung to my skin as I burrowed beneath the heavy duvet, its weight anchoring me to the bed, yet no amount of warmth could banish the icy dread that gripped my heart.

I had always been sensitive to the dark – a trait my parents often worried about – yet this was a different kind of unease. Upon moving into the house on Serlby Rise, I found myself grappling with an irrational fear of sleeping alone in my own bedroom, and this was before we had experienced anything supernatural. It baffled me; I had never experienced such trepidation at Wray Close. Yet, as soon as I stepped foot in this new home, the unease began to take root. This unnerving sensation lingered throughout my entire time there, an unwelcome companion that tainted my nights. In hindsight, I can't shake the feeling that there was something else at play – some intangible presence within those walls exacerbated my fears and my psychic abilities were quietly (and unknowingly) developing. It wasn't until many years later that I began to make sense of those experiences and the chilling sensations that accompanied them.

I recall countless nights spent wide awake, staring into the depths of my bedroom. Now, with the perspective of time, I believe that fear was not merely a figment of a child's imagination but rather whispers of intuition that I had yet to fully comprehend. My parents' bedroom, enveloped in total darkness, became my refuge and prison. Despite being with them within the room, the walls seemed to close in on me as I lay wedged between Mum and Dad. Hours would slip by – time marked only by the shivery sense of impending doom that crept over me. I often found myself staring, wide-eyed, at the corner of the room near the window where the streetlight scarcely penetrated. I knew there was something there, lurking just beyond the veil of deep shadow. I sensed it, knowing it was there, watching ... waiting. My heart would race, a frantic drum solo in the stillness, each beat echoing my mounting terror. I gripped the quilt, feeling the soft fabric against my palms, wishing it could shield me from whatever looming threat hovered just beyond the edge of my vision.

Then there came that dreadful moment, the time I can still to this day never quite shake free from my mind. It was an ordinary night – cold, as usual, with the frost creeping over the windows, creating intricate patterns that seemed to dance in the dim light. I lay there for what felt like eternity, stiff with frightened anticipation, when I sensed a movement. Within the folds of darkness, the thing shifted. I didn't see it but I sensed it. It stood by that window, for what felt like hours, watching, until eventually it slithered down the edge of the bed, and I could feel it moving closer. My breath caught in my throat as the form leaned over my mum, prevailing over the gentle rise and fall of her body. It was as if the very air had thickened around me, each inhalation becoming a struggle as panic clawed at my chest. I squinted, trying to discern some shape, some indication of what I was up against, but it remained unseen and the darkness remained impenetrable, a thick smog that thwarted my attempts at clarity.

I was beyond terrified – frozen, unable to scream or shake my parents awake. Something unseen held me captive. Instead, I lay utterly still, each muscle tensed, an unwilling and scared observer.

The moment felt like hours. The entity I could sense inched closer, leaning over her – it was as if it were sniffing her. A primal instinct told me to protect her; my mind raced. What was I going to do?

Then, just as suddenly as the presence had come, it receded, slipping back into the shadows that cloaked the room. As I lay in that eerie silence, my heart hammering, I couldn't shake the feeling of being watched. The heavy feeling left, yet the fear persisted, festering in the corners of my mind, curling around my thoughts like weeds in an untended garden.

That night was just the beginning. Days turned into weeks, and the pattern continued: I slept poorly, my days a haze of exhaustion and terror, my nights punctuated by the anticipation of the lurking threat, the dark embrace of the unknown. In the daylight, it was easier to pretend the shadows were just that – nothing more than a trick of the mind. But as evening fell, and the creeping coldness seeped into my bones, I knew the truth: I was never truly alone.

A Welcome Break

Even though the haunting on Serlby Rise could be relentless at times – dark, disturbing, and emotionally draining – there were also periods where things would ease off. Sometimes it was just for a day or two. Other times we'd get lucky, and it might be a few weeks or even months where nothing out of the ordinary would happen. No creaking floorboards in the night, no icy air drifting through closed rooms, no strange figures appearing at the window. Just normality. Peace. Or at least something close to it.

But even during those quieter spells, the fear never really left me. Not completely. It was always there in the background, like a silent passenger. Even when things felt normal, I still expected the strange to return. I lived in a kind of heightened awareness, always waiting for the next bang, the next chill, the next moment when everything would suddenly turn on its head again. The breaks were a relief – a welcome one – but they never erased the dread. They just gave it a place to rest.

In August of 1994, during one of those quieter periods, my mum and dad had planned a caravan holiday to the East Coast of Lincolnshire – one of our favourite parts of the country – staying near Skegness, Ingoldmells and Chapel St Leonards. We'd booked a static caravan at Robin Hood Holiday Park in Chapel, and I was counting down the days with proper childhood excitement. What made it even better was that Mum and Dad had said I could take Warren with us. That sent my excitement into overdrive. A full week by the sea with my best mate, away from the weirdness of home – it sounded perfect.

The plan was to leave on the Saturday morning. Bags were already packed, and we were just about set. On the Friday night, I stayed over at Nana and Grandad's while Mum and Dad went out to The Alcester with Sandy and Den – Warren's parents – for a few drinks. When I say 'a few drinks', I mean it in the Nottingham sense – several pints, a few shorts, and probably a Chinese takeaway to finish. By the time they all rolled back up Serlby Rise in the early hours, they were merry to say the least! And like a lot of folks who'd had a good night at the local, they didn't go straight indoors. They stood outside their houses, cackling and chatting, dragging out the night for as long as possible. That's when Sandy casually mentioned that Sasha was gutted about him going away without her. She was really upset, apparently in tears about it.

Now, most people might sympathise, offer a pat on the shoulder, and leave it at that. But not my mum and dad – not after a night at The Alcester. Drunkenly and without hesitation, they told Sandy, 'Ah, let her come too! There's room!'

That was that!!

Come Saturday morning, we were meant to be heading off bright and early – but instead, they were frantically trying to pack a suitcase for Sasha. It was chaos. Clothes were being thrown into bags, towels folded, toothbrushes chucked into zipped-up side pockets. I was still waking up at my grandparents', blissfully unaware, when Mum came to collect me. She turned up beaming, clearly still amused by the night's spontaneous decision.

'Guess what? Sasha's coming too!' she announced with a grin.

I was thrilled. Having her on the trip made it feel even more special.

But the story didn't end there.

As we were loading the car, Claire appeared from across the road. When she found out that Sasha was going away too, she burst into tears. Full-on heartbreak. She hadn't been invited. She didn't want to be left behind. So what did my mum and dad do? They invited her too! Within the space of twelve hours, our little holiday had gone from two adults and two kids… to four kids, two adults, oh, and the dog!

I couldn't believe it. I remember thinking it was the best thing that had ever happened. Our whole little gang, by the seaside, for a full week. Not only was it a break from the strange and frightening goings-on at home, but it felt like a proper adventure – like something out of a film. I couldn't wait to get there.

The holiday itself turned out to be one of the best weeks of my entire childhood.

We all crammed into the static caravan like sardines, clothes and belongings spread out across every available surface, someone always tripping over someone else's bag or sleeping arrangement. The beds were narrow, and there were nowhere near enough for everyone, but we made it work. That was part of the fun. There was laughter every night, whispered conversations by torchlight, and hushed giggles as we tried not to wake the grown-ups.

The budget – which was originally meant to stretch between just me, Warren and my parents – now had to cover six people, and we felt it. Meals were simple: kids specials at the chip shop. But none of us cared. Even the smallest treat felt like a feast. In the evenings, we went over to the Maid Marian Club on the caravan site. My parents couldn't afford to keep us all supplied with overpriced drinks from the bar, so they smuggled in cheap pop from the local shop, hiding them in handbags and jacket pockets like it was some secret mission. We'd sit at the back with our plastic bottles of Panda Cola, watching the entertainment – usually some cabaret act or cheesy disco, playing in the kids area – and laughing until our sides hurt.

We spent our days playing on the arcades, building sandcastles on the beach, paddling in the cold North Sea, and trying our luck on the 2p push machines. I can still remember the sound of the seagulls, the smell of chips and vinegar in the sea air, the feel of the wind on our faces as we raced along the promenade. That week, we were free. Not just from school, not just from routine – but from the weight of everything strange and dark that hung over our lives back home. Serlby Rise and its ghosts felt a million miles away. For once, I wasn't looking over my shoulder; wasn't jumping at shadows. We were just kids – loud, daft, sunburnt and happy.

And it was a feeling I've never forgotten.

That holiday gave me something I didn't even realise I needed – a breather. A chance to remember what normal felt like.

Because deep down, I think I knew it wouldn't last. The strange and the sinister would come back, as it always did.

But for that one week in Chapel St Leonards, we got to be kids again. And that, to me, was magic.

Back to Normality

Coming home from that week in Chapel St Leonards was bittersweet. We'd had one of the best holidays of my childhood. For those seven days, the darkness that had clung to us back home had been lifted. It was as if Serlby Rise had never existed – as though the ghosts had finally loosened their grip and let us breathe.

But of course, real life doesn't stay on pause just because you go on holiday. We returned to Serlby Rise to find the house exactly as we'd left it. But the air felt different again. It was like stepping back into a room you hadn't visited in a while, and realising it had been waiting for you the whole time.

The activity resumed almost straight away, though not with the same terrifying edge it had carried before the holiday. The poltergeist, or whatever it was that plagued our home, hadn't disappeared – but it seemed ... subdued. The energy was still there, the disturbances still happened, but they felt less aggressive somehow. Less malicious.

The same things kept happening. We'd walk into the living room to find the cushions scattered across the carpet in strange positions, even when nobody had been in the room. The curtains would draw themselves shut in the middle of the day, plunging the room into an unnatural gloom. Doors still had their way of opening on their own, unseen. But it had, strangely, become the 'norm'.

We stopped reacting as much. I think deep down, we were tired of being terrified. The fear hadn't gone – not really – but we'd adapted. You get to a point where something happening so often becomes just another part of your day, like hearing the post drop through the letterbox or the dog barking at the telly. When something unexplainable happens every other day, it stops being shocking and just becomes your life.

Then new things started to happen.

The loft hatch, set into the ceiling on the upstairs landing, became its own source of drama. My dad would get up on the ladder to push the hatch closed – it had no real reason to open on its own – and yet, time after time, we'd find it open again. Fully ajar too, a gaping hole, inviting you to look up into the blackness. He'd roll his eyes and close it again, only for it to be back open the next day. There was no wind in the loft. No fault in the latch. But it just kept happening. We tried to ignore it. Pretend it was just one of those things. But I think Dad and I knew it was part of something.

And then came the whispers. It started subtly – at first. But the more I focused on it, the more I realised that it was coming from right next to me. Right by my ear. Not loud, not clear – but present. Whispers. Low, unintelligible, like someone was trying to speak but couldn't quite form the words. They would come when I least expected them. Usually when I was sat quietly, watching the telly with my parents – half paying attention to *The Bill* or *Boon* – and then I'd hear it: that soft, breathy sound, like a voice just grazing the edge of hearing.

And yet, oddly, it didn't scare me the way it might have done before. Maybe I was becoming numb to it. Or maybe I was just starting to understand that I was somehow connected to it all. That this wasn't just something happening to our house ... but something happening around me. My sensitivity – my awareness – was starting to grow. What I now recognise as my psychic ability was beginning to develop. I was starting to sense things away from the house too. Serlby Rise wasn't the only place where strange things happened anymore. At school – Blue Bell Hill Primary – things took a turn for the bizarre.

Our class was located in a separate little building away from the main school. A small, standalone structure that had always felt a little out of place, tucked away from the bustle of the other classrooms. And it was there, in that detached unit, that something began to stir. Most days, after lunch, we'd gather outside the classroom, waiting for our teacher, Mrs Livingston, to unlock the door and let us back in. And that's when it started. From inside the locked, empty classroom, we began to hear the sounds of movement. Chairs scraping. Tables shifting. The unmistakable sound of children laughing and playing – even though there was no one in there. We'd look at each other, confused but fascinated. Sometimes we'd joke about it, trying to explain it away. But none of us could ignore it. The sounds were real. Clear.

On more than one occasion, we'd return to the classroom to find items had moved. Things placed in different spots than where we'd left them. Pens missing, only to reappear in someone else's tray.

One day, we returned to find a nail had been driven right through one of the panes of glass on the classroom window – nailed through the glass. But the glass hadn't shattered. There was no crack, no damage. The nail just sat there, impossibly embedded, as if it had always been that way.

It was baffling.

And while no one ever said it outright, I think the other kids felt something too – that sense of being watched, of something unseen moving around us. But for me, it all felt familiar. The energy I sensed at school was similar to what I'd felt at home. Like something was following me.

Or maybe drawn to me. It left me with a question that, even now, decades later, I still don't fully know the answer to:

Was it the places that were haunted? Or was it me? Was I just in the wrong place at the wrong time – or was I the common denominator? I began to wonder whether my presence, my energy, was fuelling these events.

Giving the spirits permission.

Giving them power.

Or maybe … they were drawn to me because they knew I could sense them.

It's a question that has stayed with me ever since.

☽✧†✧☾

Gerry & Delia's Story

The Son

Ouija boards.

Just the mention of them is enough to divide people – some dismiss them as harmless, nothing more than a parlour game, while others warn they're a gateway to something darker. I've heard the arguments a thousand times – it's just a board, just letters and numbers, how can it possibly do anything? But the truth is, it's not about the board itself. It's about the intention behind it – the energy, the mindset of those who use it, the focus they pour into the act.

I've always said that, under the right conditions, in the hands of someone who understands the risks, a Ouija board can be a powerful tool for communication. I've used them myself on investigations – carefully, with proper protection, respect and a clear purpose.

But the problem is, too many people jump in headfirst. They don't think about the consequences. They don't set boundaries, don't cleanse the space, don't protect themselves. They approach it like it's a game, or a quick fix for grief or curiosity. And when you open a door like that – without care, without preparation – you don't always know what's waiting on the other side.

And sometimes…

What comes through isn't who you think it is.

That's exactly what happened in the case I'm about to share. A story that still haunts me, because it's a chilling reminder of how easily grief can be weaponised – how something dark can slip into the cracks left by loss, wearing the face of someone you love.

☽✧✝✧☾

Weymouth, early 1990s. It's a place I know well. Growing up, it was one of my family's go-to destinations. We spent many happy holidays there – me, my parents, and my grandparents, Don and Audrey. The beaches, the pier, the smell of fish, chips and vinegar in the air, the sound of seagulls overhead … It was a place that felt safe, almost timeless, like nothing bad could happen there.

I have so many fond memories of those trips – playing on the sand, sitting on the wall eating ice creams, visiting the amusements. One year, I even brought Warren along for the ride. It was a place where I felt happy, where the world seemed simpler somehow.

Another little memory that sticks with me about those Weymouth holidays is how our relatives from Bristol would often pop down for the day while we were staying there. It was a proper family affair – my grandparents, Don and Audrey, Mum and Dad, and then the Bristol lot would arrive, and we'd all spend the day together on the beach. Buckets and spades, sandwiches wrapped in foil, sand sticking to everything. I remember how much laughter there was, the way everyone just seemed to relax, like the sea air washed the worries away for a little while. Those were the days when family felt like everything.

But Weymouth wasn't just a place for sandcastles and fish and chips for me – it was also where my lifelong love of horror was born. I was only 10 years old, on one of those family holidays, when it happened. I remember it vividly. We'd been walking along the seafront, and I spotted a small, slightly shabby bookshop tucked between a souvenir shop and a café. The window was full of paperbacks – some old, some new – and something about it just drew me in.

Inside, the shop smelled of musty paper and old wood, that comforting scent of books waiting to be discovered. My eyes scanned the displays, but it was a shelf tucked away in the corner that caught my attention – Point Horror.

I'd never seen anything like it before. The covers were bold and striking, with those classic fonts and the promise of chills inside. One title stood out: *Trick or* Treat. It had a creepy haunted house on the front, and I remember standing there for ages, reading the back cover, feeling a little shiver run down my spine.

I bought it with my pocket money – my first horror book. And from that moment on, I was hooked. Looking back now, it's eerie to think that while I was getting lost in those stories, a real-life horror was unfolding in a quiet house just a few streets away.

So when I first heard this story – when I realised that while I was down there having the time of my life, just a few streets away, a couple were going through the worst time of their lives – it hit me hard. This wasn't just a haunting in some far-off place. This was Weymouth.

My Weymouth.

☽✧☨✧☾

My dad was the source of this story. Dad had a friend – Gareth – who worked within the Catholic Church. They'd known each other for years, ever since my Dad's church days. They had been involved in a charity car wash for the church funds and Gareth was helping to organise. Gareth was well-connected, and through him, Dad had once been introduced to a bishop who lived in Dorchester. I won't name him, out of respect for his privacy, but I will say this – he was an ordained exorcist.

Gareth told Dad a story, one that the bishop had shared with him in confidence. It was something Gareth never forgot, and when Dad told me, I never forgot it either.

It was about a couple from Weymouth.

Their names were Gerry and Delia. In 1993, they were in their mid-fifties – Gerry was 56, Delia 52. They'd been together for thirty years. They were a classic seaside couple – he'd worked in the fishing industry for years, a quiet, dependable man; she'd been a part-time cleaner, warm-hearted, chatty, always the one to make a fuss of the neighbours' kids or bring round a casserole if someone was under the weather. They weren't wealthy, but they had a nice little home not far from the seafront, a modest two-bed terrace with flower pots by the front door and a small, well-kept back garden where Delia grew herbs and flowers.

They had one child – Aiden – born in 1973, their pride and joy. Aiden was a quiet lad, who grew into the kind of teenager who kept to himself, happy to tinker with his motorbike in the shed or listen to music in his room. He wasn't a troublemaker, not by a long shot – he was thoughtful, shy, a bit of a homebody. He still lived at home at 19, working part-time at a local garage. He had a few close mates, but mostly it was just him, Gerry and Delia – a tight little family unit. Growing up, Delia had a special nickname for Aiden – 'Poppit'. She'd called him that since he was a baby, a little family pet name that had stuck through the years. Even as a teenager, he'd let her use it now and then, usually with a shy, embarrassed smile. It was just their thing – Mum's little Poppit.

They doted on Aiden. He was their whole world.

And then, one awful day in 1992, that world was shattered.

☽✧†✧☾

It was a Sunday afternoon in May of that year when it happened. A warm day, with the kind of blue sky that made you think summer was on its way – one of those lazy, quiet days where the air feels soft, like nothing bad could possibly happen. Gerry had been pottering in the garden, pulling weeds from the flower beds, while Delia was inside, folding the washing in the living room with the radio humming in the background.

Aiden had gone out that morning on his motorbike. He'd only had it a few months – an old Yamaha 125, second hand, but his pride and joy. Gerry had been cautious about it from the start, worried like any dad would be, but Aiden was careful; not the sort to go tearing around at speed.

They didn't know exactly where he was heading that day – somewhere in the countryside, maybe down the lanes near Upwey or Chickerell. He'd mentioned it in passing over breakfast, his voice soft and casual, 'Just going for a ride, Dad. Back later.' And that was that.

Later never came.

It was just after three in the afternoon when the knock came at the door. Gerry wiped his hands on a rag and answered it, expecting maybe an unwanted visit from a neighbour – but it was worse than that. It was a stranger, a young man in his twenties, pale and wide-eyed, motorcycle helmet tucked under one arm. One of Aiden's biker friends.

'Mr *****,' he said, voice trembling, 'there's been an accident … Aiden … on the road near Radipole. I think you need to come.'

Delia came rushing out of the living room, her face crumpling before the words were even fully spoken. Gerry drove. He couldn't tell you how he got there – he just remembered the blur of hedgerows flashing past, the thud of his heart like a drum in his chest. Delia was beside him, gripping his arm, whispering No, no, no, no over and over like a mantra.

When they arrived, there were flashing lights – an ambulance parked on the verge, a police car angled awkwardly across the road. The smell of hot tarmac and engine oil hung in the air.

And there was Aiden's bike – smashed, bent, the front wheel twisted at a sickening angle. Aiden lay on the grass, a paramedic kneeling beside him, another standing nearby, shaking his head slowly, his lips tight. They'd done all they could, but it wasn't enough.

Gerry remembered that moment in fragments – Delia's cries, the way her knees buckled, the officer holding her upright as she sobbed into his shoulder. The way the world seemed to go silent, like someone had switched the sound off. He stood frozen, watching the paramedics pack up their kit, the stark, clinical way they worked, and he thought: This isn't real. This can't be happening.

But it was.

Aiden was gone. Just like that.

The days that followed were a blur of disbelief, a nightmare from which they couldn't wake. The house felt wrong. Too quiet, too still. His jacket was slung over the back of a chair, as if he might walk through the door at any moment, call out 'Mum, I'm home', and laugh at them for being so worried.

Delia couldn't bring herself to touch his things. His bedroom stayed exactly as it was – the unmade bed, the posters on the wall, a half-empty mug on the bedside table. She would go in and sit for hours, holding his jumper in her hands, breathing in the faint scent of him, tears slipping silently down her cheeks.

Gerry tried to be strong, for her, but the grief gnawed at him in a way he couldn't put into words. He'd sit in the garden, staring at the flowerbeds, hearing the distant roar of a motorbike engine and feeling his stomach twist into a knot. He found himself waking up in the middle of the night, expecting to hear Aiden's footsteps on the stairs.

And every time, the same awful, gut-punch realisation hit him all over again: Aiden wasn't coming back.

The quietness of the house became unbearable. Meals were eaten in near-complete silence, the clink of cutlery sounding unnaturally loud in the small kitchen. They stopped watching the TV together – Gerry would sit in the lounge, staring at the screen without taking anything in, while Delia lay on the bed upstairs, staring at the ceiling.

They were trapped in their own separate cages of grief, orbiting each other in the same small house, unable to reach out, unable to speak about what had happened. And in that silence, in that aching void, something else began to creep in.

Three months passed after Aiden's death, and for Gerry and Delia, the world might as well have ended. The house became a tomb – silent, heavy, as if it was holding its breath. The blinds were kept drawn most days, the television left off, the clock on the wall ticking too loud in the quiet. They stopped answering the phone. Stopped opening the post. Neighbours knocked at first, offering condolences, dropping off food to try and help – but after a while, the visits stopped too.

Gerry barely spoke. He sat at the kitchen table most days, staring at the surface as if waiting for something to happen. His mug of tea would go cold in his hands, untouched. Delia drifted between rooms like a ghost herself, hair unbrushed, clothes hanging loose on her frame. She'd sit on the edge of Aiden's bed, running her fingers over the crease in the duvet, whispering his name under her breath, like a prayer.

They were drowning in it – grief, deep and all-consuming, wrapping itself around their lives like a fog.

And then...

The whispers began.

It started one evening in the kitchen. Delia was standing at the sink, rinsing a plate, when she heard it – soft, so soft she almost thought she'd imagined it.

'Mum.'

She froze, her heart lurching in her chest. Slowly, she turned to Gerry, who was sitting at the table, but he was looking down at the newspaper, his face blank. She waited, holding her breath… but nothing.

But the next night, she heard it again. This time it was clearer.

'Mum…'

The voice was unmistakably Aiden's, that gentle, slightly shy tone he always had when asking for something. It came from the bottom of the stairs, just outside the kitchen door.

Delia's hands trembled as she gripped the edge of the sink.

A few days later, Gerry heard it too. He was in the lounge, staring at the muted TV, when he caught it.

'Dad…'

A whisper, faint but so real it made his blood run cold. It seemed to come from the hallway, from the direction of the stairs. He froze in his chair, the air around him suddenly heavy, the familiar scent of Aiden's aftershave – a sharp, citrusy smell – filling the room in an instant. It was so strong, he swore it was as if Aiden had just walked past him.

Then little things started to move.

Aiden's keyring, the one with the worn-down Yamaha logo, which had sat untouched on the side table since the accident – Delia found it on the stairs one morning. His battered old trainers, tucked under his bed for months, appeared by the door as if ready for him to slip them on and leave.

Gerry swore he'd left Aiden's leather jacket folded over the banister, but one morning it was draped over the back of the kitchen chair, just as Aiden used to leave it when he came in from a ride. At first, it terrified them. They were afraid to say it out loud, afraid that if they acknowledged it, it might stop.

But after a while, the fear gave way to something else – relief. They started to believe – really believe – that it was Aiden. That their boy hadn't left them after all.

It was Delia who saw him first.

She was coming up the stairs one evening, a mug of tea in her hands, when she glanced up and saw a figure – a fleeting glimpse of someone moving along the landing, just ahead of her. Tall, slim, dressed in a familiar dark tracksuit – Aiden's favourite, the one with the fraying cuffs.

'Aiden…?'

She called his name, the mug slipping from her fingers, spilling tea on the carpet. But the figure didn't stop. It walked into Aiden's bedroom, right through the door, and then … nothing.

Gerry heard the mug drop and came running. She could barely speak, tears streaming down her face, her hands shaking.

'I saw him, Gerry,' she whispered. 'I saw him.'

☽✧✝✧☾

A few nights later, they were in bed – Delia curled up on her side, Gerry sitting up reading, though the words blurred on the page. The room was dim, the only light coming from the hallway beyond the slightly ajar bedroom door.

And then Gerry both saw it.

A face, peering through the gap in Aiden's bedroom door across the landing – just a sliver of his features visible in the dark. His soft brown eyes, the faintest hint of a smile.

Aiden.

Gerry reached out and gripped Delia's hand, gesturing her to look. She gasped. Both of them were frozen, afraid to breathe in case the moment shattered. Delia wept softly, her chest hitching with the weight of it.

'He's here,' she whispered. 'He's still here.'

And at that moment, they believed it. With everything they had left, they believed. Their boy had come back to them.

☽✧✝✧☾

For Gerry and Delia, it wasn't just grief anymore. It was hope. They believed, with all their hearts, that Aiden had come back to them. Every whisper, every faint scent of his aftershave, every fleeting glimpse of his shape moving around the house – it all became proof that he wasn't really gone.

A week after, they began holding little candlelit séances in Aiden's bedroom, sitting together at a small round table that they'd dragged into the centre of the room. They'd sit there for each night before bed, the single candle flickering between them, casting tall, shivering shadows on the walls. Delia would sit with her hands folded tightly, her eyes closed, whispering, 'Ady … Poppit … if you're here, give us a sign.'

And the signs came.

They'd hear soft taps on the table – one for yes, two for no, just as they'd asked. Sometimes the tapping was faint, barely a tap at all; other times it was sharper, a distinct, deliberate knock right beneath their hands.

The room would fill with the unmistakable scent of Aiden's aftershave – that sharp, citrusy smell that had clung to his skin after he'd been out on his bike. It seemed to seep from the walls, as if the air itself remembered him. Sometimes they'd hear his voice – so soft, almost drowned out by the sound of their own breathing, but there.

'I'm here,' it would whisper, a gentle, loving sound that made Delia weep with gratitude.

And every night, without fail, they saw him. Just a fleeting figure, standing in the dark corner of the room near the window – half in shadow, half in the faint glow of the candlelight. It wasn't a full, clear vision, not quite solid, but enough for them to know it was him: tall and slim, his outline unmistakable. His head tilted slightly, just like Aiden used to do when he was embarrassed, that shy, lopsided smile barely visible in the gloom, his floppy hair parted down the middle. He would stand there for a few moments – sometimes up to half a minute – watching them in silence. Then he would fade, melting back into the darkness, leaving only the scent of his aftershave behind. This led to an almost unhealthy obsession with the séances. Sometimes they would sit there at night for hours on end.

They felt comforted. They believed, without question, that Aiden was still with them.

☽✧☦✧☾

But over the weeks, the need for more grew inside them like a hunger. The taps, the whispers, the fleeting glimpses – it wasn't enough now. Delia would lean across the table, her voice breaking, pleading with the shadows.

'Aiden … please, poppit … talk to us. Just say something. Let us hear you properly.'

But no full words came. No proper conversation. Just the occasional whisper, or the sound of his name echoing softly from the darkness. The frustration gnawed at them – this constant, aching almost of it all.

And that's when Gerry had an idea.

One night, as they sat together in the dim candlelight, his voice low and hesitant, he said, 'Maybe … maybe we need something else. To help him speak.'

Delia blinked at him, her eyes glassy, tears catching in the candlelight. 'Like what?'

Gerry hesitated, his gaze drifting to the dark corner where they'd seen Aiden's shape so many times.

'A Ouija board.'

Delia was silent for a long moment. The idea hung in the air like a spark waiting to catch. Then, slowly, she nodded.

'Yes. If it helps us speak to him … we'll do it.'

☽✧✝✧☾

They bought one the very next day.

It was almost laughable, the way it happened. Of all places, they found them in a toy shop – tucked away on a bottom shelf, among board games and jigsaws. Gerry picked it up, turning the box over in his hands. It felt wrong somehow, this plastic board with its alphabet and numbers, but it also felt … like a sign.

They took it home, the box resting on Delia's lap like a fragile treasure.

That night, they set it up in Aiden's room. They placed the board on the table where they'd held their séances, the candle flickering beside it, casting its trembling light across the letters. The planchette, smooth and cheap, sat waiting beneath their fingertips.

They began, their voices barely above a whisper.

'Aiden … are you here?'

The planchette moved.

'Mum. Dad. I'm here.'

Delia sobbed, clutching Gerry's arm as the tears streamed down her cheeks. The next night, they tried again. This time, the messages came faster.

'I'm cold.'

'I miss you.'

'Let me in.'

They asked Aiden if he was in pain, if he wanted to come home, if there was anything they could do. The planchette slid swiftly under their fingers:

'Yes. Please. Let me come in. Invite me…'

Gerry swallowed hard. Delia's voice trembled as she said it aloud, tears spilling over her cheeks. 'Come in, Aiden. Come to us. Be with us again.'

They meant it with all their hearts. They thought they were opening the door for their son.

But I have no doubt – none at all – that what they were really inviting in was not Aiden. I've seen it too many times. Grief has a way of blinding people, of making them desperate enough to believe in anything. And when you reach out blindly into the dark … sometimes it's not who you hope for that answers.

The Ouija sessions would turn sinister.

And the mask would soon begin to slip.

☽✧†✧☾

After they allowed the spirit to come into their lives, it didn't take long for the change to come. At first, it was subtle – so subtle they might not have missed it if they weren't already so invested. The planchette on the Ouija board began to move faster, jerking in sharp, erratic motions instead of the smooth, measured slides they'd seen before. The messages started to feel …

different. The words came faster, less like Aiden's careful tone and more like something pushing through, something impatient.

The voice that whispered in the dark – Aiden's voice – shifted too. It was still soft, but there was a rasp to it now, a dry, hollow edge that hadn't been there before.

'Mum… Dad… listen to me…'

It was a voice that didn't sound quite right. Then, the physical changes started slowly. The temperature in Aiden's room dropped sharply – so cold they could see their breath, even with the heating on. They'd wake in the middle of the night and feel it too, a sudden, unnatural chill that clung to their skin like damp fog.

The smell came next. At first, it was faint, a slight tang of rot in the air – maybe a dead bird in the chimney, Gerry thought, though they never found one. Then it grew stronger. It was a foul, putrid stench, thick and choking – like dog excrement, a sharp, acrid scent that burned in the back of the throat. It clung to the house, soaking into the carpets, the curtains, the very walls. They tried everything – air fresheners, candles, scrubbing the floors – but nothing shifted it.

And the sounds…

Footsteps. Heavy, deliberate footsteps on the landing at night. Slow, creaking steps that paused outside their bedroom door, as if waiting. Sometimes they'd hear a soft, wet dripping sound, as if something was leaking in the ceiling – but there was no leak. There were awful growling, breathing sounds that came from unoccupied rooms.

Things began to move on their own. The framed photo of Aiden on the mantelpiece was found smashed on the floor one morning, the glass shattered, the smiling face beneath cracked down the middle. The kitchen chairs were dragged out from under the table, their legs scraping across the floor in the dead of night. Delia's collection of delicate porcelain ornaments – gifts from friends over the years – were swept from the shelf one by one, shattering in the darkness while they huddled in bed, too afraid to move.

And every night, without fail, they saw him. Standing in the dark, across the landing, watching them.

But it wasn't Aiden. Not anymore.

The shape was still the same – tall, slim, the familiar outline of their boy. But the details were wrong. His features were twisted, stretched into a grotesque version of Aiden's face. His smile…

That smile was the worst of it.

It wasn't shy, or warm, or loving. It was too wide, too sharp – hungry. His teeth looked wrong, jagged, too large for his mouth. His eyes were dark; too dark. He would stand there, just outside their door, his head tilted at that same angle – but the way he held himself was unnatural. His shoulders hunched, hands dangling loosely at his sides, fingers too long, twitching.

Delia clutched Gerry's arm one night, her voice a hoarse whisper.

'That's not him. That's not our boy.'

But by then, it was too late.

They tried the Ouija board again, desperate for answers. The planchette flew under their fingers, spelling out words in a fevered rush: 'Come with me. Be with me. Join me.'

Delia's breath hitched, her voice barely a whisper. 'Aiden, poppit … what do you mean?' The planchette jerked.

'Come. You can be with me if you… leave this place. Cross over.'

Gerry stared at it, his face pale, a cold sweat on his brow. 'Leave…?' he asked, his voice breaking.

The board spelled it out, slow and deliberate this time, each letter a hammer blow:

D-I-E

Delia let out a choked sob, pulling her hands away as if burned. Gerry sat frozen, the colour drained from his face. They stared at the board in stunned silence. The air in the room felt thick, suffocating.

That night, as they lay in bed, wide-eyed and sleepless, they heard laughter.

Low, cruel, echoing through the house.

Delia turned her head and screamed.

Standing at the foot of the bed was Aiden – or what looked like him. He was dressed in his biking gear, the same jacket, the same scuffed boots. But his face was pale, waxy, and his body was covered in blood – dark streaks smeared across his chest, dripping from his hands. His eyes gleamed in the dark, and the smile…

That smile was a snarl.

He lifted a hand. It was broken, hanging in an impossible angle.

Then he laughed – a horrible, wet, gurgling sound that didn't belong in a human throat.

Gerry scrambled out of bed, heart hammering in his chest, but by the time he turned the light on, the figure was gone. Nothing but the stench of rot lingering in the air, and a faint, sticky smear of something dark on the carpet by the door.

Delia sobbed into her hands, rocking back and forth, whispering 'This isn't him … this isn't our boy'… over and over until her voice cracked.

The darkness had truly taken hold of them. The thing that wore Aiden's face had made itself known.

And Gerry and Delia, trapped in their grief, had been the ones to let it in.

☽✧✝✧☾

By the time they reached breaking point, Gerry and Delia were hollowed out. The house had become a prison – each creaking floorboard, each shifting shadow a reminder that they were no longer alone in their own home. They barely slept, barely ate. They jumped at every sound. The thing that wore Aiden's face seemed to know exactly how to keep them on the edge, pushing them closer and closer to madness. In their desperation, they turned to the place they thought would offer sanctuary – their local church.

Gerry had never been particularly religious, but Delia had been raised in the faith, attending Sunday service as a girl. It felt like the right place to turn – after all, if they were dealing with something dark, wasn't that the job of the church?

They made an appointment with the vicar, a soft-spoken man in his late fifties, who welcomed them into the church office with polite smiles and folded hands.

But as they told him their story – the Ouija sessions, the twisted figure of Aiden, the laughter, the smell, the foul presence – his expression shifted. His eyes narrowed. He sat back in his chair, arms folded across his chest, nodding politely but offering little in return. Delia pleaded, her voice cracking, 'Please, reverend ... we're begging you. There's something in our house. It's not our son. We know that now.'

But the vicar just gave them a tight, awkward smile.

'I'm sure it feels that way, but these things have a tendency to fade over time. I'd suggest prayer, perhaps counselling ... have you thought about speaking to a grief support group?'

Gerry clenched his fists, a cold fury rising in his chest. They left the church feeling small, humiliated, as if they were being dismissed as silly, grieving fools.

Let me just say this – I've seen this happen far too often. People in genuine need of help, reaching out to the church, only to be met with polite smiles, vague reassurances and the unspoken message that they're imagining things. The truth is, many religious figures don't want to get involved in cases like this. Either they don't believe in the paranormal, or they're afraid of what might happen if they acknowledge it.

And that's when people like Gerry and Delia are left to fend for themselves.

Out of options, they turned to the only other avenue they could think of – some local paranormal investigators. They got in touch with a team – Mick, John, Russell and Caroline. They arrived one evening in late October, their van pulling up outside the house just as the last light of day was fading. They were an ordinary looking bunch – jeans, jumpers, warm jackets – but they carried an air of quiet focus, a seriousness that suggested they'd seen things they couldn't explain before.

They brought tape recorders, camcorders, and a few pieces of equipment – things to measure temperature. They set up cameras in the lounge, on the landing, and in Aiden's bedroom, positioning them carefully to cover the whole space.

Russell set up a trigger object – a small toy motorbike from Aiden's shelf, placing it on a sheet of white paper marked with a pencil outline, to see if it moved. They dimmed the lights, lit a single candle in the centre of the table, and settled in for the night.

But the house … the house seemed to go quiet. It was as if whatever was in there had decided to hide – lurking just out of sight, making Gerry and Delia look like fools. The investigators heard nothing unusual that night. No footsteps, no tapping, no moving objects. The temperature dropped once or twice, but not dramatically enough to be conclusive.

They played back the recordings the next day – faint clicks, the occasional pop of the heating, but nothing they could point to as definitive.

Gerry felt the hope drain from him. Delia sat on the sofa, wringing her hands, whispering, 'It's making us look mad … it hid from them.'

☽✧✝✧☾

A week later, the investigators tried again. This time, the team brought in a medium – a woman named Maureen, in her early sixties, with short, white-blonde hair and a calm, focused presence. She sat quietly in Aiden's room for a long time, her eyes closed, her breathing steady, as the investigators watched.

And then she spoke.

'There's something here,' she said softly, her voice low and measured. 'It's … not a person. It isn't your son. It isn't a spirit in the way you'd think. It's … old. Very old. It's what we'd call an elemental.'

So, what is an elemental, I can hear some of you asking yourselves. You see, people tend to think of spirits as the ghosts of the dead – humans who've passed over, maybe hanging around because they've got unfinished business. But Elementals are different.

They're not human, and they never were. They're ancient forces – dark, primal energies that feed on certain emotions. Grief. Fear. Rage. They can be born of trauma, of bloodshed. They don't just haunt a place … they infest it. And they're clever – far cleverer than most people give them credit for.

When I talk about elementals, I often point to the case of Leap Castle in Ireland – probably the most infamous example of an elemental spirit I've ever come across. Leap Castle, nestled in the wilds of County Offaly, is a place steeped in blood and history. It's been the site of murders, executions, and all kinds of dark, brutal events across the centuries. It's said that a priest was killed during mass there – stabbed to death in front of his own congregation. The castle even has an oubliette, a deep, hidden chamber where prisoners were thrown in and left to die.

But the thing that sets Leap Castle apart isn't just the bloodshed. It's the dark, inhuman presence that's said to haunt there.

The elemental at Leap Castle is a strange being. The people who've encountered it describe it as a shadowy figure, sometimes appearing as a hunched, hairy, bestial shape. It's said to give off an unbearable stench of sulphur and decay – a foul, choking smell that fills the air when it's near. Witnesses have felt a sense of overwhelming dread in its presence, a paralysing fear that grips them tight, as if the air itself has turned hostile. They report feelings of being watched, of being drained, and some have even described being physically attacked – scratched, pushed, or left with strange, burning marks. It seems to feed on the energy of the place – on the violence, the fear, the suffering and the negativity. It thrives in that atmosphere, growing stronger the more people are affected by it.

They manipulate the people who live there, feeding off their emotions, using their vulnerabilities against them. They twist grief, anger and pain into a kind of fuel, and just like the elemental at Leap Castle, the thing in Gerry and Delia's house had found exactly what it needed – grief, raw and unguarded, pouring from a wound that hadn't healed.

It wore Aiden's face, spoke in his voice, and used every ounce of their heartbreak to tighten its grip.

That's the nature of an elemental – it doesn't care about the person you lost. It cares about the energy you give it. And once it gets its claws in, it doesn't let go without a fight. The elemental had taken the form of their son, Aiden – because it knew that's what they wanted to see.

And now… it was in.

☽✧☨✧☾

The investigative team returned the following weekend, determined to catch something concrete. They set up again – more cameras, more sensors, more recorders.

And this time … It didn't hide. Almost immediately, they felt it – the oppressive atmosphere, the weight in the air like a storm about to break. The temperature in Aiden's room dropped sharply, breath misting in the cold. The temperature gaige registered the drop.

Caroline felt a sudden, sharp scratch down her back as she stood by the window – three long, burning lines that left angry red welts across her skin.

John heard footsteps pacing on the landing, slow, deliberate, heavy. Russell, sitting alone by candlelight in Aiden's bedroom, stared into the gloom … and saw something. It swore he saw a figure, stood in the open door, barely visible for a half a second, so quick that he wasn't even sure he had seen anything. He couldn't see much with his eyes, as the room was dark, barely visible in the light from the candle.

Russell's hands shook as he lifted his camera, snapping a single photograph in the dim light. Then he suddenly felt a wave of nausea crash over him, cold and sour, rising from the pit of his stomach. He barely made it to the door before he doubled over, vomiting onto the carpet.

When they reviewed the photo weeks later, their breath caught in their throats.

There, standing by the door in the grainy image, was a figure that looked like Aiden – or rather, something wearing Aiden's shape.

Its face…

Smiling.

I want to take a moment to talk about the photograph taken during that investigation – because, quite honestly, it's one of the most disturbing images I've ever seen in my years researching the paranormal. What it shows is chilling. When you compare it to the photos of Aiden, it's impossible not to see the resemblance. The shape of the face, the build, even the hair – it's Aiden.

But it's not.

The longer you look, the more wrong it feels. There are marks on the face – subtle at first, but unmistakable when you really examine it. A strange, sinister smile stretches across his lips, just a little too wide, almost like a leer. The eyes are hollow, empty pits that seem to swallow the light. The scars across the nose, faint but visible, add to the sense that you're looking at something that isn't quite human.

This picture ... it's one of the best ghost photographs I've ever seen in terms of evidential value. It's rare enough to get a clear image of an alleged spirit – but to capture something that matches the family's description, down to the unsettling details they experienced? That's powerful. This isn't just a vague blur or a shape in the mist. It's a face – a recognisable face. And that face matches everything Gerry and Delia saw.

But it's not just the evidence that makes this photograph so chilling – it's the feeling it gives you. When I look at this image, I feel it in my gut. A wave of sickness, like a cold, heavy weight settling over me. The kind of feeling that makes your skin crawl, that makes your stomach twist, that leaves a bitter, metallic taste in your mouth.

I've enhanced the photo – brought out the details, sharpened the features. And it's even worse. You can see the twisted expression more clearly, the way the mouth is pulled into that awful, unnatural grin. It reminds me of the horror film Smile – that same eerie, too-wide smirk that feels more like a threat than a smile.

This photograph haunts me. Even now, when I think about it, I feel a shiver run through me. It's a reminder of how close the dark can get – how it can stand just feet away, smiling at you in the dark, wearing the face of someone you love.

It's Aiden ... but it's not Aiden.

It's something else.

After Russell's sickness, the team ended the investigation there, shaken and rattled to their core. They promised Gerry and Delia they'd come back and that they would find them help.

But the thing in that house...

It wasn't finished.

Not yet.

If you want to follow the trail beyond these pages, the author keeps their updates here – including the photographs of the ghost. https://www.facebook.com/share/1CvaPZtKAk/

But Mick and the team weren't ready to give up on Gerry and Delia. After that night – after the photograph, the scratches, the sickness – Mick knew they were dealing with something dark. He had seen plenty in his years investigating the paranormal, but this case left a pit in his stomach. It was personal, intimate, manipulative. He was convinced the couple were telling the truth. So he pressed on. He made phone calls, drove miles to pay visits. He tried to get the church involved – really involved. But, as is often the case, he was met with that all too familiar wall of polite scepticism and awkward silence.

'It's probably just grief, Mick,' one priest told him over the phone. 'It happens sometimes – people think they see things, hear things. It's not our place to intervene in such matters. We can't help every family that claims to have a ghost in their house. These situations tend to resolve themselves once people stop feeding into them.'

And so, people like Gerry and Delia are left to fight battles they're not equipped for – alone, afraid, and at the mercy of something they never asked for.

☽✧✝✧☾

Back in Weymouth, the terror only escalated. Every night, the visions returned. The figure – Aiden's shape, standing in the corner of the room, or at the foot of the bed, or halfway up the stairs. Always watching. Always smiling. But now it spoke every night. In the darkness, they would hear it – that voice, soft, familiar, wrong.

'Poppit… Poppit… why are you scared, Mum? Don't be scared of your little Poppit,'

Delia's heart would twist every time she heard it, that cruel mockery of the pet name she'd used for her son since he was a baby. It wasn't just a name – it was theirs, a word wrapped in love. And now, it was being used against her, weaponised.

Gerry grew sunken-eyed, grey-faced. He stopped going into work altogether, telling them he was sick. Delia called in sick more often than not, her voice hoarse on the phone, making excuses she could barely remember afterwards.

They were falling apart.

Then one night, after a particularly bad episode – where the figure had stood at the foot of the bed for hours, just smiling while they huddled under the covers, too afraid to speak – Gerry snapped. He got up the next morning, made a cup of coffee and stared out of the kitchen window for a long time, his hands trembling. Then, quietly, he said, 'We need to leave. We need to get away from here.'

Delia didn't argue. She just nodded, tears running silently down her face.

That afternoon, Gerry did something drastic – he went out and booked a holiday to Italy. A whole month away, in a rented apartment in an old, converted villa in a quiet little town. He used nearly all the money they had in savings. But he didn't care. He just wanted to take Delia as far from that house, from Weymouth, from the nightmare, as he could.

They left within days, their bags packed in a rush, the house locked up tight behind them.

And for the first time in months ... there was peace.

The villa in Italy was old, stone walls and terracotta tiles; a little weathered, but filled with warmth. The quaint little town stretched around them, olive groves and dusty roads, the scent of sun-baked earth and lemon trees in the air. For the first few nights, they lay awake, tense, waiting – half-expecting the figure to appear in the dark corner of the room, to hear the voice calling 'Poppit ... Poppit...'

But nothing came.

No smells. No taps. No whispers.

Just the sound of people walking the dimly lit streets, the relaxing buzz of the bars and bistros, the distant hum of cicadas, the soft clatter of plates in the apartment below. They were relieved. Overwhelmed, really, by the absence of it all.

And they started to relax. They walked together through the little markets, sat in cafés with tiny cups of bitter coffee and wandered down narrow streets in the fading light. They began to feel like themselves again – like Gerry and Delia, the couple who had been before all of this, despite one with a heavy grief still weighing them down. For a while, they even let themselves believe they could stay there forever.

But they couldn't.

They had to go home.

☽✧✝✧☾

When they returned to Weymouth, the house felt cold, unfamiliar. A pile of mail lay on the doorstep, stuffed through the letterbox in a crumpled heap. Delia gathered it up absentmindedly, flipping through bills and leaflets with numb fingers. Then she spotted it – a letter from Mick. He'd been trying to contact them for a couple of weeks, not realising they'd left the country. They called him immediately, and when he answered, they could hear the relief in his voice.

'Gerry, Delia – thank God. I've been trying to get hold of you.' Mick sounded breathless, excited. 'I've managed to arrange something ... something big. We've got the church on board. I found a bishop – local, respected, experienced – and he's agreed to help. He's going to perform an exorcism.'

Gerry's hand trembled as he held the phone. For the first time in months, they felt the smallest flicker of hope.

An exorcism. A bishop.

Maybe, just maybe, they could take their lives back.

☽✧✝✧☾

The bishop arrived on a grey, drizzling morning – nothing dramatic, no booming thunder or eerie omens, just a quiet knock at the door around 10 am.

He was an older man, well into his seventies, with thinning silver hair, a lined face, and a calm, almost serene presence. He wore a simple black suit with a small white collar, and when he introduced himself, his voice was soft, measured, with a slight Dorset lilt.

'This won't take away your grief,' he told them gently, 'but it may give you peace.'

He had brought two colleagues with him – both younger, both quiet, respectful men. They carried small bags containing what they needed: holy water, a crucifix, a thick, well-worn Bible. There was no fanfare, no drama. They didn't rush in waving crucifixes or shouting at the devil to leave. They took their time, moving quietly from room to room, saying quiet prayers, sprinkling holy water in the corners, marking the doorways with small signs of the cross in blessed oil. It wasn't like the movies. There was no screaming, no thrashing furniture, no demonic howls. Just a calm, methodical ritual – prayers of deliverance, Psalms, the Litany of the Saints, and the Prayer to St Michael.

For three days, the bishop returned each morning, leaving in the late afternoon, with his two younger colleagues. They spent long hours in quiet prayer, sitting in Aiden's bedroom with the door open, reading aloud from the Bible in calm, steady voices. Sometimes the bishop would walk the house slowly, praying under his breath, his fingers moving over the beads of his rosary. Gerry and Delia would sit in the lounge, listening to the gentle cadence of the bishop's voice drifting through the house. It was strange, but comforting – a sense that something was being lifted, slowly and carefully, like layers of dust being brushed away.

On the third day, just as the bishop was finishing his final prayers, the house felt … different. Lighter. The air didn't feel heavy anymore. The oppressive, choking cold was gone. The smell of dog muck had lifted, replaced by a faint, clean scent, like freshly cut grass. The bishop packed up his things, shook their hands warmly, and offered a final, quiet blessing at the front door.

'May you have peace now,' he said, his eyes kind, steady. They said their thanks and he left.

☽✧✝✧☾

That evening, Gerry and Delia lay together in their bedroom, the silence feeling strange, almost alien after so many months of terror. They talked quietly, holding hands, still processing it all, when suddenly…

The room seemed to shift.

A bright, white light filled the space, soft and warm, like moonlight shining through a window. It wasn't harsh or blinding – it was gentle, almost like a glow from within. And standing in that light…

Aiden.

Not the twisted, mocking figure they had seen before – but their real Aiden. His face was soft, peaceful. His eyes were warm, the same shy, lopsided smile on his lips. He looked just as he had before the accident – healthy, whole. He didn't speak, but they felt it – an overwhelming sense of love, gratitude, forgiveness.

And then … the scent of peonies filled the room. Delia gasped, tears spilling over her cheeks. Peonies – her favourite flowers. Aiden had always bought them for her on Mother's Day. The vision faded gently, the light dimming, and they sat in the quiet, weeping – not in fear, but in relief. They knew now, deep down, that their boy was safe.

He had moved on.

The house stayed peaceful after that. No more whispers, no more footsteps, no more twisted smiles in the dark. But of course … the grief didn't vanish. They still missed Aiden – every day. The ache of losing him never fully healed. But they carried it differently now. There was a sense of closure, of knowing that he was at peace.

They learned to live again. They took walks by the sea, sat in the park with a flask of tea, and went on holidays when they could. They laughed together, sometimes through tears, and they spoke about Aiden often – his kindness, his shyness, the way he used to bring Delia peonies, their little Poppit.

They lived the rest of their days as best they could, knowing it's what Aiden would have wanted.

And in that quiet way, they honoured him.

☽✧✝✧☾

The case of Aiden is, without a doubt, one of the most disturbing cases I've ever come across. It's a story that stays with you – not just because of the terrifying events that unfolded inside that house, but because of the raw, human pain at its core. This wasn't a simple haunting, or a cold, impersonal entity floating around in the dark. This was something far more cruel – evil, wearing the face of someone loved, someone lost.

Evil, as I've said before, doesn't always come crashing through the front door with flashing lights and thunderclaps. It creeps in quietly, slips into the gaps where the grief seeps through. It waits for you to be at your weakest, at your most broken. And when it finds that opening, it feeds.

That's exactly what happened here.

Gerry and Delia were two parents, utterly devastated by the loss of their only son. Their grief was so heavy, so all-consuming, that they would have done anything for just one more moment with Aiden. And that's when it came for them – something dark, manipulative, wearing their son's face like a mask. It twisted Delia's pet name, Poppit, into a weapon. It smiled that horrible, empty smile, and it took every ounce of their pain and turned it into fuel.

But despite the horror, despite the heartbreak, I think there's something positive here too. Because they fought. They didn't give up. They sought help, they reached out, they faced the darkness head on – and in the end, they found peace. They saw the real Aiden, just once more. They knew he was safe.

And they carried on.

Not without pain – because the pain of losing a child never truly goes – but with the strength to live the life their son would have wanted for them.

And so we come to the end of the stories of others. These cases – Gerry and Delia, Vanessa, Patricia, Steven, Carly and all the rest – are just a glimpse into the world I've walked through. They are true, every one of them. They are stories of people who never asked for this, never wanted the dark knocking at their door.

But the truth is … these stories are just the beginning. These cases have only scratched the surface of what I have to share. It's hard to believe, I know, but these aren't even the worst cases I've encountered. There are files in my archive that make these look like the tip of the iceberg. Stories that are darker, more dangerous, more … unexplainable. But those will have to wait – until next time, and the next book. For now, we return to conclude my own story.

The hauntings of Serlby Rise; the haunting of my life.

Because the thing I've learnt is that sometimes, the darkest cases aren't the ones you hear about.

They're the ones you live through…

My Haunted Life

Part Eight

The End……?

Disturbing Incidents

It was a warm, lazy spring afternoon on Serlby Rise, sometime in March 1995. Saturdays had settled into their familiar rhythm by then – Warren, Sasha and Claire always disappeared off into town with their mums, a little weekly ritual of wandering the Victoria Centre to do clothes shopping. I usually spent those times at home, cocooned safely in my room, passing the hours away with video games or sketching in my drawing pad.

I remember this day clearly: I was sitting on my bed, game controller in hand, idly glancing out of the window between levels when I saw her. Christine Adams from next door. She was crossing by the hedge between our houses, her black clothes catching the sunlight in a way that made her seem almost smoky, ghostlike. She walked right up our garden path and knocked on the front door. Seconds later, my mum's voice echoed up the stairs.

'Adam! Come down!'

Curious, and a little wary, I put the controller down and headed downstairs. When I reached the hallway, there she was – Christine – standing awkwardly by the door, her pale hands fidgeting with the sleeves of her jumper. She asked if I wanted to come round to hers to 'hang out'. in her room.

I froze. We barely knew each other beyond the odd nod or muttered 'Ey up' on the way to school. And, truth be told, she unnerved me. There was something … off about her. An energy, a feeling that prickled the back of my neck every time I saw her. Even then, at 12 years old, I sensed there was more to her than just the moody 16-year-old teenage goth aesthetic. It was something deeper. Something darker.

I shot a pleading look to my mum, desperate for her to save me from this awkward situation, but she missed it completely. Smiling, she practically ushered me towards Christine, delighted that I was making 'new friends'.

Reluctantly, heart pounding with a kind of primitive fear I couldn't explain, I agreed.

The short walk to their front door felt like an eternity. Every fibre of my being screamed at me to turn back, to get away, to run back to the safety of our house. But I couldn't bring myself to say no.

We stepped inside. At once, I was swallowed by a suffocating heaviness. The entrance hall was a claustrophobic mishmash of peeling wallpaper, dark green paint, and heavy, faded curtains that seemed to sag under their own weight. The smell was an odd mix of stale florals, damp wood and something else – something faintly metallic, almost like blood. The walls up the staircase were crammed with old framed photographs and paintings, their sepia-toned faces staring down blankly like the forgotten dead. It reminded me immediately of the Bates Motel from *Psycho*. I had only ever seen the outside of their house before; now, inside, it was everything I feared – and worse.

Caroline appeared, beaming a greeting at me, her bulk framed awkwardly in the doorway as she bent down to tend to some weeding outside. I mumbled a nervous 'hello' in return, hoping – praying – that Dana would be around too, someone familiar to balance the unsettling energy.

But no. Dana was out with her dad.

I was alone. Alone with Christine.

She led me upstairs.

Her room was at the end of the corridor – the master bedroom, she said, shared with Dana. But it didn't feel like a normal room. The moment she opened the door, a shock of cold air hit me full in the face. It wasn't just cooler than the rest of the house; it was freezing. I instinctively hugged myself as I took in the scene.

The walls were plastered, floor to ceiling, with posters of East 17. No gaps. No windows visible. Just an endless collage of the boy band staring down, their faces distorted and wrinkled by overlapping tape and old glue.

The bedspreads were black, the curtains were black, even the lampshades were black. It didn't feel like a teenager's bedroom. It felt like a shrine. A crypt.

Christine flopped down onto her single bed and motioned for me to sit beside her. I steered away instead, perching uneasily on the edge of Dana's bed. An hour passed – an hour that dragged like wet cement. She talked endlessly, feverishly, about East 17, rewinding and replaying the same cassettes over and over again until the tinny sound of their songs became a kind of maddening background buzz. I nodded along politely, barely hearing her words, just counting the minutes until I could leave.

Eventually, she asked if I liked them. I shook my head slightly, murmuring that they weren't really my thing. It was like flicking a switch. Christine's face twisted in rage. Before I could react, she lunged forward and slapped me hard across the face.

The sting of it was sharp, shocking. I just sat there, frozen, stunned into silence.

And then, as quickly as the rage had come, it vanished. She smiled again – an unsettling, glassy-eyed smile – and carried on talking as if nothing had happened. I sat rigid, sick with fear, my mind racing. Every instinct in my body screamed that I needed to get out, to run, to escape this girl and this house. But I couldn't move. I was rooted to the spot.

The cold in the room deepened. It was bone-deep, an unnatural cold that didn't match the warmth of the day outside. I recognised it. It was the same oppressive, unnatural chill that sometimes filled our own house at night.

Something was here.

Christine moved across the room to a battered chest of drawers. She rummaged inside and pulled out a small, gleaming object – a penknife.

Then she produced something else: a crucifix. But not a normal one.

This crucifix was blackened, twisted, carved with strange shapes that made my stomach churn just to look at it. It was grotesque, almost mocking.

Christine returned to her bed and stared at me with wide, fever-bright eyes.

'Do you want to call up the Devil with me?' she asked casually, as though suggesting a game.

I blinked at her, sure I had misheard. But no – she asked again. Slowly. Deliberately.

I stammered something incoherent, but she only laughed – a soft, chilling laugh – and sat down closer to me.

'I do it all the time,' she whispered. 'He comes here, in my bedroom. He talks to me. He has sex with me. In this bed.'

The words slithered into my brain like snakes.

She leaned in closer, her breath icy against my cheek.

'Do you want to take me, Adam?' she said. 'Do you want to touch my tits?'

I was 12 years old, sheltered and innocent in the way only a child of that era could be. I didn't even really understand what was happening, but I knew one thing: it was wrong. Everything about this was wrong.

I wanted to cry.

And then, it got worse.

I felt it.

A presence.

A crushing, unseen presence that filled the room like invisible smoke, thick and suffocating. It was as if something monstrous was perched in the shadows above us, hanging from the ceiling like a spider, watching, drooling, waiting.

The Devil? I wasn't sure of it, but my innocent brain told me that it was him.

Christine's grin widened as she dragged the penknife across her own finger, drawing a bead of blood. She dripped it onto the black crucifix with grim reverence.

'I sold my soul to him,' she said, almost singing. 'Satan owns it now. He wants others too.'

Something inside me broke free then – some final fragment of survival instinct – and I stumbled to my feet.

Mumbling something, anything, I backed away, edged towards the door. Christine just sat there, smiling at me, her finger bleeding freely, the black crucifix soaking up her blood.

I turned and fled.

I nearly slipped down the staircase in my panic, heart hammering against my ribs, vision blurring with tears I refused to let fall. I yanked open the front door – and was greeted by the sight of Caroline outside, screaming in agony on the front path. The huge, moss-streaked gravestone that she had propped against the wall – her mother's gravestone – had toppled over and crushed her foot. She clutched at it, shrieking, her cries of pain cutting through the heavy summer air like a knife.

And above it all, from somewhere behind me in the house, I thought I heard Christine's laughter.

After what happened with Christine next door, I was left … shaken.

No, shaken isn't the right word. I was terrified. The kind of terror that settles deep in your bones and stays there, gnawing at the edges of your thoughts long after the moment has passed.

I cut all contact with the Adams family after that day. I didn't go near the place ever again, only when passing it to go to school or to play at Warren's. I didn't ask how Dana was doing. I didn't even glance in their direction when I saw them in the garden. I just couldn't. But there is one thing that's always haunted me…

I never told anyone.

Not my friends. Not my parents. Not even a whisper in the dead of night when I couldn't sleep. I never uttered a single word about what I experienced in that room – about what I felt breathing down my neck as I stood frozen by her bed. I kept it locked inside, like some dark, festering secret that felt too dangerous to speak aloud.

I told myself it wasn't my problem. Because the truth was, I had my own house to worry about. Because whatever had been waiting in Christine's bedroom, whatever had watched from the shadows … it wasn't the only thing out there. The awful things that lurked in my own home were still waiting for me…

☽✧†✧☾

By the summer of 1995, a few months had passed since the incident with Christine. For a while, things at home went quiet. The strange occurrences – the footsteps, the voices, the heavy air of dread that seemed to linger in certain rooms – began to ease. Not disappear, not completely. But ease.

I was suspicious of the silence.

Because in this house, peace never meant peace. It meant the storm was gathering.

And deep down, I knew that.

Still, I tried to enjoy the quiet while it lasted. I distracted myself with a way I had always enjoyed – by drawing. Art was a refuge for me. I could lose myself in my sketchbook for hours, pencil gliding across the paper, shaping monsters and faces and strange little worlds. I was never short of imagination.

But even that small comfort wasn't safe. There were many times I'd get up to leave the room – to grab a drink, go to see mum when she'd call me from the kitchen, to just stretch my legs – and when I came back, I'd find something written on the paper. Scrawled words, quick and jagged, almost illegible. Not mine. Not written in my hand. And never anything I could fully decipher – just strange markings, jumbled letters, like someone trying to speak through me but not quite getting the message out. I started tearing those pages out. Quietly. Hiding them. I didn't want to scare Mum and Dad.

But deep inside, I knew what was happening. I just didn't know what it meant.

As the weeks passed, something inside me was beginning to shift. I started to notice things more. Not just the typical bumps and creaks that came from the old house, but the spaces in between – those quiet moments where the air would change. Thicken. Moments when the hair on my arms would rise and I'd feel that awful prickling sensation on the back of my neck, as if something was standing behind me. Watching me.

I found myself staring blankly into corners of rooms – particularly near the stairs, or the hallway just off the entrance – drawn to them by a feeling I couldn't explain. It wasn't curiosity. It was instinct.

There was something there.

I couldn't see it, but I could feel it. A heavy presence, like a silent onlooker pressed just beyond the veil of the visible. My sensitivity was growing stronger. I didn't know the word for it back then, but I was becoming psychic.

It wasn't something I ever asked for. But I couldn't deny it. The more time I spent in that house, the more it rooted itself in me.

I started taking an interest in things that set me apart. While other kids were obsessed with football stickers or the latest games, I found myself drawn to the strange and unexplainable. I started watching The X-Files religiously.

I became fascinated by the paranormal – UFOs, ghosts, cryptids, anything that hinted at a world just out of reach. And for a time, that helped. It gave me something to focus on, a way to frame what I was experiencing. Maybe I wasn't just going mad. Maybe there was something more to it. Something that made sense, at least to me. My interest in the unknown gave me a strange sense of control – like if I could just understand what I was seeing, I could learn how to deal with it.

But there was always something deeper. Something I couldn't quite name.

There was a secret inside me.

I could feel it – like a locked room in my mind that I didn't have the key for. An awareness of something that wasn't just watching me from the shadows of the house … but one that had settled itself inside me. Some kind of memory that had become trapped. I didn't know what it was. I didn't even know how to think about it properly. I was still just a boy, staring into the unknown, trying to make sense of the darkness around me and within me.

But I knew this: Whatever it was … It would not stay buried forever. That key would turn, eventually.

And when it did – everything would change.

☽✧†✧☾

By the time summer rolled around in 1995, I wasn't the only one noticing that the silence in our house wasn't quite as peaceful as it seemed.

I think Dad had been hoping against hope that the church blessing had worked. That somehow, through prayer, the house had been freed.

But he knew better.

It was in the little things – the way he moved through the house with that quiet caution again, the way he paused at the foot of the stairs as if listening. I caught him staring up at the landing more than once, his mouth drawn tight, his eyes unsettled. He was hearing things. Feeling things. Just like me.

And just like me … he didn't say a word.

Until one Saturday morning.

I was watching TV in the front room when he walked in holding my drawing pad – my sketchbook that rarely left my side. It had been sitting on the dining room table, where I'd left it the night before.

'What's this, Ad?' he asked.

I looked at it, and my stomach sank. Three long, jagged scratches in black pencil ran across the top page. Deep gouges, harsh and purposeful – like something with claws had dragged them straight through the paper.

I hadn't done that. I knew I hadn't.

I just stared at it. 'I … I don't know,' I said, but my voice betrayed me.

Dad sat down in the armchair, still holding the pad. Then he said, 'You think the ghost did this?'

I hesitated, then nodded.

That was when he let out a breath like he'd been holding it in for months. The kind of breath that carries with it the exhaustion of pretending everything's okay.

'I've been hearing things too,' he said, quietly. 'I just didn't want to scare you.'

That hit me like a punch. Because I'd been doing exactly the same thing.

'I didn't want to worry you either,' I told him.

We just looked at each other for a few seconds – father and son, both haunted, both pretending for the other's sake. And both finally realising that we'd never been fooling anyone.

We sat down and had the conversation we should've had weeks ago. We both admitted that we'd known – known – that it was still there. That the thing that haunted our house hadn't left at all. It had just grown quieter for a while. Gone dormant. We'd both been pretending, keeping it from each other so the other wouldn't worry. I was keeping quiet for him. He was doing the same for me.

But it hadn't helped. Not really.

Because silence in a haunted house is never peace – it's the sound of something waiting. Dad didn't want to burden Mum with any of it. She was sceptical, and always had been. And more than that, Dad didn't want to scare her. So he carried the weight of it on his own – until one day, he didn't.

☽✧✝✧☾

Our neighbour Jed was a friendly bloke. A proper hands-on type – mechanic by trade. He and his girlfriend were the kind of neighbours my parents would chat to from across the street and have the odd drink with now and again. Jed lived directly across the road from us, in one of the better-kept houses with a nicely paved drive and a spotless Ford Sierra he was forever polishing. He was a funny guy, always cracking a joke. Dad would often chat to him out on the front drive, especially if the weather was good and one or the other was tinkering with a car.

On this particular afternoon, I remember the sun was out. You could smell the freshly cut grass from someone's garden up the road. Me and Dad were out cleaning the car on our driveway. We were scrubbing away when Jed wandered over with a cold can of Coke in one hand and an oily rag in the other. He and Dad began to chat. They talked a bit about football, cars, the usual stuff. He cracked a few jokes with me, and we were laughing and enjoying the banter. Then, as Jed turned to head back to his drive, Dad said, 'Jed – can I ask you something? Bit of a strange one.'

Jed paused. 'Go on,' he said.

'Have you ever had anything weird happen in your house? I mean … not just creaks and groans. I mean really weird. Strange things.'

Jed stared at him, the way people do when they're weighing up whether someone is having a laugh. But Dad wasn't laughing.

'I'm serious,' Dad said. 'Because something's not right in ours. Hasn't been for years.'

Jed took a slow sip of his drink. 'You mean you've got a ghost?'

Dad nodded. 'I think so. Adam's seen things. I've heard things. It's … it's not just a one-off. It's been happening for years. Some weeks are quiet. Other times, it's like living in a nightmare. The church tried to help but…' he shrugged, 'it didn't last.'

Jed was silent for a moment. Then he said something that surprised Dad: 'I believe you.'

'You do?' Dad asked.

Jed nodded, his expression now unreadable. 'I've never had anything happen here,' he said, motioning to his own house. 'But I had something happen to me a few years back. Somewhere else. It was … well, it's stayed with me, let's put it that way.' He looked Dad in the eye.

'Something disturbing. Something I've never told many people.'

Dad didn't push him for details. Not yet. Jed promised he'd tell him the full story when he had time.

But even just hearing those words – 'I believe you' – meant a lot. It made him feel better that someone outside of the church believed us.

☽✧✝✧☾

It wasn't until a few weeks after that conversation on the drive that Jed finally told his story to Dad. The timing was casual, but the conversation would be anything but.

It happened one Friday night, down at The Alcester. Mum had gone along too, as had Jed's girlfriend. The four had met up there for a drink a few times – friendly laughs, warm lighting, and the gentle drone of '90s pop playing through a slightly dodgy wall speaker.

That night, Mum and Jed's girlfriend had taken over a table in the lounge and were deep in conversation. Dad and Jed drifted over to the bar area and got stuck into a game of darts – just the two of them, a pint each, the soft thud of the dartboard, and the occasional banter with the old fella perched near the fruit machine. It was at the end of their second game when Jed threw a particularly bad dart and muttered, 'I never did get round to telling you that story, did I.'

Dad nodded. 'Mate, I've got enough of my own to deal with.' he joked.

Jed gave a half-hearted laugh and sipped his pint. Then he leaned back against the bar and said, 'I've been thinking a lot lately. About what you said. About the stuff happening in your house.'

Dad just nodded. He didn't say anything, let Jed speak in his own time. He took a breath, deep and long. Then he told Dad his story.

☽✧✝✧☾

The year was 1989. Jed had been seeing his girlfriend Dee for about six months. Things were going well. Jed had been through a rough divorce previously, and he was finally beginning to feel settled again. Dee was warm, kind, and, most importantly to Jed, she got along well with his teenage daughter from his first marriage. He also got on well with Dee's family. Her mother, Pam, was what he described as 'a proper character' – your classic Nottingham matriarch – no nonsense, always calling people 'duck'. Pam would regularly invite them over for Sunday roasts, and Jed had started to feel like he was part of the family.

Dee's job occasionally took her abroad on business trips. It wasn't a frequent thing, but every so often she'd be gone for a few days. That autumn, she was away in Ireland for four nights. Nothing unusual. She was due back on a Saturday afternoon, and Jed decided to surprise her with a romantic meal. It wasn't something he often did, but he wanted to make the effort.

So that morning, he headed to the local Co-op supermarket to get what he needed. Steak, potatoes, a few vegetables. Just the basics. As he was approaching the entrance, he happened to bump into Pam. She was just leaving the shop, carrying two heavy bags of shopping, and greeted him in her usual warm way. 'Ey up, duck,' she said cheerfully. She looked perfectly fine. Normal. Healthy. She opened one of her bags and showed him the contents: a few bits and bobs. Lettuce, tomatoes, cornflakes, milk. Standard stuff.

Jed told her about the surprise meal he was planning for Dee.

'Oh Jed, you are a romantic, aren't you?' Pam said with a soft laugh. Then she added something that stuck with him later. 'When you see her, please tell her how much I love her. You take good care of her, Jed.'

With that, she smiled, turned, and walked off up Carlton Road. Jed went inside and did his shopping, thinking nothing more of it.

That afternoon, he was home in the kitchen, steaks sizzling, table laid, candle lit. He was genuinely looking forward to seeing Dee. When the knock at the door came, he assumed it was her and he was right. But something was off the moment he saw her face. She stepped in, quiet, pale. Her arms were wrapped tightly around her torso like she was physically holding herself together. Jed greeted her warmly and told her about the dinner, trying to lighten the mood.

But Dee just stood there, staring blankly. Then she broke. She started sobbing, uncontrollably. Jed led her into the living room, sat her down, and held her while she cried. Eventually, through trembling lips, she got the words out.

'It's Mum,' she said. 'She's had a heart attack. She died.'

Jed, stunned, shook his head. 'I'm so sorry. God, Dee, I can't believe it. I only just saw her today. At lunchtime. She looked fine.'

That's when things turned strange.

Dee pulled away, confused and suddenly angry. 'What do you mean you saw her today?'

Jed explained. About the Co-op. About their brief conversation. About the shopping and what she'd said. But Dee wasn't having it.

'Jed, you couldn't have seen her. She's been dead since yesterday afternoon. The ambulance found her at home. She's been gone over twenty-four hours.'

Jed didn't know what to say. He swore on everything he knew that he had seen Pam, had spoken to her, laughed with her. But the timeline was impossible. Pam had already been dead.

And yet, he had seen her. Clear as day. Her raincoat, her bobble hat, her shopping bags, her voice, her familiar laugh.

For whatever reason, Pam had chosen to show herself that day, reaching out to him as a final farewell, to make sure that he looked after her daughter.

☽✧☨✧☾

To this day, I still think about Jed's story. What he saw that day wasn't some misty apparition or half-glimpsed shadow. He saw a woman. A person. Pam looked exactly as she always had. She talked to him. She laughed. She carried shopping bags filled with real, tangible items. It wasn't just a vision – it was an encounter. Physical. Interactive.

And that's the part that rattles me the most. How does that work? How does a spirit not only appear, but appear so fully, so vividly, so convincingly, that a man who knew her well had no idea she was already dead? What were those shopping bags? Could a spirit really project such a perfect illusion? Could Jed's mind have conjured those details somehow? I don't think so. There was too much consistency, too much clarity. He remembered what was in the bags. He remembered the weight of her presence. There was nothing dreamlike or vague about it.

This story has always stayed with me because it shatters our idea of what ghosts are. They're not always translucent figures floating at the end of a hallway. Sometimes, they look like us. Talk like us. Smile like us. They are us.

For my dad, it was a moment of comfort too. Knowing that Jed had gone through something so strange, so inexplicable, reminded him he wasn't alone. Other people had experienced the unexplainable. Other witnesses. Other lives touched by the paranormal. Jed's experience is one I often repeat when I speak to people about how spirits sometimes return to us. It's one of the clearest examples I've ever come across of a ghost that wasn't just seen – but engaged with. A full-bodied, intelligent, purposeful return. If you ever needed proof that something lingers after we go, well ... Jed's encounter might just be it.

But back at our house, our real, tangible haunting continued. Oh, it wasn't like it was previously. Things really started to quieten down. By the summer of 1996, life inside Serlby Rise had grown pretty quiet – but it was the kind of quiet that makes your skin itch. A heavy, watchful silence. It wasn't that the house had suddenly turned tame. If anything, it felt like it was biding its time, crouched somewhere just out of sight. But for now, the incidents tapered off. For once, things almost felt normal.

But I didn't trust it.

By now, I'd learnt that lulls in activity were never to be celebrated. The house played games, and calm was just a mask it wore when it wanted you to drop your guard.

Still, we had other things on our minds – real-world problems that demanded attention. My Grandad Frank's health was declining, and it cast a long shadow over everything else. I loved him dearly. He was a tough man, strong-willed and sharp, the kind who didn't suffer fools. But he had suffered plenty himself.

Back in the 1970s, he'd been outside a pub one night and saw a fight break out. Most people would have walked the other way. But not Grandad Frank. He stepped in to break it up – and paid a terrible price. One of the men, wielding a broken bottle, stabbed him in the neck. He survived, somehow, but it damaged his heart. The trauma of his stabbing had a lasting impact. Throughout the late '80s and early '90s, he suffered a series of angina attacks and heart problems, some of which were serious enough to hospitalise him. But he always bounced back, always seemed to return home a little thinner, a little paler, but smiling and joking as if nothing had changed. And now, in 1996, his heart health was catching up with him. My parents were consumed with worry. Every phone call brought tension and set hearts racing. The haunting faded into the background – not gone, just out of focus.

There had been serious conversations being had behind closed doors. One of those was about moving. Not out of fear of the supernatural. This wasn't a panicked escape. It was about family. Love. Responsibility.

There was talk of going back to Wray Close to be nearer to Grandad Frank and Nana Joan. That street had history for us. I'd lived there until I was 5. My mum and dad had lived in their first homes there. It still felt like the place we were meant to return to. Plus, my dad's parents weren't the only ones who lived there. A few years before, my other grandparents – Don and Audrey – had already made the move. They'd swapped their house on Ranby Walk with my dad's cousin Maria and her family. We really like to keep it in our family, us lot!

As Grandad's health worsened, Dad seemed more and more set on going back. Even Mum, who usually held her ground, didn't push back. She wanted to be near her parents again, and maybe part of her was ready to leave Serlby Rise behind.

But if we thought the house would let us go quietly, we were mistaken.

Not long after the death of Rupert the canary, my mum decided to bring another pet into our home, a budgie she named Monty. At first everything seemed perfectly fine, and the joy of having a new companion brought a sense of normalcy back into our lives. However, it wasn't long before tragedy struck again; in a hauntingly similar turn of events, Monty was discovered lifeless in his cage, mirroring the fate that had befallen Rupert. The sequence of events left a profound sense of unease in me, and the echoes of loss seemed to linger in the air around us. It was as though it was reminding me that it was still around. Even with all my efforts to lead a normal life, the essence of the house lingered, entwined with my every thought.

With hindsight, I think it knew we were getting ready to leave. Houses like that … they feel things. They react. And as the idea of moving grew stronger, the atmosphere inside the house changed again. The stillness twisted.

It became a kind of pressure, like walking into a room where someone's been crying – or worse, seething with rage.

In the summer, when I was 13 years old, we finally made the decision to leave Serlby Rise behind and return to Wray Close. On the surface, it felt like this haunting chapter of my life had closed. But as you'll come to learn… it was anything but over.

Death in the Family

I will always remember the day Grandad Frank passed away. There are certain moments in life that etch themselves deeply into your memory that even decades later, you can recall them with perfect clarity – the light outside, the smell in the air, the tone in your parents' voices. That day in September 1996 was one of those moments for me. It also, in a way I didn't understand at the time, opened the door to a new period in which the strange, the sorrowful, and the supernatural seemed to weave themselves more tightly into our story.

We thought Grandad Frank was indestructible in some strange way, as if he'd always manage to pull through from his heart problems. But that September morning proved otherwise.

It happened in the early hours. I didn't know at the time. I was just a kid. I was, coincidentally, staying overnight at the house of my other grandparents, Don and Audrey, who lived only a few doors away. I had been woken by my grandparents, got dressed for school, eaten my breakfast and left the house without any inkling that something awful had happened during the night. They hadn't said a word. I suppose they didn't want to upset me before school.

The day at school was normal in that surreal way days often are when something life-changing is happening just outside your awareness. I remember sitting in class, fiddling with a pen, talking to friends at lunch, thinking about nothing in particular. If there were signs, I missed them. But when I walked back to Don and Audrey's after school, and walked through the front door, everything felt off. My mum and dad were there, something that automatically made no sense since they usually didn't come to pick me up after work until 5 pm. The atmosphere was strange – heavy, almost like the air itself had thickened. Mum and Dad were sat in the living room, quiet and pale-faced. I could see something in their eyes even before they said the words.

'Grandad's passed away,' Mum told me gently.

I just stood there, not quite knowing what to say. A hot sting welled up behind my eyes. I nodded, and then, I think, I asked how. They explained it had been his heart. A heart attack. He'd gone in the night.

We went to my Nana Joan's flat a few minutes later. She lived in a modest ground floor place at the top of the close. I remember walking down the corridor towards her living room, hearing muffled crying from within, and knowing that life wasn't going to be the same again. Nana Joan was a mess, as you'd expect – her face blotchy, her eyes red-rimmed. My Auntie Diane was there too, along with Eleri and Nathan. Normally, we'd be over the moon to see each other. But not that day. That day we just sat in silence in Nana's living room, on her well-worn sofa and faded armchairs, the television humming low in the background with the sound turned down. She had just lost her beloved husband, yet somehow she was still putting on a brave face for the sake of us kids. That was the kind of woman she was. Strong in ways that didn't always show, but always present when we needed her most.

Nobody really spoke. There were no words. Just the occasional sniffle, the odd comforting pat on the shoulder or hand. Even as kids, we understood what had happened. We felt the grief in our bones. It was like something had been taken from all of us – some foundation that had always seemed solid, gone overnight.

I remember Nana putting the kettle on to make the adults cups of tea, trying to busy herself, trying to take care of everyone the only way she knew how. Isn't that the unique British way to deal with a death in the family? Stick the kettle on. A cuppa always made things better....

Grandad Frank was a man full of stories, laughter and life. He'd always had time for us. Whether it was telling us daft jokes or making us laugh with the mildly insulting nicknames he gave his neighbours (one unfortunate old lady named Clara, who had quite a prominent nose, was referred to by him as 'Clara Concord'!), he had a presence that made you feel safe. Losing him left a silence that couldn't be filled.

We were all still trying to make sense of it. The weight of what had happened was too heavy for any of us to carry alone. Together, we were processing it. No one really knew what to do with themselves. The room felt full, but not in a comforting way – more like everything was swollen with emotion, tension, grief. The adults whispered or wept quietly in the living room while us cousins hovered on the edge of it all, unsure of our place. Nathan, Eleri and I were all just kids. Not small children, but not quite old enough to know how to hold grief properly either. We felt it keenly – we really did – but we didn't understand how to behave in the face of it. Do we cry? Do we sit still? Do we speak?

Nana was doing her best to hold things together. She kept trying to smile for us. She wanted to protect us, I could see that. Her heart was breaking and yet she was still playing the role of guardian, like she always had. Then, out of nowhere, one of the old pop vans turned up outside – those little travelling shops that used to come round the estates selling lemonade, cola, dandelion and burdock. Nana reached for her purse and, through tears, handed us a couple of quid. I can still see the tremble in her hand as she pressed the coins into mine.

'Here y'are, kids,' she said, voice wavering, her eyes glistening. 'Go get yourselves something to drink off the pop man.'

It was such a small gesture, but it meant everything. She was trying to give us a moment of normal. A break from the heaviness.

So the three of us went outside. The autumn air was cool but not unpleasant, the light flat and colourless. We got our bottles – mine was cola, always was – and we stood outside for a few minutes, talking quietly. It was easier out there. There weren't adult eyes watching, no one trying to hold it together for us. We didn't say anything profound – just shared how weird it all felt. We were heartbroken, but also awkward. None of us really knew how to grieve in front of the grown-ups, especially not in front of Nana. We didn't want to be seen as disrespectful or thoughtless, so inside we mostly stayed quiet, saying nothing. Just absorbing.

Eventually we went back in and made our way into Nana and Grandad's bedroom. That was something we'd always done, even when things were normal. We'd hang out in there together, sit on the bed, mess about with bits and bobs in the drawers. It felt like our little sanctuary inside the flat.

That day though, it was different. The room felt hushed. We didn't mess about or chat much. We sat on the edge of the bed, sipping our drinks in near silence. I was so thirsty I finished mine quickly, and after a few minutes I decided to go and get another. I stood up and left the room, heading down the narrow passage to the kitchen. The flat was oddly still. Just the low hum of voices from the living room, broken by the occasional sniffle or sigh.

I filled my glass, the pop fizzing softly, and turned to head back to the bedroom. As I passed the doorway to the lounge, I paused. I could see my mum, my dad, Auntie Diane and Nana all sitting there. They looked tired, bruised in a way only grief can bruise you. Dad noticed me and gave me a soft, reassuring smile.

'You alright, son?' he asked gently.

I nodded, not trusting myself to speak. Just as I was about to carry on walking –

I heard it.

From the hall, behind me. A voice. Just one word.

'Joan?'

It wasn't quiet – it was clear and loud enough that it echoed down the passage with a strange, hollow clarity. There was a questioning tone in it. Almost confused. A sense of someone calling out into the dark, lost and unsure.

But I knew that voice. Instantly. Unmistakable. It was Grandad Frank.

My heart thudded once, hard – but I wasn't scared. Not even a little bit. I was shocked, yes. Frozen for a moment, just listening. But there was no fear. Only a kind of calm awareness.

I looked back into the living room. Nobody else had reacted. Not Mum, not Dad, not Nana, not Diane. They carried on, oblivious. No one flinched, no one even looked up.

I was the only one who'd heard it.

Something shifted in me at that moment. I stood there, holding my drink, and felt a strange kind of comfort settle over me. The voice had come from beyond wherever he'd gone – but it had come to me. And only to me. That was when I truly started to realise that something was different about me. It wasn't just chance, or coincidence or imagination. There was a reason I'd heard him and no one else had. The reason strange things always seemed to happen around me. A reason I'd always felt a little out of step with the world. That was the moment I began to understand who I was.

Psychic.

Not just someone who believed in ghosts – but someone who could hear them. And Grandad's voice – clear as day, just one last call for his wife – was the beginning of everything that would follow.

This was just the beginning of my life of paranormal adventures.

☽✧†✧☾

Epilogue

The Shadows Stay with You

The truth is, you never really leave a haunting behind.

You might move house. You might grow up, grow older, tell yourself that chapter of your life is over. But it lingers – like smoke on clothes, like old wallpaper beneath fresh paint. The shadows stay with you. Not always in ways you expect. Not always in ways you can see. But they do.

I've spent most of my life chasing ghosts – mine, and other people's. What began in a council house in Nottingham has taken me into some of the darkest corners of people's lives. I've stood in cold bedrooms, basements, abandoned halls, listening to voices that shouldn't be there. I've held the hands of terrified strangers. I've heard things, felt things, seen things – things I still struggle to explain, even after all these years.

And what I've learned is this: hauntings aren't just about old houses or creaking stairs. They're about people. About trauma. Loss. Regret. Unfinished business. Whether it's a voice calling out for someone long gone, or a shadow standing silently at the edge of a child's bed – these phenomena are always tied to emotion. Always rooted in something deeply human.

Some might dismiss the stories in this book. Some may dismiss my story. They'll say it's just the wind, or the wiring, or an overactive imagination. And maybe for them, that's true. But for those of us who've lived through it – who've seen lives unravel and families fall apart under the weight of something unseen – there's no need for explanation. We already know it's real.

Not every case ends with closure. Not every spirit moves on. Some stay. Some want to be heard. Others just want to be left alone.

And some … well, some never were human to begin with.

I don't claim to have all the answers. I never will. But I believe in listening. I believe that when someone tells you they're afraid in their own home, you believe them. You sit with them. You bear witness. Because sometimes, that's all we can do.

Thank you for walking with me through these stories, and sticking with me through mine – for braving the dark with me. Whether you read this with a sceptic's mind or an open heart, I hope something here stayed with you. Maybe a detail. A whisper. A shadow at the edge of the page.

And if you ever find yourself alone in the quiet, and the air shifts, and something moves just out of sight – don't be too quick to dismiss it.

You never know what might be watching.

Until next time…

Keep watching the shadows.

☽✧✝✧☾

The End
Not…

☽✧✝✧☾